Roe v. Wade

LANDMARK LAW CASES

AMERICAN SOCIETY

Peter Charles Hoffer
N. E. H. Hull
Series Editors

Titles in the series:

N. E. H. HULL AND PETER CHARLES HOFFER

Roe v. Wade

The Abortion Rights Controversy

in American History

UNIVERSITY PRESS OF KANSAS

Published by the University Press of Kansas (Lawrence, Kansas 66049),
which was organized by the Kansas Board of Regents and is operated and
funded by Emporia State University, Fort Hays State University, Kansas
State University, Pittsburg State University, the University of Kansas, and
Wichita State University.

Library of Congress Cataloging-in-Publication Data

Hull, N. E. H., 1949–

Roe v. Wade : the abortion rights controversy in American history /
N. E. H. Hull and Peter Charles Hoffer

p. cm. — (Landmark law cases & American society)

Includes bibliographical references and index.

ISBN 0-7006-1142-8 (cloth : alk. paper) —

ISBN 0-7006-1143-6 (pbk. : alk. paper)

1. Roe, Jane, 1947– —Trials, litigation, etc.   2. Wade, Henry—Trials,
litigation, etc.   3. Trials (Abortion)—Washington (D.C.)   4. Abortion—
Law and legislation—United States—History.   I. Title: Roe versus
Wade.   II. Hoffer, Peter Charles, 1944–   III. Title.   IV. Series.

KF228.R59 H85 2001

342.73'084—dc21   2001001785

British Library Cataloguing in Publication Data is available.

Printed in the United States of America

10 9 8 7 6 5 4 3 2

The paper used in this publication meets the minimum requirements of the
American National Standard for Permanence of Paper for Printed Library
Materials z39.48-1984.

TO OUR BROTHERS,

DRS. LESLIE A. HULL AND BARRY J. HOFFER,

WHO UNDERSTAND HOW SCIENCE AND SOCIETY MUST

AND DO COME TOGETHER

CONTENTS

EDITORS' PREFACE

Long ago, when one of the coauthors of this book (and coeditors of this series) was in graduate school, he proposed to do a seminar paper on a topic that included recent government decisions. "Nonsense," retorted the instructor, a wizened and honored historian, "that's current events, not history." Any history of *Roe v. Wade* must touch current events and so runs the risk of offending such scholarly purists. It is true that distance from events and people often gives passions a chance to cool and perspectives the opportunity to broaden. The events' true significance may become clearer in the passage of time. But *Roe* is the exception that tests this rule, for not only has the topic of abortion remained highly politicized over the course of the past 150 years, but the terms in which the people in our study characterized the law of abortion over those years (hence the language of our primary sources) are invariably moralistic and partisan. Distance in and of itself has not lent enchantment or enlightenment to this topic.

In the latter sense, it is perhaps most fitting that *Roe* appear in the Landmark Law Cases and American Society series. The series has been graced by scholarly studies of a wide variety of topics whose resolution was not clear when the books were published and in some cases was not likely to be resolved, at least to everyone's satisfaction, in the near future. Insofar as these cases are likely to be contested further in the courts, books like *Roe* tie the present and future to the past. The legal maneuvers and intellectual claims of abortions rights and anti–abortion rights litigants are not new. Instead, they are part of a dialogue over gender, law, medicine, politics, and religion going back to the beginning of the republic.

The authors of the book that follows are, respectively, a law professor who also holds a doctorate in history and teaches both subjects and a history professor who has long had an interest in legal themes. They have collaborated on two other books, the first on infanticide and the second on impeachment. In those works and this, they bounced ideas and arguments off one another and shared the duties of research, writing, and refinement of the text so thoroughly that it would be difficult now to reconstruct precisely who did what. They can say that their personal views on abortion rights differ, and that they have tried in the book to show respect for and give hearing to a wide spectrum of arguments on abortion rights.

ACKNOWLEDGMENTS

The authors acknowledge with gratitude the suggestions of the participants in the New York University School of Law legal history seminar, the Rutgers Law School–Camden faculty workshop, and the University of Georgia department of history faculty colloquium, to whom the manuscript was presented in the fall and winter of 2000–2001. Thanks also to James Mohr and Sarah Weddington for their fine readings of the entire manuscript, and Mark Tushnet, Sarah Igo, and Linda Kerber for specific information. Both authors assigned the manuscript to their legal history classes and benefited from the students' comments. In addition, Williamjames Hoffer, invariably our most severe critic, gave us the benefit of his training in both law and history. Sherree Dendy copyedited the preliminary draft of the manuscript and Carol A. Kennedy copyedited the final draft.

The library systems of Camden County, New Jersey, New York University, the University of Pennsylvania, Rutgers University, and the University of Georgia provided on-line aids as well as access to their shelves, for which we are grateful. Rayman Solomon, dean of the law school at Rutgers–Camden, and James Cobb, head of the department of history at the University of Geogia, arranged teaching schedules and facilitated research funding, without which aid this book would remain unfinished.

Michael Briggs, the editor-in-chief of the University Press of Kansas, has worked with us for almost a decade on the Landmark series, in addition to encouraging us in the present labor. It has been a model collaboration. Other series authors' acknowledgments have just about exhausted the vocabulary of praise for Mike. We are left with a simple, heartfelt, "thanks."

Introduction

Early one evening in February 1970, at Columbo's Pizzeria in Dallas, three women sat at a table and talked. One—small and slender, with a hint of Cherokee and Cajun ancestry in the set of face—was pregnant. Her name was Norma McCorvey. Twenty-three, poor, and by her own admission "not a gentle woman, or a sophisticated one," she had abused herself and been abused by her society. Divorced and without family she could rely on, she wanted the pregnancy terminated. Under Texas law the only legal reason for an abortion was to save the mother's life, and McCorvey could not find a doctor who would perform the operation. All they would do—could do under the law—was tell her who to contact to arrange an adoption.

Opposite McCorvey sat the other women, dressed, McCorvey recalled, in two-piece business suits. One, tall, dark-eyed, with a round attractive face and shag-cut brown hair, had arranged the meeting and listened attentively. The other, blond-haired, with an almost ivory complexion and a sympathetic manner, drew McCorvey out. In other cities and other times, the two might have been undercover policewomen whose jobs it was to find and arrest abortionists. Or they might have been agents for an abortionist, arranging the illicit abortions that were many women's alternative to attempting to perform an abortion on themselves. Or they might have been abortionists, as were women from time immemorial.

Abortion was still a crime, and Dallas's district attorney Henry Wade prosecuted abortionists. But the three women discussed McCorvey's desire openly, for the dark-haired woman was Linda Coffee and her blond companion was Sarah Weddington, both newly minted practicing attorneys and both looking for a plaintiff to bring a lawsuit that would challenge the Texas anti-abortion laws.

Perhaps it was not surprising that McCorvey found two lawyers to help her in the heart of Texas. The University of Texas Law School admitted women from its founding in 1883, and the first woman enrolled there in 1911. The law school remained among the top ten nationally in admission of women, and when Coffee and Weddington entered in 1965, there were twenty other women in the class. The state bar admitted its first woman lawyer in 1910, and by the middle 1960s, Dallas ranked sixth among major American cities in the number of women practicing law. Still, of Coffee's and Weddington's graduating class, all but they had decided to postpone practice until they married and had children, for in the 1960s mainstream culture pressured women to follow that course. Women comprised less than 2 percent of the total number of lawyers in the state and did not hold any partnerships in the major law firms.

Coffee and Weddington knew from their work with women's groups and their lobbying efforts in the Texas legislature that the "reform" abortion laws sweeping though the country simply expanded the list of doctor-approved exceptions to the anti-abortion rule. Only a handful of women gained the privilege of hospital abortions through these exceptions, and McCorvey would not have qualified for them. Coffee and Weddington wanted to abolish the laws and base abortion on a woman's choice, not a doctor's discretion. They knew the struggle would be long, hard, and impossible without a named plaintiff.

Thus, that blustery winter Texas morning, all three women had much to gain as well as to lose in their crusade against the abortion laws. McCorvey could not support a child and did not want to face the peril of a back-alley abortion. Coffee and Weddington knew that an expensive and wearying diversion into an uncertain crusade could cripple their careers. But if they won, women all over the country might take heart in their victory, and more important, the forty-two states that like Texas restricted abortion to the few cases where a woman's life or health was in peril would have to recalibrate their laws to allow women the right to choose when and if to have children.

McCorvey was enthusiastic but unsure what would be required of her. She did not want to appear in court. Coffee and Weddington were worried that McCorvey might not be the best plaintiff. They were still looking for a married couple who wanted the right to an abortion and a doctor who wanted an end to the restrictions on abortion to join in the suit. Yet Norma McCorvey would become the center of the litigation—for her case was the one that raised the central issue of a pregnant woman's right to have an abortion. To protect her reputation, the lawyers agreed that she would become anonymous: Jane Roe.

Roe v. Wade and its companion cases remain the most divisive and controversial judicial decisions of the twentieth century. As we write this introduction, nearly thirty years after *Roe,* states continue to legislate regulations for hospitals and clinics, doctors, and family counselors with the avowed purpose of discouraging abortion. Are these legal under *Roe?* Do these place an undue burden on women seeking abortions? Courts have issued a bewildering variety of answers. The raised voices of advocates and opponents of *Roe* in judges' chambers and legislative halls have spilled into the streets, causing state and federal lawmakers to debate and federal courts to adjudicate rules separating pro–abortion rights and anti-abortion demonstrators from one another. Police forces continue to search for the sniper who killed a doctor in his own home because the doctor, whose private life and professional conduct was otherwise unblemished, performed abortions. He was not the first doctor to die for that act, nor will he be the last. While most anti–abortion rights activists have called the murder of doctors immoral, more than a few have called the murderers heroes, arguing that they saved thousands of lives of unborn children by taking the life of the abortionist.

For the legal scholar and the historian, these passions must be banked if not entirely stilled. While we have our personal opinions, we should be above the clamor of the partisans. Yet we too face a kind of dissociative or fragmenting sensation in the face of *Roe,* for it brings together so many—almost too many—disparate fields of history and legal study. Roe implicates vital questions of gender, law, medicine, politics, and religion.

———

Roe was a watershed event in American women's history, coming at a time when feminism had developed but not yet established the legal basis for its reform program. Indeed, law had yet to catch up to the gains that women had made in the marketplace, academe, and the media. *Roe* added to economic and political aspirations a more intimate sense of the differences between women and men and the legal debilities inherent in those differences. But to see *Roe* as part of a separate women's history misses what is perhaps the most important point: it was the legal relationship between men and women that law mirrored and compounded that gives to *Roe* its complexity and drama. For *Roe*'s declaration that abortion was no longer a crime made the case into a symbol—for advocates of abortion rights a symbol of autonomy, of choice, and ultimately women's control of their reproductive lives; for women faced with the choice of an abortion, a source of soul searching and often of guilt, for no one knows more immediately than the pregnant woman that abortion ends a potential life; and for opponents of *Roe* a horror, not just for the violence it portended to a generation of "unborn," but for the disruption of the home, the family, and the duties that women owed—or should have owed—to fathers, husbands, and children.

In the late 1960s, advocates of women's legal right to abortions selected the word "choice" to promote their cause. The word became the centerpiece of a new paradigm of women's place in the law, in which women's rights grew out of women's experiences, and therein the differences between women and men, rather than being privileges granted by men to women. Feminists argued that access to a safe, legal abortion was all about choice, about women's right to determine what happened inside their own bodies. Choice went hand in hand with the concept of privacy, a legal right that was almost one hundred years old by the time it was featured in the *Roe* opinions, but one that had only recently been applied to women's reproductive experience.

When used to describe abortion rights, choice translated into "consent." Some feminists argued that in a nonconsenting pregnancy—for example in incest and rape—the fetus was an intruder in a woman's body, and she had a right of "self-defense" against it. Citing the extreme changes that pregnancy inflicts upon a woman, including a 400 percent increase in certain hormones and changes in heart rate and other organ functions, these feminist theorists asserted that pregnancy is akin to an invasion. Courts and Congress have regarded these "wrongful pregnancies" as exceptions to general rules limiting funding for abortions, but the extreme language of some advocates of abortion rights in these cases gave opponents of abortion evidence to argue that the pro-choice stance is inherently anti-children, anti-family, and anti–traditional women's roles, turning a dispute over a medical procedure into a much broader controversy over lifestyles and moral obligations.

In the long course of women' s rights agitation in America, *Roe* has a special place, but the case was just as much a part of the history of gender—of men's and women's relations to one another. As opponents of *Roe* correctly argue, women's reproductive choices do not concern women alone. Some men performed abortions or cooperated in them, while other men decried abortion as a danger to the future supply of soldiers and workers a nation needed, or worried about the loss of numbers among the "better sort," the "ruling race," or God's chosen people. Men who opposed abortion employed legislatures, pulpits, hospital board rooms, police forces, and the courts to condemn, uncover, and criminalize abortion, but other men, including doctors and lawyers, sympathized with the motives of women who sought abortions and joined in the effort to legalize abortion.

Indeed, women's history and the history of gender come together in our study. As a private act, concerning only the mother, her family, and her helpers, abortion belongs to women' s history. Insofar as abortion became a matter of public concern—a story of the evolution of legislation and law enforcement, of the changing professional status and standards of doctors, lawyers, clergymen, and political leaders—abortion, and *Roe,* require the analysis of gender.

Moreover, the private and the public stories of abortion that lead into and out of *Roe* do not have a linear or parallel relationship. Instead, the private act and the public enactment have a cyclical interrelatedness. Abortions increased in number when families found they could not afford additional children, in times of want and need. When more children meant greater chance for family success, abortion numbers waned. Public response to abortion followed this curve as well, as public officials, usually men, reacted to perceived threats from increases in numbers of abortions. Protests against abortion may well have reduced the number of abortions sought, but the burden that denial of safe abortions placed on some young women became denial of the pregnancy itself, with horrific consequences—unacceptably high rates of death in childbirth and tragic neonaticides.

No legal historian or constitutional scholar can doubt that *Roe* is now a centerpiece of our constitutional history, in particular the constitutionalization of the rights of women and the right of privacy. In addition, *Roe* raised questions of federal-state relations (federalism), the doctrines of due process and equal protection under the Fourteenth Amendment, and the very nature of "fundamental rights." In the hundreds of lower-court hearings and nearly two dozen Supreme Court cases on *Roe*, the courts have had to refine the notions of statutory interpretation, injunctive relief, and other basic concepts before the courts even got to the "merits" of challenges to states' restrictions on abortion practice.

Roe was also a milestone in the relationship between (most often male) doctors and their female patients and thus becomes an important part of the history of the medical profession in America. From condemning abortions in the nineteenth century, the elite medical practitioners came to champion therapeutic abortions in the early twentieth century and then (with a few exceptions) joined with women's advocacy groups to argue that the decision for first-trimester abortions belonged to the woman and her doctor.

Seen from doctors' perspective, as a part of the rising profession of medicine, *Roe* was one chapter in the story of the politicization of the doctors. From the beginning of the republic, abortion involved not only the relation of doctors to patients but doctors' views of their professionalism (for example, concept of medical ethics), the medical doctors' struggle against alternative medicine and folk practitioners, and doctors' status in the society as a whole. As abortion discourse over the years in general and the decision in *Roe* particularly was based on medical distinctions about viability, so doctors' stance on abortion brought them and their profession into the public eye.

In politics, the local, state, and national elections and legislative sessions since the early 1970s have featured harsh rhetoric and determined campaigning on both sides of the abortion rights issues. Apparently, *Roe* sits on a fault line, a fissure between right and left, traditional and modern, running through our national politics. Although not all Democrats favor choice and not all Republicans are right-to-life advocates, many leading Democratic candidates have reaffirmed their commitment to the pro-choice rulings in *Roe* and subsequent cases, while as early as 1976 leading Republican spokesmen called for a return of abortion law to the states, and some wish the states to again make abortion illegal.

Abortion partisanship has long captured the attention of the political media, and astute political observers regard candidates' positions on abortion rights as a "litmus test" of their prospects for success at the polls. Thus it was no surprise when conservative leaders like Paul Weyrich of the Free Congress Foundation and Phyllis Schlafly of the Eagle Forum asked prospective Republican presidential candidates, in a closed-door session on February 3, 1999, to answer the question "What commitments, relative to abortion, would you require from appointees to the Supreme Court?" If the interest of the electorate in the abortion controversy lags, the media reignites it. When on the anniversary of *Roe,* January 22, 2000, fifty T-shirt-clad anti-abortion demonstrators braved freezing weather to ask, "Mr. Clinton, stop killing children" at the gates of the White House, they were almost outnumbered by television crew members recording the event for posterity.

The politics of the cases takes the historian into the rhetoric of the parties in the abortion story. Even the selections of the most basic of terms—are we speaking of a "fetus" or an "unborn child"—are ringed with subtle political connotations. Weddington reminded the Supreme Court when she came before it that she was not advocating abortion, but a woman's right to terminate a pregnancy. Counsel for the state of Texas replied that the unborn had "rights" as well, which the state was obligated to protect. Faced with the myriad of gender, legal, religious, and political meanings of the these terms and the motives of all the parties, students of *Roe* must be especially sensitive to the nuances of political speech.

Roe also impels an inquiry into religious belief and practice in America. From the first, the question of abortion called forth religious and religiously originated moral judgments. While it may be true, as poet and scholar Adrienne Rich has warned, that "the absence of respect for women's lives is written into the heart of male theological doctrine, into the structure of the patriarchal family, and into the very language of patriarchal ethics," some men and women cleave with deep respect to the subordination of woman to man found in the Bible. The "right-to-life" credo of the Roman Catholic Church and the evangelical ministry is sincerely and consistently held and led opponents of abortion to stress the importance of protecting the unborn from what one Supreme Court justice called the "whim and caprice" of women. Because of the First Amendment ban on the establishment of a state religion, anti–abortion rights advocates had to efface these tenets from their arguments in court, but in the public debate, religion is central to much discussion of abortion.

Inspired by religious ideals, anti-abortion advocates responded to the "pro-choice" label by selecting their own key word: "life." The concept that the soul entered the fetus at conception was a relatively new one in Christian thought, dating no more than a century before *Roe,* but by expanding upon it, opponents of abortion in evangelical Protestant sects, the Roman Catholic Church, and other religious groups found a moving anodyne to the pro-choice rhetoric. The linking of life to traditional maternal roles further argued that abortion violated the most basic of women's duties to children.

———

As wide-ranging as we must be in our attempt to capture all of the story, there are subjects here not covered, and for good reason. We have not considered in detail the many ways in which women and men won for women the right to vote, to participate in organized labor, to go to college and graduate school, to enter the professions, and to hold high political office—the whole panoply of civil and economic rights that people of color had achieved in these same years. These surely set the stage for *Roe,* but rest upon other lines of narrative and are already well recounted. More important, perhaps, abortion rights are fundamentally different from civil rights and civil liberties for women, even though they involve legislatures and courts. The Nineteenth Amendment and the Civil Rights Act of 1964 brought women more fully and equally into a world that had been the preserve of men. Abortion law reform did not bring women more fully into the world of men—not in the same way at least. Abortion rights gave to women a legal right to be different.

That might sound incongruous, for the constitutional basis for abortion rights was due process and equal protection in the Fourteenth Amendment, the Ninth Amendment's "rights ... retained by the people," and other provisions that did not distinguish between men and women. Yet by its very nature, abortion distinguished between men and women, for men never did have abortions, nor bear children. Under an old regime of law and politics exclusively male, supported by a worldview that regarded women as the inferior sex and praised the ideal woman as wife and mother, men played a major role in the abortion story. Men made laws against abortion, enforced them, then argued against them and repealed them, dictating women's access to legal abortion. But when, and for so long as, women have a right to abortion, men play a diminished role in the tale. Thus the abortion story, despite the absence of gender in the constitutional language on which abortion rights rest, differs from the many other stories we can tell about women's rights in the twentieth century.

We have divided the book into six chapters, following the story chronologically. The first two chapters trace abortion law until *Griswold v. Connecticut* (1965), in which the U.S. Supreme Court found unconstitutional a state law forbidding the use of contraceptives and the dissemination of information on their use. The next two chapters lead up to and through *Roe*. The final two chapters focus on the politics of abortion after *Roe* and the two cases that were supposed to explain *Roe*, but in fact came close to reversing it, *Webster v. Reproductive Services* (1989) and *Casey v. Planned Parenthood* (1992). An epilogue traces the cases and congressional acts during the administration of President Bill Clinton.

Our conclusion asks whether the controversy over *Roe* can have a resolution. In all, we have tried to place *Roe* in the long curve of history rather than isolate it as a self-contained moment. Although it is a landmark case in itself, its continuing influence on American law and politics prove that landmark cases live long beyond their formal resolution in courts of law.

CHAPTER I

Abortion Becomes a Crime, 1800–1900

Why in the space of a single century from 1800 to 1900 did one of the most intimate and private acts, a woman's decision to abort a pregnancy, become the object of intense public scrutiny and calumny? How did conduct that had for millennia primarily involved women become in those same few years a major preoccupation of men? How did an event in which governments professed little interest become such a notorious offense against the state? These are the first quandaries the student of abortion law encounters in a subject whose history is filled with irony and contradiction. One cannot understand what *Roe v. Wade* meant to women or to men without understanding how abortion became illegal, and that story begins in the nineteenth century.

The laws that first made abortion a serious crime reflected profound changes in social and political relationships, in particular increasing complexity and tension in the associations between men and women; new sources of moral authority and new ways of expressing that authority; and a hitherto unprecedented degree of governmental intervention in private life. In an era of rising middle-class domesticity, growing professionalism of doctors and ministers, the popularization of science, and new kinds of state-imposed social controls on everyday life, abortion became a way of redrawing boundaries of deviance that extended into the confines of the bedroom and the doctor's office.

But the relevant history of abortion does not begin with its criminalization. Instead, one must understand that before abortion became a crime it was one of the many choices that women made on the reproductive continuum from conception to birth. These choices were rooted in local custom and domestic mores and monitored not by the state but by ordinary women and men in the course of their lives, by families and communities, and by religious institutions. Indeed, although attempted and completed abortions were often secret acts, neighbors and family often knew about or suspected an abortion, and the community shared folk wisdom on how to procure an abortion and harbored abortionists. Women who were the victims of incest or rape, women who feared the exposure of an illegitimate child, women who could not take care of the children they already had, women whose mental and physical health would have suffered from continuing a pregnancy, and women whose lives were at stake often turned to family and neighbors for aid. "Cunning men" and women, folk healers and herbalists, and doctors might be summoned. Midwives sometimes doubled as abortionists. Other women were so desperate that they took matters into their own hands, using a wire to puncture their own uterine walls or ingesting combinations of noxious herbs or poisonous chemicals to force their organs into violent contractions. Thus before abortion became the object of law it was a subject of everyday life.

When Abortion Was Legal

Definitions of abortion vary, but the common ground among them is that an abortion is the premature end of a pregnancy. Spontaneous abortions, often called miscarriages, occur naturally in over one-half of all pregnancies. Induced abortions, using herbal potions to induce a mother to expel the fetus, or mechanical means to remove the fetus, are as old as human society's records. In societies where exposure and other forms of infanticide were widely practiced, for example in ancient Egypt, Greece, and Rome, abortion was not a crime, but a common form of birth control. Upper classes practiced it to avoid unwanted childbearing. Lower classes used it to limit family size when one more child would so stretch family resources that existing family members were endangered.

According to the most recent study of abortifacients, Roman couples used the juice of the silphium plant, a giant fennel now extinct, to induce abortions. Apparently it worked (silphium contains ferula, which prevents pregnancies in test mice). Queen Anne's lace (wild carrot) was another ancient favorite, and is still used in folk remedies. The

Greeks preferred pennyroyal, which contains pulegone, a natural abortifacient. Greek doctors sometimes helped administer the drug. Egyptian texts mentioned acacia gum, recognized today as a spermicide. In these societies, abortion was part of a wide spectrum of intimate activities rather than a uniquely amoral exception to accepted norms.

Abortion in the ancient and early modern worlds also was tied to a cleansing of the reproductive system—so closely tied that supposed abortifacients were commonly used by folk healers to restart the menstrual cycle when it had stalled. Such menstrual stimulants/abortifacients appeared in most lists of early modern herbal folk remedies . In English botanist John Goodyear's 1655 translation of one of these herbal handbooks, there were nine herbs that supposedly ejected dead fetuses, forty-nine others that expelled the embryo, eighteen that killed the fetus, and six more that (somewhat redundantly) "caused abortion." Some of these potions were taken alone, others in combination. Many of the herbs assumed to produce abortion, for example savon, were also used to bring on menstruation and so to improve the chances of conception. The same nurse who watched over the pregnant woman and helped birth the infant, might, on another occasion, "gather rew [rue], savine [savon] and the flowre of camphora, and calamint, and dill" to concoct and administer an abortifacient.

Well into the nineteenth century, English and American home remedy and medical manuals listed common abortifacients as ways of restoring the normal menstrual cycle, not because the euphemistic phrasing was necessary to avoid legal prosecution, but because abortion was simply one of the many ways in which women dealt with gynecological and obstetric matters. All the authors denied that they were promoting abortion, and warned women against violent exercise, blows to the belly, or jumping off high places, and then turned around and enumerated the pharmacopeia of herbal abortifacients. Iron and quinine administrations along with a small portion of black hellebore would cause violent bowel spasms and expel fetuses; doses of calomel and aloes would induce diarrhea; juniper extract, a staple of the folk abortionists' herbal garden, and snakeroot were well-known Native American remedies for menstrual cramps—but like hellebore, iron and quinine, calomel, and aloe, juniper and snakeroot were equally effective in causing abortions.

Advertisements for juniper and snakeroot in nineteenth-century newspapers extolled their ability to relax the female organs, though the advertisement warned that "it has frequently been successfully employed for the (generally unjustifiable act) of procuring abortion." After indexing, in detail, all of the folk cures for unwanted pregnancies, one manual writer deplored "the horrid depravity of human weakness" that would lead a woman to employ such means to abort a fetus, but surely readers caught the obverse, subliminal message as well. (A correspondent reported to the authors a patent-medicine advertisement reading, "Absolutely must not be taken by pregnant ladies, as it is sure to cause an abortion." The warning's purpose, betrayed by the "sure to" phrase, could not be mistaken.)

Some methods for the restoration of fertility (or the inducing of abortion) were mechanical. One manual recommended electrical shocks to the uterine area to accompany a pint or so of a solution of pennyroyal, taken every night before bedtime, to promote menstrual flow. Alternatively, one might "boil five large heads of hemp in a pint of water" and take these before bed to restart the menstrual cycle. Another mechanical method of "unblocking menses" was the use of douches, spraying vinegar or strong brine into the vaginal cavity. All three of these procedures would also cause an abortion.

The so-called water cure, a fad popular in the nineteenth century, urged women to sponge the vaginal cavity with cold water, as well as indulge in frequent cold water baths, to remedy sluggish reproductive systems. The same method would, as it happened, prevent conceptions, at least according to early-nineteenth-century medicine. One must bear in mind that until the middle of the nineteenth century, basic processes of human reproduction were poorly or wrongly understood. The motility of sperm, for example, was a mid-nineteenth-century finding. Thus one should not be surprised to see such "heroic" or extreme herbal and mechanical programs prescribed for obstetric health—or to prevent pregnancy.

The dual nature of so many of these medical administrations suggests that the authors knew well that their readers did not always see abortion as unthinkable or detestable. It was merely one of the many possible outcomes of sexual activity. As the writers of the manuals hinted and readers undoubtedly understood, such steps were left to the discretion of women, in private. Their reproductive bodies were their own.

As were the reasons women had for seeking to terminate a pregnancy. Undoubtedly women whose families were already so large that additional children could not be easily fed or clothed and women who did not want another child availed themselves of abortion. In addition, unwed mothers, to hide the shame and avoid punishment for the bastardy, might attempt abortion. Colonial law prosecuted unwed mothers with fines, whipping, and public shaming. Abortion would avoid these penalties and protect the reputation of the woman. There was in addition a psychological component of abortion for such young people. From the court records in infanticide cases historians have found evidence that poor, unmarried female defendants regarded the fetus as a foreign body, to be purged from their wombs. Often, the records reveal, such women had already tried and failed to abort the fetus.

For the same reasons that women tried to keep illegitimacy private, they kept abortions secret. Nevertheless, cases in the colonial judicial records demonstrate that neighbors knew about the pregnancy and its termination. Sometimes the pregnant woman called upon family members and friends, or networks of older women and midwives, for help. On occasion, the family would hire a "cunning man" or folk healer. Still, recorded cases were rare, for the pregnant woman was unlikely to complain about a procedure that she sought and willingly endured; nor were midwives, the presumptive accomplices in such a procedure, likely to report their complicity. Most midwives knew perfectly well how to abet an abortion but did not report such cases, even in private. For example, Martha Ballard, a midwife in Hallowell, Maine, at the end of the eighteenth century and a dozen years into the nineteenth, recorded her presence at hundreds of births and sickbeds over the course of a thirty-year career, and never mentioned abortion, although there must have been some abortions rumored in the neighborhood. She was a skilled herbalist herself and often administered folk herbal remedies, such as tansy, a well-known abortifacient. She drily noted that she favored it for "worms."

When reports of abortion did appear, they were usually part of a pattern of serious accusations. For example, in 1668, New Haven authorities heard testimony from midwives that Ruth Briggs had not aborted her illegitimate child, but the child had been born alive and then killed. Briggs was executed for infanticide. When the pregnant woman did not want the abortion or the abortion was botched, a case would come to court. Colonial Maryland authorities probed one case of unwanted sexual intercourse leading to an abortion in 1663. Rumors reached the magistrates that a Portuguese doctor named Jacob or John Lombrozo had forced his attentions on his maidservant, Elizabeth Wild. Alternating promises of marriage with violent exhibitions of his amour, he impregnated her, but when she conceived, he administered an abortifacient. Neighbors reported her complaints against him, but by the time that the magistrates began to inquire, the doctor and the maid were married. She recanted her earlier accusations, but the gossip continued until Lombrozo sued his neighbors for slander.

Botched abortions also led to prosecutions. One such case, from the northeastern Connecticut village of Pomfret, in 1742, caused a considerable stir, for it involved a man already well known and mistrusted by the authorities. John Hallowell, a self-taught "practitioner of physick," used both an abortifacient and a "manual operation" to rid nineteen-year-old Sarah Grosvenor of her "conseption." Over the next month, Sarah struggled valiantly against a "malignant fever," then she died. Despite his ill-repute, Hallowell escaped prosecution for five years— the same secrecy that had concealed the pregnancy veiled his contribution to Sarah's death. At last rumor—the same unofficial source of accusation that had brought Dr. Lombrozo to heel—induced the Connecticut magistrates to pursue Hallowell. Convicted and sentenced to twenty-nine lashes, he fled to Rhode Island, followed by a trail of suspected crimes and escapes. Rumors that a woman had sought or gained an abortion, or that a woman or man had performed one—leading to suits and countersuits for slander—were far more common than prosecutions for abortion.

The Laws Against Abortion

When early modern English and colonial law took note of abortion, it was to protect the potential mother from the abortionist. She was the victim. Attempted or successful abortions that killed the mother were felonies. If an abortion killed a viable fetus, it was a serious misdemeanor. But how was the court to know that the violence done the woman was not either a common battery or an accident having nothing to do with the pregnancy, or that the administration of the abortifacient was not, on the one hand, an attempt to restart the menstrual cycle, or, on the other, an attempt to poison a woman who happened to be pregnant? In such cases, the pregnancy itself had to be proven before the prosecution could frame a charge around the attempted abortion.

But proving that there was a fetus in the uterus and that the fetus was alive (or "quick") was not easy. In the first place, a woman who procured an abortion, whether it succeeded or not, was not likely to testify to her complicity—it would reveal the very fact that she was trying to conceal. Abortion of a fetus in the earliest stages of pregnancy was the most easily concealed of crimes, for the victim (under the law the woman) conspired in her own victimization. Nor would the abortionist testify to his or her own crime. In the second place, the state of medical knowledge at the time made it difficult for the authorities to determine whether the pregnancy was terminated by the abortion or the injury to the woman caused by the actions of the alleged abortionist. The civil courts required proof of quickening, that is, that a live fetus existed.

The best evidence of quickening was the independent motion of the fetus in the womb. But this evidence was problematic for two reasons. First, the woman victim was the best and frequently the only source of this evidence—that is, of the precise time when such motion could be detected. Second, motion of this sort had religious implications that civil courts could not ignore.

Judeo-Christian teachings asserted that God implanted the soul when the infant was alive, and quickening was conventionally assumed to be the moment when such life began. In the Bible, a fine was levied on anyone performing an abortion, and an abortionist faced death if the woman died. Talmudic scholars decided that the harm had to befall the woman, not the fetus. The rabbis also concluded that there was no crime unless the fetus had quickened, but abortion was still permitted if the pregnancy endangered the mother's life. Some Jewish jurists went so far as to allow abortion if the pregnancy hurt the mother's reputation. Medieval European medical writings referred to the early fetus as a toad or a parasite, not as an unborn child, but the same writers saw abortion after quickening as a mortal sin, for from that time the fetus had a soul. Early Islamic medical writers like Avicenna discussed abortion in the context of birth control methods, but by the early modern period, the Roman Catholic Church frowned on contraception of all kinds.

Thus once again, the law conceded what local knowledge had long abetted: abortion of the fetus before quickening, on the assumption that the fetus was not "in life," that is, was alive but not human yet, was one of the many choices that women could make along that reproductive continuum. Comparing the law on abortion to that on infanticide illustrates how this early modern attitude toward abortion functioned. Neonaticide—the killing of a newborn—might in fact be a kind of delayed abortion (in which the mother denied the fact that she was pregnant and then through neglect or rejection of the infant allowed it to die), but the courts did not treat neonaticide with the same leniency as they did abortion precisely because the newborn was alive when it was killed or allowed to die. For example, a 1624 English law adopted in most of the colonies made concealment of the suspicious death of an infant "in life" presumptive evidence (that is, rebutable evidence) of murder, although the defendant who could prove she had delivered a stillborn child or the child had died from misadventure (accident) would escape conviction.

Even this harsh law was mitigated by juries' growing willingness to accept the defendant's testimony that the infant was not born alive and that the defendant had no intention of killing the infant. Almost all of the defendants in these infanticide cases were poor, unwed, young women—the very targets of the 1624 law, for such women had (in the eyes of the law) the strongest motives for wanting to hide the shame of their illegitimate pregnancies. But in the eighteenth century, all the defendant had to do was prove that she had made some provision for the child, for example by laying aside swaddling, to persuade a jury that the concealment of the corpse (and the pregnancy) was motivated not by the desire to hide a crime but by the desire to hide the shame of bearing an illegitimate baby.

It may well have been the declining rate of convictions in neonaticide cases that led to the first English act outlawing all attempted abortions, at whatever stage of the pregnancy. The 1803 statute was the work of the chancellor of England, Lord Ellenborough. Although he was a traditionalist and a moralist, abortion was not the focus of the bill. Instead, he proposed to codify the already dizzying list of capital crimes, including picking pockets and stealing clothing worth more than one shilling, and close loopholes in the criminal law. In one of the sections of the law, abortion or attempted abortion upon a pregnant woman became an offense whose punishment was transportation to a penal colony. The death from abortion of a quick fetus was manslaughter. The provisions on abortion in the bill were poorly drafted. There was no mention of mechanical methods of abortion and nothing was done—perhaps nothing could have been done, to be fair to the law—to provide a sure guide in court that the victim of the abortion would otherwise have borne a live child.

One suspects that the new provisions on abortion had as much a hortatory and admonitory purpose as a prosecutorial one. The law declared abortion a crime against the state. The crown prosecutors knew that they would never be able to bring many cases of the new crime to light, except in the most egregious and tragic fact pattern: an attempted abortion that led to the death of the woman. Then the law, as revised, shifted the burden to the defendant to prove that the woman had not been pregnant—evidence that few defendants could have provided. If the deceased had not thought she was pregnant, why would she have asked the defendant to assist in an abortion?

The English law making abortion after quickening a manslaughter did not immediately come to the United States. Quite the reverse was true. Here a reform movement led by luminaries such as Thomas Jefferson was busy codifying state laws to prune them of the brutality of the English criminal code. In many of the new state codes, punishment for petty larcenies, pilfering, and other crimes against property was reduced from the gallows to jail terms. But in the course of this general reform of the criminal laws on the books, state legislators encountered the same problem as had Lord Ellenborough—multiplicity, redundancy, and confusion. In the course of clarifying and liberalizing criminal laws, states recognized that statutes on battery, poisoning, and murder overlapped abortion. Some attempt to define the latter was thus necessary, if only to bar prosecution when there was no evidence of quickening.

The first reported abortion case—thus precedent—under this liberal American legal regime occurred in Massachusetts in 1812. The Supreme Judicial Court there dismissed a charge of attempted abortion against Isaiah Bangs because the prosecution could not prove that the woman was with child, in other words, that she had quickened. In one sense, then, the precedent was that the fetus was not a human being until quickening, a legal rule that conflated pre-1803 English precedent with established religious concepts of life, but in another sense the question was the vexing one that without proof of quickening—that is, motion of the fetus—one could not tell if the fetus was alive or had for some other reason died in the womb, or indeed, if the woman had been pregnant at all.

In 1821, Connecticut became the first state to explicitly criminalize abortion. The primary purpose of the law was to spell out the conditions under which the state could prosecute the abortionist for an abortion. The provisions appeared in the middle of an omnibus crime bill and penalized anyone giving poisons, "maliciously," to a woman quick with child, intending to cause the miscarriage of the pregnancy. The law did not apply to attempted abortions or successful abortions before quickening, nor did the law make the woman, despite her complicity in some cases, an accessory to the crime. In fact, prosecutions occurred only when a woman died or suffered grievous harm through the abortionist's recklessness or negligence.

From 1828 to 1829, Missouri, Illinois, and New York legislators adopted statutes similar to Connecticut's, but with one major difference: the first two states did not mention the quickening doctrine. Judging from the handful of prosecutions, the reason for this change in law was not to treat the newly conceived embryo as a victim of the abortion, but to protect women who were hurt by attempted abortions early in the pregnancy. The law warned abortionists that they practiced at their peril whatever the stage of the pregnancy. Women were still not made liable for the crime, and without their testimony the number of cases remained small and the conviction rate minuscule.

Thus one may surmise that the first round of state anti-abortion laws had the same purpose as the 1803 English law: to announce that the state would protect women against the misconduct of abortionists. The woman who attempted her own abortion was not the object of the law, nor was the protection (at least explicitly) of fetal life before quickening. Such hortatory laws were common features of early American criminal jurisprudence. Coupled with the fact that there were few documented instances of abortion and even fewer indictments for it, these first statutes seem to fit the hortatory model, colonial precursors of which included statues that penalized blasphemy and disrespect to parents.

The 1828 New York anti-abortion act had one unique clause legalizing abortion when "the same shall be necessary to preserve the life of such woman, or shall have been advised by two physicians to be necessary for such purpose." This "therapeutic exception" to the anti-abortion law was an elastic one, for doctors might (and in later years did) argue that mental health and future physical health could be considered acceptable reasons for abortions under the therapeutic exception. Again, the clamor of the medical community for such "doctors' acts" suggests that their purpose was to protect women from quacks and herbalists whose ministrations might endanger the women's lives. As such, it was a paternalistic piece of legislation in which men told women what was best for them. Women who sought abortions were not liable to any penalty. Doctors who performed an abortion had notice that they would be held accountable, as they would for any other professional misconduct.

This wave of abortion-control laws spread in the 1830s and 1840s to Indiana, Iowa, Mississippi, Arkansas, and Maine. Again, in all of these the state had to prove intent—that is, that the purpose of the administration of the drugs (or the use of the mechanical devices) was to cause an abortion. Without this element the charge failed, and without evidence that a fetus had been aborted, it was difficult to prove the requisite intent. In general, before quickening, attempts to procure the abortion were made misdemeanors. After quickening, that is, when the prosecution could present evidence that the pregnancy had entered its later stages, the abortion became a more serious offense. In effect, all of these statutes assumed that the fetus was a person only after quickening.

In part the reluctance of American lawmakers to broaden the definition of the offense or to include women as defendants in the early years of the nineteenth century may be laid to the fact that there were few abortions reported. This reasoning reflected a kind of circularity, for procuring or performing an abortion was no crime if no one was harmed (that is, attempted abortion was not criminal), and most abortions were performed before quickening. Even those after quickening were secretive events, in which the "victim," by law the woman, took an active role and was thus unlikely to complain. What is more, the manner of passage and the language of the first anti-abortion provisions in the states indicated that there was no great swell of popular opposition to abortion. The laws were generated by an internal process of refinement of the criminal law.

Early antebellum American legal authorities may have had another reason to look the other way in cases of abortion. In 1798, Thomas Malthus, an Anglican minister, published his *Essay on the Principle of Population*. It was a startling and disturbing piece of demographic theory, for he reckoned that while food supplies tended to increase arithmetically, population was rising geometrically. Epidemic diseases like smallpox that had controlled population rises were coming under control through public health measures. War, always a reliable reducer of populations, had grown tamer, or so it seemed in 1798, before the Napoleanic Wars. Malthus concluded that the masses were doomed to perpetual existence on the edge of famine. In later editions, Malthus suggested that only moral restraint (in other words, voluntary abstinence from sexual activity) could forestall the cycles of poverty that overpopulation caused. Nevertheless, his was a sobering warning to an English nation already concerned with agricultural rioting and urban unrest by large numbers of very poor people. Early-nineteenth-century demographers and moral reformers in England and France suggested that artificial contraception was the only answer to the Malthusian crisis, and contraception (birth control by artificial means) verged on abortion.

Malthus's work was read and quoted in the United States with approval, although his influence here was never as great as in Europe. Given that most abortions that came to the attention of American courts involved the same social class of people whose population growth had so concerned Malthus, it would not be surprising if abortion was, if not condoned, at least overlooked by early national lawmakers. When abortion among the middle and upper classes spread, or at least grew more visible, such indifference would change.

The Rise of Abortion and
the Changing Shape of the Family

The most striking shift in the history of nineteenth-century abortion was that by the 1840s, an event that was discussed only in whispers had become a subject of common conversation. Charles Knowlton, a western Massachusetts doctor and freethinker, made the case for the medical profession's intervention in unwanted pregnancies in social terms, a forerunner of medical opinion on birth control and abortion in America a century later. His *Fruits of Philosophy*, first published in 1832, when Knowlton was thirty-two, and revised by him until his death in 1850, had the prescient subtitle *The Private Companion of Young Married People* (anticipating the privacy right that became the basis for birth control in America). Influenced by Robert Dale Owen's pioneering *Moral Physiology, or a Brief and Plain Treatise on the Population Question* (1831), a Malthusian argument in favor of limitation of population to conserve diminishing natural resources, Knowlton argued that the health of the people depended upon the health of mothers. "How often is the health of the mother, giving birth every year to an infant . . . and compelled to toil on, even at those times when nature imperiously calls for some relief from daily drudgery—how often is the mother's comfort, health, nay even her life thus sacrificed?" In a nutshell, this was the argument for informed medical intervention to prevent danger to the mother through an unwanted pregnancy.

Knowlton was not writing to support abortion, but to ensure that pregnancy resulted in well cared for and healthy children as well as satisfied and happy parents. He reviewed common methods of birth control such as abstention, partial withdrawal during intercourse, complete withdrawal, and sponging or washing out (douching) the vagina with cold water or various solutions of alum, zinc, pearl ash, or household items like vinegar after sexual concourse, trying to be as matter-of-fact as he could. He offered prescriptions for fertility and renewal of the menstrual cycle should it become sluggish.

But there was still only a short distance on the reproductive continuum between herbal remedies used to stimulate the menstrual flow and those used to induce abortion in early pregnancy. For example, Knowlton's prescription to remedy "torpor of the genital organs"—open air, good food, removal of constricting dress, strict temperance in all things, and "some scales which fall from the blacksmith's anvil, or some steel filings . . . put into old cider or wine . . . standing for a week or so . . . taken two or three times a day" along with pills "of four parts of aloes, two parts of myrrh, and one of saffron, by weight"—certainly sounds like a common folk potion to induce abortion.

Knowlton was not an abortionist, nor did his books cause women to choose abortion, but the same romantic sentiment that pulsed in his writing was spreading through the land, and it powerfully changed women's and men's attitudes toward family, love, and gender. In this era, a wave of sentiment, sometimes associated with romanticism, swept through American middle-class culture. Affective marital relations, based upon choice, mutuality, and a rise in the status of women within the family, flowed on this tide of sentimentality. In books and short stories, poetry, newspaper editorials, plays, manuals for marriage and manner, women's natural virtues were stressed, instead of (as in previous centuries) women's natural lasciviousness. Unwanted pregnancies in this context could have no good end. As Henry Wright wrote of them in 1858, "no words can express the helplessness, the sense of personal desecration, the despair, which sinks into the heart of woman when forced to submit to maternity under adverse circumstances. . . . Her whole nature repels it." The abortion of such an unwanted child was a blessing to it as well as to the mother, for such a child "is conceived in weakness, is developed in joyless, lifeless imbecility, or intense anguish."

Wright was one of a number of male and female advocates of women's emotional and physical liberation who supported birth control (though few defended a woman's right to an abortion as openly as Wright). Other champions of "free love" among men and women might disavow abortion, but they did argue that women had the right to refuse as well as accept marriage and childbearing responsibilities. Male and female freethinkers produced and disseminated tracts on women's reproductive organs that further gave women control over childbearing. As Harmon Knox Root wrote in his *The People's Medical Lighthouse* (1858), "we want the liberty that allows each one alone to judge conscientiously for himself, in regard to matters pertaining to his affectionate nature." Lest readers think that only men had such affective motives, Root extolled "the affectionate mind of a young and passionate woman. There is within her very soul a love for the opposite sex as such, and in her physical organization an amative passion." For such a couple, birth control was not a sin but a way to ensure that natural sexuality did not incur unwanted complications.

The view that the new culture or sentiment took of children was just as novel as the depiction of love. Children, once regarded as miniature adults capable of sin, became innocent as little angels. Novel educational schemes like Bronson Alcott's Temple School and European systems like the "kindergarten" assumed that the development of children's moral faculties required love and gentle tutelage rather than corporal punishment and the threat of eternal damnation. Books and toys for children became major consumer items, children's clothing was redesigned for comfort and mobility, and entire communities began to invest in schemes of public education, so that all children might learn to read and write. (This was true for immigrant children, children in the cities, and children on the frontier, but not for slave children—in this respect, the South lagged behind the rest of the nation, although the wave of sentiment and the chivalric idealization of [white] womanhood did reach the South.)

But the growing fondness for children did not lead to larger families. In fact the reverse was true. As the investment in love and family funds in each child increased, and the mortality of children declined, parents opted for fewer children. At the start of the century, the average number of live births to a family was over seven. By the end of the century, it was under four. This drop in family size was not due to the influx of immigrants—they tended to have larger families at the start of their residence than native-born. Nor was the change in family size due to epidemic diseases, famine, or war. Middle-class married couples were consciously practicing strategies of family limitation.

Within the new ideal of a companionate family based on romantic love and affectionate childrearing, women and men decided together on the number of pregnancies and the ultimate size of the family. They used a wide variety of methods for preventing conception, including douching, sponging, male prophylactics such as the condom (particularly after rubber condoms replaced animal skin varieties), and the newest importation from France, the pessary (a primitive form of diaphragm). Voluntary birth control and voluntary abortion did not lie in opposition to one another, but were decisions to control family size made at different moments on the reproductive continuum.

Responding to and advocating the new autonomy that women exercised in reproduction, defenders of the liberation of women connected their spiritual fulfillment to control of the reproductive process. Elizabeth Cady Stanton, whose feminist activities included a wide range of causes, toured the lecture circuit to advance "enlightened motherhood" and "a gospel of few children and a healthy happy maternity." Another promoter of women knowing about and having control of their own bodies, Sarah Blakeslee Chase, openly urged the use of contraceptives. A homeopathic physician, she sold douche syringes in her office. Arrested five times for performing abortions, she was routinely acquitted by juries until one patient in her care died. After serving six years in prison for performing an abortion, she was released and went back to helping women prevent unwanted pregnancies.

Given this cultural climate, it should come as no surprise that abortionists began to compete for business openly. The introduction of rotary newspaper presses allowed publishers to reduce the cost of newspapers and increase their size. Newspaper publishers added more advertisements, including those for abortifacients and abortion practitioners, to fill their pages. The best known of these practitioners, Ann Lohman, an English immigrant to New York City who called herself Madame Restell, opened abortion referral agencies in a number of cities and an abortion clinic in New York City. Arrested repeatedly, she defied the prosecutors until conviction in the 1870s. Her rivals included a Dr. Carswell, who guaranteed in his advertisements to "remove the difficulty in a few days" and swore that "strict secrecy is observed." A Dr. Dow promised "good accommodations for ladies" in addition to refusing payment unless the procedure was successful. Private female clinics opened in a number of cities, and treated "all diseases peculiar to women." None admitted to performing abortions, but local prosecutors and sensationist newspaper reporters told a different story about some of them.

There also rose a brisk trade in over-the-counter and mail-order abortifacients, including pills, powders, and solutions for douching. A Dr. Peters offered "French renovating pills" by mail, direct from France (where new birth control methods were the rage) via a Boston accommodation address. These "charmed pills" were accompanied by certificates of success. Of course one must, Dr. Peters warned, always be on the lookout "for counterfeits." If one was wary of imported pills sold by strangers through the mails, local druggists also supplied the trade. One of the more imaginative homemade abortion devices was a suction pump whose inventor pledged "it can scarcely fail."

Although advertisers offered inexpensive abortifacients, women who could were willing to pay considerable sums for an able abortionist. Estimates of the costs vary, from under ten dollars to as high as one hundred dollars. These were significant amounts of money at the time. Nor was abortion confined to cities where Madame Restell and her counterparts lived. Observers reported that every town and village seemed to have its abortion practitioners, evidence convincing one historian that in the 1850s and 1860s the rate of abortion had risen to the range of one per every five or six live births.

The Doctors React

Even before the Connecticut statute was passed, doctors had played a role in abortion cases as witnesses or parties. Under the new laws, which made evidence of quickening crucial to prosecution, the doctors' role increased in importance. Their credibility as experts for the state was vital to conviction of the abortionist. Thus doctors' legal status and professionalism became tied to these cases. In the 1840s, a cadre of young and well-trained professional physicians in the northeastern states took the lead in campaigning against abortion. Most had either testified in court in abortion cases or written treatises on women's health. All had treated women who suffered from botched abortions, and some of the abortions ended in the deaths of the women. In speaking out they may have been motivated by fear of loss of patients to the swarming numbers of homeopaths and herbalists who provided abortions, but this is a cynical conclusion. The vast majority had the interests of their patients at heart, and the apparent explosion of abortion practice by nonlicensed doctors appalled these mainstream physicians.

As Hugh Hodge, a Pennsylvania doctor, reported in a widely reprinted 1869 lecture on obstetrics, "In 1854, I attempted to have the subject [of criminal abortion, that is, abortion induced by criminal means] presented to the legal profession, hoping through them to procure some more severe legislative enactments." He failed at the time, but did not surrender. "Since this period, nothing has been wanting on the part of the profession to illuminate the public mind on the nature of this crime." For, despite the first wave of laws criminalizing abortion after quickening, "the profession had in former times, from the imperfect state of their physiological knowledge . . . undervalued the importance of foetal life."

For Hodge, as well as for the other advocates of criminalization of abortion, the doctor's patient was the fetus as well as the mother. "He must regard the infant, as well as the mother, from the period of conception to delivery." Anticipating the terms of the dispute in later years—a substantial portion of the language of the mid-nineteenth-century attack on abortion reappeared in the mid-twentieth-century debates—Hodge used terms such as "unborn child" and "infant" to describe the fetus even in its earliest state. The mother was only a nest, and "similar to the chick in ovo, [the fetus] is, therefore, not only a living, but an independent being. . . . It has a spiritual existence . . . it is capable of thought . . . it knows and feels its spiritual existence."

Hodge may have reckoned that the success of the anti-abortion campaign would go far in establishing the professional status of the doctors, for he argued that only those purveyors of medicine who saw as he did regarding abortion could be considered professionals. "Under this representation of the subject, the elevated character and immense importance of obstetric science to the welfare of a community must at once be apparent." That is, unlike Knowlton, who clung to the somewhat romantic notion that the welfare of the community depended upon the health of its maternal nurturers, Hodge argued for a more modern, scientific, and (at least implicitly) misogynistic conception that the welfare of the community depended upon the authority of its experts—here the "obstetric scientists." Hodge conceded that women might be the repositories of republican virtue—the angel of the home—but only when they conformed to the highest standards of motherhood as defined by experts. Even the most refined women, who might, "in other respects," have a moral character without reproach, and "be devoted, with an ardent and undying affection, to the children who already constitute their family," were unfit to make a decision about abortion because they did not understand that the fetus was fully alive from the moment of conception. The degraded mothers of "the lower classes of society" also must bow to the authority of the professional doctors on this matter.

The doctors asserted that authority by detailing, from their own experience (the authority of eyewitness experience was among the strongest and most persuasive forms of authority in this era), the horrific nature of abortions gone wrong. The number of women who died from such abortions cannot be known, but doctors saw many such cases in their final stages. Horatio Storer, a Boston physician, published accounts of these tragedies in the late 1860s, and circulated his reports to medical associations all over the country. He spoke at their meetings as well. Storer and his allies won over the members of the American Medical Association, and they joined him in demanding stricter laws against abortion.

Revelatory accounts of "criminal abortion" popularized the doctors' crusade. Typical of these reports was Ely Van de Warker's. Van de Warker was a Syracuse, New York, practitioner, who not only recounted his own experiences with botched abortions but reported on laboratory experiments he performed with domestic animals. He gave doses of various abortifacients to dogs and recorded their progressive symptoms. There was nothing in his presentation that practitioners of abortion, including midwives, did not know, but by publicizing the damage that these methods incurred, he hoped to promote even more stringent legislation against them.

If correct—and all evidence suggests that his descriptions were based on firsthand evidence—the methods that some mothers used, or that were used on some mothers, were indeed horrific. To the list of violent emetics and purgatives Van de Warker added cotton root, supposedly used extensively by slaves to induce abortions. But the staples remained aloes, commonly found in all abortion pills, which left the users exhausted and feverish, rue, which caused vomiting, tansy, and savon. The theory of all of these was that by causing violent contractions of the gastrointestinal system, they would also cause the uterus to contract and expel the embryo. Van de Warker also recited the mechanical methods that women used to perform abortions on themselves, including inserting pieces of whalebone, iron wires, knitting needles, and stylets into the uterus to puncture or tear the amniotic pouch.

In a clinical prose that was both deeply moving and obviously sincere, Van de Warker recalled having to stand by the bedside of a patient and try to stop the hemorrhaging or prevent the spread of infection. But the tone of his lecture, typical of the genre, saw not the mother's anguish or the social forces acting on her, but her immorality in seeking the aid of abortionists. Thus, instead of concerning himself with the reasons why, in one case, "a young female, dreading her second labor, took three fresh roots of rue, boiled them in water, and dranke the potion," he railed that "the cool effrontery of young girls and women in speaking to strangers, non-professional, upon this most secret function of her sex is astounding."

As for the doctor who performed abortions out of misplaced compassion or for ill-gotten gain, the reformers' scorn was unmitigated. By the end of the century, about the worst charge one doctor could make against another was that of taking part in an abortion. When Brooklyn gynecologist and obstetric surgeon Mary Dixon Jones aroused the envy and enmity of other, male New York City doctors, they claimed that she performed abortions at her clinic. Although she was able to defend herself against criminal charges, she could not win a libel suit against the newspaper that printed the abortion claims, and her career was ruined.

The combination of moral superiority and medical concern in the elite doctors' campaign against abortion—a campaign joined by just about every elite practitioner who wrote on the subject—folded into a much wider campaign by public health officials and physicians against infant mortality of all kinds. By the late 1840s, using recently published statistical compilations, doctors and sanitary reform advocates had discovered an appalling infant mortality rate in the eastern seaboard cities. They ascribed the crisis to the incapacity of immigrant mothers to care for their children—what one observer in 1894 termed "the race traits and tendencies" of the newcomers—as well as to the poverty in which the immigrants lived. Thus it was moral fault as much as economic want that exposed these infants to disease, hunger, and cold. Public health officials demanded that sickly and fragile infants so endangered must be protected against their own parents—the same kind of argument that the elite medical profession deployed against the mother and father of an unborn child who sought the aid of an abortionist. One consequence of this reform effort was the establishment of public and private foundling hospitals and orphanages for abandoned infants. Ironically, though no surprise, the mortality rate in these institutions was as high as the mortality rate among families in the bowels of the urban ghettos.

The ties between the two campaigns demonstrate that the motives of the doctors were as humanitarian as they were self-serving, and that the assumption behind both was that experts—professionally trained doctors and public health officials—knew what was best for the unborn and the newly born. Wise parents who cared for their future offspring would do best to defer to such experts. So would the lawmakers.

The Second-Stage Legal Attack on Abortion

From the late 1840s to the end of the century, Storer, Hodge, Van de Warker, and others in the anti-abortion medical cadre sought and found potent political allies in the church and the state. After the Civil War, anti-abortion ministers made "this horrid crime" the object of scathing sermons, some viewing abortion to be "a greater evil, more demoralizing, and destructive, than either intemperance, slavery, or [civil] war itself." Other ministers warned against the husband and wife who fell into the sin of abortion "thoughtlessly." They must be made to see that abortion was "MURDER." Episcopal Bishop Arthur Coxe, in 1869, saw abortion as a "sacrifice to Moloch" that would deny the kingdom of heaven to any who practiced it. In the same year, the General Assembly of the Presbyterian Church made abortion the subject of universal condemnation—those who counseled it or performed it were committing a "crime against God and against nature."

The Roman Catholic bishops of Boston and Baltimore agreed that the crime of abortion was on the rise. The church, at first adhering to the doctrine of quickening, had not openly condemned early abortion. By 1869, following a papal encyclical attacking all birth control, leading Catholic spokesmen condemned abortion at any time in a pregnancy. By the end of the century, the Catholic hierarchy had concluded that even therapeutic abortions were a sin. In Catholic hospitals, doctors were instructed that abortions were not to be performed even to save a mother's life, for killing the fetus would destroy a soul in being. It was better, one cleric wrote, that a thousand women might die than one innocent soul be lost. As a second Catholic spokesman warned, "Birth restriction [by artificial means] will never meet the approval of the Catholic church."

The doctors and the clergy turned to state and federal lawmakers, and more anti-abortion statutes appeared in the period from 1840 to the 1880s. At first, despite the perceived increase in abortions, state legislatures retained the idea that an attempted abortion upon a woman whose fetus had not quickened was no crime. The key cases upholding that view came from Massachusetts, where in 1845 Chief Justice Lemuel Shaw, perhaps the leading legal thinker of his day, dismissed a case against abortionist Luceba Parker. There was no evidence that the fetus had quickened, hence no way to tell that an abortion was intended. In a second case, the woman, Maria Aldrich, died from a botched abortion by a Boston doctor. The pregnancy was advanced when the doctor operated, but the victim was unmarried and determined not to have the child. Without evidence of intent, the jury could only acquit under the law as it stood. The outcry led to a revised state law that for the first time in the United States made attempted abortion, at any time in the pregnancy, punishable by one to seven years in jail and fines. But juries still resisted the idea that one could indict for a crime when the victim—the woman (not the fetus)—wanted the procedure. Over the next decade there were thirty-two trials in Massachusetts under the new law and no convictions.

New York also revised its anti-abortion laws in 1845, for the first time making the death of the fetus (as opposed to the death of the woman) a criminal offense. Attempted abortion at any time in the pregnancy, as in Massachusetts, was a crime. New York added a second novelty to its laws. Women who sought an abortion or attempted to perform one on themselves were subject to a fine of up to one thousand dollars. This portion of the act, almost unenforceable on its face (for the best evidence was the testimony of the mother), was in fact never imposed. It must be regarded as another of the admonitory type of criminal law.

One historian has argued that the law also reflected concern about who was committing or seeking abortions. Desperate, poor, unwed, immigrant women would not be deterred from seeking or performing abortions by the new provision in anti-abortion laws. They would not likely know of it. Instead, it was the middle-class, educated woman whom the legislators feared would abort an unwanted child. These were not the women who took a wire hanger or piece of whalebone to themselves, but women who patronized the pharmacies, read the advertisements in the newspapers, and obtained the aid of physicians.

In the following years, the example of Massachusetts and New York (the two states were regarded as leaders in many areas of law) influenced other states to add statutes against abortion to their codes or to revise their earlier laws. In 1846, Michigan and Vermont adopted the New York law but retained a therapeutic exception clause and refused to indict mothers. Two years later, Virginia, followed by California, New Hampshire, New Jersey, and Wisconsin, passed laws against abortion. New Jersey, California, and Wisconsin refused to punish abortion attempts before quickening, Virginia penalized attempted abortions at any time in the pregnancy, but New Hampshire made women liable to criminal penalties, like New York. In the 1850s, territorial legislatures in Minnesota, Oregon, and Kansas passed anti-abortion acts, but intent, hence quickening, had to be proved. In a series of anti-abortion laws, Texas made any attempted abortion a felony. If the woman died as a result, the charge was changed to murder, even if the woman consented to the procedure.

In the same decade, states like Alabama, Connecticut, and Maine revised their abortion laws, but these altered statutes still strove to protect the pregnant woman against the abortionist (that is, made her the victim) rather than prosecuting her for seeking the abortion. Indiana and Iowa added laws in the 1850s that were clearly directed against the advertisers and producers of abortifacients—in the paternalistic rather than the misogynistic tradition. Other states, for example Wisconsin in 1858, followed New York's course.

By the next decade, the doctors' campaign against all attempts at abortion bore fruit in almost all state legislatures. In 1860, Connecticut and Pennsylvania lawmakers made women who sought abortions or performed them upon themselves guilty of a felony, although the Connecticut Supreme Court still viewed the law as a paternalistic measure that limited "the power of a woman to injure her own person." There was also a fine for advertising or otherwise disseminating information on abortion. Pennsylvania criminalized all attempted and completed abortions, but the law was rarely enforced, causing the state's mainstream doctors to complain, with the support of Storer and the American Medical Association, that the state was doing too little to protect women from themselves. After the Civil War, northern states like Illinois and Ohio banned the sale or advertisement of abortifacients. Married women who took such drugs, except under the advice of a physician (presumably to restore fertility rather than end a pregnancy), were to go to jail for at least three months. It may be that behind the new regulations was the fear that northern states needed to replace the men lost in the war—at least that is what the inclusion, for the first time, of the modifier "married" before women suggested. The purpose of marriage, the statutes implied, was to produce children. Using drugs to obstruct that outcome was what concerned the lawmakers.

Throughout the 1860s and 1870s, in state after state and territory after territory, sometimes with doctors packing the galleries and shouting encouragement, legislatures made all attempts at abortion, all practitioners and accessories to abortion, and all providers or advertisers of abortion paraphernalia liable to criminal penalties. The old distinction between before and after quickening vanished from the law books, and the protection of the fetus, rather than the woman, became a theme in many of the new laws. In the 1880s and 1890s, penalties for aiding an abortion at any stage, including providing abortion counseling, grew stiffer. The rate of convictions grew apace. An offense rarely prosecuted and even more rarely leading to a guilty verdict before 1850 became commonly prosecuted and was often followed with a conviction after 1870.

In aid of the goal of conviction, judges loosened the rules for admissibility of evidence in abortion cases. Before the new set of laws, judges had refused to let juries weigh purely inferential evidence (for example, that a defendant could have performed an abortion). In the 1870s, judges opined that not only could speculative evidence be admitted, it could in and of itself determine the outcome of the case. The absence of eyewitness testimony and confessions (remember that attempted abortions were offenses in which defendant and victim conspired to evade the law) had been a barrier to conviction before the passage of the new laws in the 1860s, as had defendants' arguments that the woman had not been pregnant at all, or that the operation was necessary to save the woman's life in a pregnancy gone wrong. After 1870 it became the burden of the defendant to prove that the pregnancy had gone wrong and abortion was a medical necessity.

The inversion of the common formula that the defendant was innocent until proven guilty reflected judges' desire to drive abortionists from the land. Indeed, courts allowed police and prosecutors to carry on searches and seizure of evidence without warrants in order to catch and convict suspected abortionists. Massachusetts, whose courts had in 1845 explicitly dismissed a case when the prosecution could not prove that the woman had been pregnant, ruled in 1882 that the prosecution did not have to establish that the woman was pregnant. The attempt (and with it the parties' assumption of pregnancy) was sufficient.

Not only did the anti-abortion forces find allies in the state legislatures; the Forty-second Congress also aided their cause. In March 1873, Congress passed an amendment to the 1872 federal obscenity law, for the first time prohibiting the importation into the United States or dissemination in Washington, D.C., or United States territories (a good portion of the trans-Mississippi West) of "any card, circular, book, pamphlet, advertisement, or notice of any kind stating when, where, how, or of whom, or by what means, any of the articles in this section

... whether for the prevention of conception or for causing unlawful abortion ... can be purchased or obtained, or shall manufacture, draw, or print or in any wise make any of such articles." A final section prohibited the sending of any such materials through the United States mails. Punishment could include one to ten years at hard labor in a federal prison and or a fine of one hundred to five thousand dollars. In the following years, federal courts ruled that even those who did not actually mail the offending literature or drugs were guilty under the statute if they began the process, and that mere slips of paper (thus, presumably, personal letters) fit the description of proscribed mailings.

The 1873 Act for the Suppression of Trade in, and Circulation of Obscene Literature and Articles for Immoral Use was in its time and remains to this day the nation's most sweeping intrusion of government into private conduct, excepting the requirement of compulsory public school education for young children. Like the latter statutes, the act was supposed to improve the morals and protect the spiritual strength of the nation, but unlike the public school laws, turning birth control information into pornography was sex-specific. The intended audience for birth control literature was predominantly female.

The federal act spawned a legion of state imitators. Within a little more than a decade after its passage, over twenty-four states passed their own obscenity laws banning the dissemination of birth control information. Connecticut barred the use of all contraceptives, even in the privacy of a married couple's bedroom, along with all private discussion of birth control (even between a doctor and a patient). New York's law made it a criminal offense to possess instructions for birth control or abortion. Fourteen states, including New Jersey and New York, went beyond the federal law to criminalize private communications and conversations among individuals about contraceptive methods. These repressive statutes gave state authorities a power to enter and search as well as to prosecute that verged on the "black codes" that southern states passed after the Civil War to deny newly freed men and women full rights under the law.

A few of the states excepted doctors and druggists from this ban on possessing birth control information, but most imposed it on all their citizens. In seventeen states and the District of Columbia, no doctor might advise on birth control even in the course of treatment of a patient. In effect, birth control and abortion became taboo subjects, mentioned in whispers behind closed doors. Against First Amendment challenges to the new laws ("Congress shall make no law . . . abridging the freedom of speech," a precept that in later years was applied to the states through the Due Process Clause of the Fourteenth Amendment) in federal courts and similar claims to free speech under state constitutions, federal and state courts deferred to the legislative branches.

The man behind the federal law was Anthony Comstock, not himself a member of Congress but one of the many middle-class morals reformers of the age. Born in 1844 in Connecticut, he became the epitome of the Victorian moralist, vigorously transforming religious ideals into statutes. A devout Protestant, he opposed all kinds of pornography, including all forms of literature that included sex scenes, as well as birth control and abortion information.

After service in the Union army during the Civil War, he became a dry goods salesman in New York City, where he daily witnessed street scenes of immorality for which his strict New England upbringing had not prepared him. Married to an older woman, fastidious in habits and dress, he appointed himself the guardian of his neighbors' morals. With financial backing from Morris K. Jesup, a well-to-do New York City banker, founder of the Young Men's Christian Association and charitable donor to museums and conservationist projects, Comstock promoted his ideas widely. Both men, restless with ordinary pursuits, campaigned against the vices of the city that corrupt politicians supposedly had allowed to flourish.

Comstock parlayed the battle against vice and pornography in the city into national prominence, made friends among New England legislators who shared his views, and influenced the passage of the first obscenity law under which he served as an enforcement officer. New York City was a center of risqué publications, and Comstock did not want for targets. When some members of Congress wavered during debates on the 1873 law, Comstock convinced them that birth control and abortion information was pornography and must be banned from newspapers and advertisements sent through the mails. Comstock's influence prevented an amendment to the text that would have excepted doctors' communications on birth control from the blanket ban.

Comstock was also partly responsible for the severity of the New York State version of the anti–birth control information laws. He must have taken pride in the evidence that his campaign, along with the new state laws and the altered attitudes of judges in abortion cases, had reduced the number of abortions among the better classes.

Comstock, named a special agent of the U.S. Post Office under the revised federal statute, used undercover agents (often acting as one himself) to ferret out birth control providers. He received a fee for each arrest. In 1874, fourteen of the twenty offenders he arrested were tried and convicted. In 1875, seven of the seven he trapped, all sending medical information through the mails, went to jail. Doctors and freethinkers protested to the courts and legislatures in vain. Soon the act was known as the Comstock Law and the campaign itself was called, by its opponents, "Comstockery."

Anti-Abortion, Racism, and Sexism

The moral paternalism of the doctors was sincere and benign, but behind it lurked a far deeper and more virulent condemnation of women's reproductive autonomy. Such radical contumely of conventions of marriage as Chase and others offered deeply worried men like Dr. Henry Gibbons. In an 1873 lecture he foretold that such ideas "have given birth to a number of anomalies, if not monstrosities, religious, intellectual, and moral." Men like Wright and Root and women like Chase had "crazed" their audiences, and hatched "the serpent that tempts the woman to put to death her unborn offspring."

Why were men like Gibbons so concerned about a radical fringe argument? The answer lies not in the experience of the medical profession per se, but in attitudes toward culture and nurture of the next generation that anti-abortion doctors shared with many other men and women. During the carnage of the Civil War that attitude gained poignant and powerful expression. For some of these observers, the sacrifice of those whom Abraham Lincoln called the "consecrated" dead raised the specter of a nation weakened by the loss of its best men. The lament might be couched in religious terms—the words of Julia Ward Howe: "as He died to make men holy/Let us die to make men free"—

or in the conventions of Romantic sentimentality. As Union nurse Hannah Ropes wrote of one dying soldier: "I was glad he was unconscious [in his final moments], for he had a wife and two pretty children. Their likeness lay under the pillow where his head rested, with the death damp drifting like tears unto the [photograph] so precious to him." Ropes knew but did not add that there would be no more pretty children from him. Howe, equally mindful of the losses, went on to promote a new holiday: "Mother's Day."

In their lament for the departed war heroes' vacant armchairs and the empty cradles that resulted, elite writers added to the sentimental rhetoric of the age a new theme, a science of race and breeding that made anti-abortion into a national crusade. Abortion among the best men and women would destroy the ruling race. The logic of the new science of race was simple. As Boston aristocrat Henry Cabot Lodge put it, "The men of each race possess an indestructible stock of ideas, traditions, sentiments, modes of thought, an unconscious inheritance from their ancestors, upon which argument has no effect." The seeds or germs of superior cultures passed through the blood from generation to generation. Scholars at leading universities agreed: in Anglo-Saxon or Teutonic "blood" lay the origins of freedom, democracy, and progress. At best, other races could learn how to adopt these institutions from the master races; at worst, hordes of inferior peoples would overwhelm their superiors and destroy civilization.

The African American and the Native American were the most worrisome of the master race's competitors. As Illinois Democratic senator Stephen Douglas avowed, shortly before the Civil War, "I am opposed to negro equality. I repeat that this nation is a white people— a people composed of European descendants—a people that have established this government for themselves and their posterity, and I am in favor of preserving not only the purity of the blood, but the purity of the government from any mixture or amalgamation with inferior races." By the latter phrase, Douglas meant the birth of children of mixed ancestries. During the antebellum period, as long as the labor of slaves grew in value, southern planters encouraged slave women to have many children. Despite all obstacles, African-American population grew swiftly. After the Civil War ended slavery, white southern intellectuals rethought their views of the growing population of their black neighbors. One of the most fearsome of the catalogue of freedmen's and women's vices was sexual excess, the supposed "habit of the majority of the colored population." A misreading of the raw census data for 1870 and 1880 convinced observers that African-American population was increasing at a rate much higher than that of European Americans (the actual figures showed the reverse).

As European Americans swept west, pushing aside native peoples, racism called itself "Manifest Destiny" and seemed to favor the master race automatically. The Native Americans had no acquired immunities to European diseases, and their population declined steeply, effectively removing them as competitors for land and natural resources. But by the 1880s, with Native American population recovering slowly from the devastation of contact with European diseases, the race theorists were again on their guard. For example, young Theodore Roosevelt, a student of these racial theories, insisted that the Indians had to make way for the Europeans, for the "spread of the English-Speaking peoples over the world's waste spaces [that is, the places where Indians, Asians, and Africans lived were wasted] had been not only the most striking feature in the world's history, but also the event of all others most far reaching in it effects and its importance."

Safety for the master race and its culture lay, in part, in numbers. As John Fiske, a young scholar who tied expansion to the Anglo-Saxon racial ideology, told audiences in 1880, America could contain 700 million Anglo-Saxons, if the parents of the master race produced sufficient children. The Reverend Josiah Strong's *Our Country: Its Possible Future and Its Present Crisis* (1885) sold over 175,000 copies, and its message explicitly tied racism to breeding. Strong opposed immigrants because they diluted the blood lines of the master race and believed that the future strength of Anglo-Saxon peoples lay in its power to multiply its numbers faster than any other race. Storer was blunt: "upon the loins . . . of our own women . . . depends the future destiny of the nation." Else the country would be flooded with "children . . . of aliens."

But simple numbers were not the only salvation for the master race. As Roswell H. Johnson, a professorial observer, commented in the course of castigating college women for having too few babies, "my argument is seriously misunderstood when it is described as seeing only numbers. Its whole weight is placed on the difference in quality among children and the serious racial consequences of a low birthrate in the superior class." Roosevelt agreed; men and women from the "strong races" who did not have children were "criminal[s] against the race . . . the greatest thing for any woman is to be a good wife and mother."

Women's Frailty, the New Feminism, and Abortion

The confluence of reproductive ideologies at the end of the nineteenth century assumed the inherent weakness of all women. They had to be protected from that weakness, lest it destroy them and the next generation. Doctors, lawmakers, and racial theorists writing in the last decades of the nineteenth century agreed that women were "lesser men," whose emotional and mental "faculties" could not stand the demands of modern public life. Pseudo-scientific accounts of the origin and progress of differences between the sexes purported to prove that women's brain capacities were invariably inferior to men's. Thus women could never engage in purely intellectual activities, the higher orders of the species' mental functions. This was supposedly truer as one climbed the ladder of civilization, so that educated women were even farther behind educated men in western societies than women were behind men in more primitive cultures.

Moreover, these observers of the second sex opined that women's "periodic ordeal" (the menstrual cycle) further diverted blood from the brain, making women even more inferior to men during a large portion of their adulthood. Following these findings, women were supposed to finish their education before their full sexual development, and before education diminished their capacity to perform as mothers (the logical consequence of the danger that higher education and lifelong intellectual employment posed to their health). Storer argued that women should not practice medicine because the menstrual cycle in adult women "unfits them for any responsible effort of mind. . . . Women's mind is prone to depression, and, indeed to temporary actual derangement, under the stimulus of uterine excitation . . . at the monthly period." The result, as one feminist critique of this reductionist pseudo-science reported in 1899, was to be a contraction of women's lives, "in place of the active laboring woman, upholding society by her toil, has come the effete wife, concubine or prostitute, clad in fine raiment, the work of other's fingers, fed on luxurious viands, the result of other's toil, waited on and tended by the labor of others." In short, the ideal woman was a queen bee, breeding the next generation.

Women who disregarded these sex-specific prescriptions would slip into uncontrolled promiscuity, or so theorized opponents of abortion. Thus doctors saw women's writing about romantic love and free expression of passions as dangerous and prescribed extreme cleanliness and godliness in sexual activity for women. Typical was the physicians' response to stays, corsets, and other forms of fashionable harnesses— not because they were restrictive, but because they would make it more difficult for women to conceive children. Like other forms of sexual expression, the wearing of corsets for mere sexual display offended the doctors' sense of women's purpose and place in society. The corset might "excite amative desires" one doctor wrote, but it also "keeps the blood from returning freely to the heart." Thus the already frail and easily misled emotions of women would be turned from dutiful wife and mother to seductress.

The more women explored their own feelings, the more uneasy some men became. This was particularly true when women wrote about cross-dressing (dressing as men), about romantic attachments with other women, and about free love. Attachments among young women at schools, passionate even if sexless, were more common, and grown women in what were called "Boston marriages" owned property jointly and traveled together, conduct at cross-purposes with what men regarded as appropriate for women. Although these expressions were confined to a small group of literary women and freethinkers, their implications were immediately suspect. Laws punished cross-dressing under the rubric of disorderly conduct.

A more direct attempt to control women's sexuality lay in the campaign to regulate prostitution in the late nineteenth century. Like abortion, prostitution was a very old institution, often condemned but widely tolerated and practiced. Prostitutes often lived and worked in brothels, but many were self-employed and went about in public soliciting business. In the last years of the nineteenth century and the opening decades of the twentieth century, men discovered in the conduct of prostitutes the same immoral themes that they suspected in respectable women's newfound autonomy in matters of sexuality and reproduction. Reformers condemned the prostitutes' open display of sexuality, their gaudy dress and apparent independent way of life.

The arguments that male reformers in the period used against prostitution derived from those deployed against birth control and abortion. Prostitutes gave diseases to men, thence to wives, limiting their ability to have children. The children they produced would be deformed, an example of physical damage following moral decay. Reformers recognized that they could not abolish prostitution, but demanded the segregation of prostitutes from the general population and the periodic inspection of brothels for violations of sanitary codes. Only then would the fathers, and then the mothers, of the race be protected.

Speculation on the threat that birth control and abortion may have posed to men's sexuality to one side, it was undoubtedly true that the crest of the anti-abortion wave came at a time when feminism was making itself a regular and forceful part of American culture, society, and economic life. By the end of the century, the efforts of the first generation of women reformers such as Susan B. Anthony, Lucretia Mott, and Elizabeth Cady Stanton had greatly expanded the sphere of acceptable women's activities, but one vignette, recalled by Stanton, suggests the depths of men's unease. She was interrupted during one of her many speaking engagements in favor of women's right to vote by a man who demanded to know why women did not find producing large families to be the most fulfilling female activity. Why, he himself had eight sons by his wife. Stanton acidly replied that she never met a man worth eight replicas.

Despite both offhanded dismissal and systematic derogation by some men, women's clubs and associations grew in membership, organization, and power from 1860 to 1900. A national association of these clubs met annually to further women's interests. Women attended colleges and universities, and coeducational schools' female enrollments mushroomed. By 1900, the University of Chicago was 50 percent female. A few women entered the medical and legal professions, and many more joined the ranks of teachers, librarians, secretaries, nurses, and social workers. Some gave public lectures or taught at evening schools, when not so long before an unescorted woman in public in the evening hours had raised respectable people's eyebrows.

Through their involvement in reform movements, women participated in public life. Frances Willard, for example, led the Women's Christian Temperance Union, and its demands for curbs on or prohibition of the sale of alcoholic spirits made its leaders admired (and feared) public figures. Women took an important if not a leading role in the organized labor movement. The Women's Trade Union League, founded in 1903, reflected the upper end of the women's labor movement, but its member organizations were not afraid to strike for women's pay, safety, and other issues of importance to all women who worked outside the home. Women's campaigns for the right to vote, begun before the Civil War, had yet to bear fruit (except in a few far-western states), but women held marches, rallies, and fund drives in support of women's suffrage that would have been unthinkable a few years earlier and that made many men uneasy about women's place in the home as well as in politics.

At the same time, as Willard put it, these reform efforts depended upon the image of women as more refined and civilized than men. Many women's participation in the movement in fact derived from domestic concerns, such as limitation of husbands' consumption of alcoholic beverages. This echo of earlier nineteenth-century notions that women were the true repositories of virtue went hand in hand with the claim that virtue began in the home, and women's reform efforts thus became, as Willard wrote, "the home going forth into the world."

As Willard knew, despite their changing place in the public eye, women's claims to importance still rested upon the superior virtue of maternal roles—the projection of a "domestic feminism" onto the larger screen of public life. In fact, much turn-of-the-century feminist activity stressed improvement of sanitation, nutrition, and child care in the home. Some of these feminists argued that the "homemaker" should be treated as a professional and equated female labor in the home with male labor in the marketplace. (Note that at this time the majority of women, particularly women of color and women in the cities, actually worked at least part of their day outside their own homes. Thus the elevation of the homemaker was a middle-class movement, even though the literature on cleanliness, food preparation, and child care was directed toward the lower classes. The paternal and condescending concern that elite men showed for elite women repeated itself in the patronizing attitudes of elite women for lower-class women.)

The very logic of "domestic feminism" led to celebration of motherhood and childrearing. The tenets of domestic feminism might be stretched to accommodate family limitation in the name of curbing sexual indulgence and better care of children already born, but domestic feminism and its ideological successors had no place for abortion. Indeed, feminists had to protect their other goals by denouncing abortion. In the nineteenth century, "female physician" was often used as a euphemism for an abortionist, but Elizabeth Blackwell, one of the first and most influential women among the mainstream medical profession, loudly denounced abortions and refused to perform them, although as a female doctor she was often approached by women who wished abortions. Instead, she wrote, women had to favor "restraint" over "indulgence." Mary Grove Nichols, whose defense of women's sexual rights included "the right [of a woman] to herself . . . the right to decide . . . who shall be the father of her children . . . whether she will have children and to choose the time for having them," still warned against dangerous abortion techniques. They might be a woman's right, "exclusively her own affair," but they were "wicked." Marriage rates among these women fell by four percentage points in the last years of the nineteenth century, and divorce rates among the middle class grew, proof that the virtuous middle-class woman controlled her "vital force" by refusing to engage in sexual relations rather than terminating unwanted pregnancies by abortion. Some, like the urban reformer Jane Addams, chose spinsterhood over marriage

Addams, from her vantage point as the head of Hull House, a refuge for the needy in turn-of-the-century Chicago, knew all about abortion, particularly among immigrant women who already had a large family. From the records of hospitals that saw the end results of these abortions—women bleeding to death or dying from infections—scholars estimate that there may have been as many as two million abortions in the United States yearly at the end of the 1800s. Among working-class people in New York City early in the twentieth century, health care professionals found that one out of every twenty pregnancies was terminated by an abortion or by the death of the mother from an attempted abortion. In Chicago alone, one doctor, whose practice included women who were the victims of their own attempted abortions, estimated six to ten thousand abortions in 1904.

These women turned to immigrant midwives and a few sympathetic doctors to perform abortions in homes and offices, as Addams certainly knew, but she did not publicize her knowledge. Instead, Addams helped finance a study of midwifery and nursing practices in the city to determine the causes of the high infant death rate, part of a campaign against midwives (in favor of regular doctors) to reduce the number of backstairs abortions. By the eve of the nation's entry into the First World War, with "the Anglo-Saxon Race" facing so many perils for which a new generation of future soldiers seemed the only answer, the anti-abortion war seemed to be won. In vain did feminists like Leta Hollingsworth protest that "We should expect . . . that those in control of society would invent and and employ devices for impelling women to maintain a birthrate sufficient to insure enough increase in the population to offset the wastage of war and disease." She bitterly noted that "men of the greatest prestige" judged women who objected to this breeding role to be "abnormal" and "decayed." Women who claimed autonomy in their lives and the right to control what happened to their own bodies were dangerous. Love of their husbands and their country dictated that they bear as many children as they could.

All manner of social institutions, including the church, the schools, and the print media pressed home the same point. Women should remain the mothers of the race. The law rewarded fecundity and penalized birth control and abortion. Hollingsworth might dream of a time when all the "most intelligent women of the community, who are the most desirable child bearers, will become conscious of the methods of social control . . . the laws will be repealed and changed; enlightenment will prevail . . . and the increased happiness and usefulness of women would, in general, be regarded as social gain." But that time seemed far away.

The circle had come almost entirely closed. As in ancient times, abortion was again a word that was spoken in a whisper behind closed doors, again a secret act, involving a conspiracy of players. But now, unlike in ancient times, the state had taken an interest in abortion to protect the future interest of the state in the "unborn child." But Hollingworth implied that men had another goal in their anti-abortion campaign. Fearing loss of power over women because of the new feminism, men used abortion as a symbolic social curb. By linking women's autonomy over their own bodies, including autonomy over their sexual relations with men, to the crime of abortion, men sought to restrict women's freedom.

————

The nineteenth century was one of immense novelty and experimentation in the law. Lawyers and judges invented the modern concepts of labor unions, corporations, anti-trust rules, torts (civil wrongs), contract, and negligence. Legislatures introduced sophisticated schemes of regulation of commerce, working conditions, and economic development. Jurists laid the foundations for the sociological interpretation of the laws. The criminialization of abortion fit into this pattern of growing legalization of private conduct, but it was never a major concern of lawmakers or legal theorists.

The relative unimportance of abortion in the larger scheme of legal development is significant. The elaboration of a visibly gendered world order, in which the subordinate place of women and women's needs was taken for granted, long preceded the nineteenth century, but the legal context in which that asymmetry functioned had changed by the end of the 1800s. Examine the changing legal rules for marriage and divorce in the nineteenth century, by comparison with abortion. By the second half of the century, statutes in family law had redressed the most obvious injustices of common-law coverture, in which wives' legal interests were entirely subordinated to their husbands', by giving married women more power to hold property in their own name, obtain divorces, and gain custody of their children. Then courts stepped in to restore the common-law rules of coverture, and legislatures recanted their liberality. Or look at lawyering: the practice of law had grown lucrative, and the size and wealth of firms had risen geometrically to service the growing legal needs of business and labor, but many states barred women from practicing law, few women trained as lawyers, and fewer still practiced. None were partners in major law firms. Women's priorities in legal reform would have to be articulated by men, in the language of Victorian paternalism. Similarly, in the tightly reasoned legal paradigm of the late nineteenth century, male-dominated activities like banking, industrial organization, and regulation of the workplace took precedence over activities assumed to be associated with women.

The criminalization of abortion fit the overall gendering of law, in which male lawgivers asserted that women must be protected against their own weakness and immorality in having unwanted children and then seeking the assistance of abortionists. Doctors and legislators agreed that the state must interpose itself between women and the dangers of such abortions. To attack the abortion laws, women would have to attack the gendered legal paradigm into which abortion laws so neatly fit. But the disparity between the importance that women assigned to the abortion issue and its relative unimportance within the late-nineteenth-century legal paradigm required that women find some collateral line of attack to open the door to the discussion of abortion, long before they could press for reform of the law. In the first half of the twentieth century, the birth control movement's efforts to legalize the distribution of contraceptives provided the opening that abortion rights advocates needed.

CHAPTER 2

Abortion and Birth Control, 1900–1965

By the early 1900s, anti-abortion laws were fully deployed and looked irreversible, a thick and well-morticed wall against women's supposed immorality. Police informants, policewomen posing as patients who needed abortions, and large-scale raids of abortionists' offices and homes ensured that abortion would remain a risky business for its providers and riskier still for women who wanted a safe operation. In the meantime, the lawgivers turned their attention to the suppression of other vices, for example, criminalizing the sale of alcohol and the use of opiates.

In the male-fashioned and male-dominated late Victorian legal paradigm, women's issues such as abortion played a minor role, and anti-abortion laws were but a small part of the campaign against vice that spilled over into the beginning of the twentieth century, but the reasons why women sought abortions had not changed, and even as the laws became more harsh, the demand for abortions again increased. Among immigrant women, pouring into the country before the First World War, among farm women, hit by a depression immediately after the war, and among a broad segment of American society during the Great Depression of 1929–1939, safe abortion again became a major concern. But the laws now forbade mention of it, much less a drive for abortion rights reform.

Abortion rights reform was liberated from the darkness into which the state laws and police raids, papal encyclicals, Comstockery, and advocates of population growth had cast it by another movement—albeit a cautious cousin unwilling to admit kinship: the birth control crusade. For promoters of birth control had similar clients to advocates of abortion rights—married women who did not want more offspring or whose husbands did not want a larger family, unmarried women who wished to avoid the shame of an illegitimate child, poor men and women who could not afford a child, women who were victims of rape, incest, and spousal abuse, and women who were too mentally and physically drained to take care of one or one more child. In the 1920s and 1930s, feminist birth control advocates made the tactical choice of an alliance with highly respectable foundations and reputable doctors, making men the patrons of the movement. The cost of this bargain was that women who led the birth control movement and personally believed that women had a right to abortions still could not speak of that right in public—indeed they elected to condemn abortion to ward off the argument that birth control was merely a form of very early abortion.

Birth control agitation that had begun as an expression of women's right to control their own reproductive lives veered away from advocacy of women's autonomy, courted eugenics (the pseudo-science of population engineering), smiled on theories of population limitation, and contented itself with court cases and legislative acts that gave doctors the right to inform their patients about birth control information rather than give the patients a right to have the information. If this decision to place women's reproductive fate under the protection of doctors seemed necessary, and ultimately proved a successful stratagem to legalize birth control, it made abortion seem all the more dangerous to society. Still, the story of abortion in this era was inextricably bound to the struggles of the new birth control movement, and because the tie could never be totally cut, when birth control enthusiasts won their legislative and court battles, abortion rights edged closer to legality.

Sex and the "Modern" Woman

In the years before the outbreak of the First World War, polite culture frowned upon mention of sex. Sensational events like Anthony Comstock's arrest of and the subsequent trial of Victoria Woodhull, a New York City spiritualist, women's rights advocate, and newspaper publisher, for printing exposés of the activities of rakes, had a chilling effect on all public discussion of sexuality. But after the horrors of the World War had brought home to men and women the frailty of so many other Victorian conceits, such as the assumption that Europe was too civilized to engage in large-scale warfare, to use chemical weapons, or to ravage civilian populations in time of war, the self-imposed ban on sexual topics in literature, newspapers, and theater relaxed. The "lost generation" of the 1920s rediscovered the pleasures of the flesh. One critic remarked that the automobile, in itself a symbol of modernity, had become a moving bordello. By the middle of the 1920s, the "true womanhood" of the ankle-skirted Victorian matron had given way to the "new womanhood" of the scantily clad "flapper." At the movies women and men could view, on a large screen and in perfect respectability, art films with titles like *Sinners in Silk*, *Women Who Give*, *Rouged Lips*, and *The Queen of Sin*. Most of these movies warned that unbridled lust led to a woman's downfall, but the frank depiction of that lust on the screen belied the clichéd morality of the movies' endings.

Sexuality in the automobile and on the big screen was not evidence in itself of women's growing autonomy—indeed it exploited more than liberated women. But the "new-style feminism," as modern writer Elaine Showalter calls it, demanded reciprocity of sexual enjoyment within the family. And women's sexuality in marriage was now celebrated by journalists, doctors, and social scientists. For a marriage to work, these pundits agreed, women and men had to find sexual pleasure in one another. Some defenders of the so-called companionate marriage, such as Judge Ben Lindsay of Colorado, argued that sexual experimentation before marriage might even be a good thing, allowing prospective brides and grooms to decide if the marriage would fulfill their sexual needs. Sexual contentment became the "centerpiece" of marriage, according to one historian. Popular books and manuals on marriage, which in the previous century had stressed the obedience of women, now made women full partners in the conjugal bedroom.

Social science, which in some ways had supplanted religion as interpreter of moral values in middle-class culture, promoted the study of women's sexuality in comparative rather than moralistic terms. George Gallup's and Elmo Roper's often cited public opinion polls applied statistical sampling techniques to everyday questions of moral conduct, and Robert and Helen Lynd's study of the "freer sex ideas" that had taken root in "Middletown" between 1924 and 1938 popularized a sociological view of sexual conduct. Instead of condemning women as the inferior sex and locating sex drives in women's supposedly weak faculties, the researchers documented gendered differences in temperament and cultural expectations. Other studies concluded that women were distinct from men in their sexual objectives, but not because God had created women to serve men. Instead, women wanted loyalty, companionship, stability, and status in their mates. (Men, according to these studies, still wanted women who were good breeding stock.)

The focus on sexuality brought women to the center of the new American culture, but the new woman was not just a caricature of sexual liberation. She was energetic, athletic, and skilled, and could say "no" to sex or to marriage or to children. She could, as feminist and journalist Mary Alden Hopkins wrote in the *Nation,* in 1926, "earn my own living, do not take my husband's name, and . . . escape the dreary common place." In a lighter vein, newspaper editorials defined the liberated woman as a person, "Who can play golf all day and dance all night, and drive a motor car, and give first aid to the injured if anybody gets hurt, and who is in no more danger of swooning than a man." Even in fields of domestic work, the new woman was changing the rules. Housekeeping became domestic engineering as women teachers pioneered the field of home economics in colleges and high schools. The older emphasis on basic nutrition and sanitation gave way to more modern concerns, like the introduction of labor-saving appliances. Comfort in the house added to the pleasure of marriage, a variant on the theme of sexual fulfillment.

To fulfill the consumer desires of the young, advertising, itself a new and rapidly growing field, catered to women. In 1911, the *New York Herald* ran its first advertisement for "maternity gowns"—hitherto, like pregnancy itself, a taboo subject in the newspapers. In 1920, the paper company Kimberly Clark put "Kotex," a disposable sanitary napkin, on the market. Its sales zoomed off the charts. By the late 1920s, estimates put women as high as 80 percent of all purchasers of appliances and modern "conveniences." Advertisers referred to the potential consumer as "she" and featured in text and pictures the "modern woman." Predictably, women's items like cosmetics soon led the way in advertising revenue.

"Modernistic" childrearing among the middle classes combined the new reliance on science with the innovative potency of advertising. Take, for example, the "better baby shows" that the glossy magazine *Women's Home Companion* began to sponsor in 1913. Advertisers and companies producing baby products joined to run the shows, using them to introduce mass-market products. The organizers gave blue ribbons to the healthiest infants in the show. At them one could purchase L. Emmett Holt's best-selling *The Care and Feeding of Children,* one of a slew of "how to" manuals featuring the latest in scientific techniques for rigidly scheduled feeding (not on demand—that would spoil the infant) and toilet training (on an even more rigid schedule, starting at age three months). And it all seemed to work—the mortality rate for infantile gastrointestinal and seasonal disorders dropped visibly.

The modern woman who married for sexual fulfillment, and had children because she wanted to, increasingly listened to the advice of experts on childrearing. U.S. government pamphlets on feeding and health care became required reading in middle-class households. But not every mother had the advantages of the personal liberty, the time, and the purchasing power of the new woman. Congressional acts in 1921 and 1924 had all but ended the flood of immigration from southern and eastern Europe and Asia, but the cities still teemed with first- and second-generation immigrant poor. After the war, the nation's economy as a whole boomed, but farmers found that prices for staples like tobacco, cotton, and foodstuffs were falling, and rural poverty became a way of life, particularly in the South, Southwest, and Great Plains states. In 1922, a series of devastating droughts and the spread of the boll weevil decimated the cotton crops in these regions. The agricultural depression fell hardest on people of color—many of them sharecroppers, whose large families had hitherto been a hedge against low wages. Poor people had been able, in the past, to find work for their children in factories and fields, but the automation of American industry, child labor laws, and depression in the farming country made large families an economic liability.

Despite the ban on dissemination of birth control information, many poor couples practiced it. Returns on a sexual habits questionnaire that Stanford University professor and student counselor Celia Duer Mosher circulated indicated that over 80 percent of the respondents regularly used some means of birth control, most often mechanical methods like diaphragms or condoms. Mosher's respondents were middle-class and upper-class women, but the steady decline of the number of conceptions among all social and economic classes of married women, most striking in the Great Depression years of 1929–1941, but evident from the beginning of the century, suggests that women's networks, older family members, supportive nurses, doctors, and druggists, and underground pamphlets privately printed and passed from hand to hand spread information on methods of contraception.

The Radical Roots and Conservative Progress of the Birth Control Movement

Consumer demand for birth control information ensured that it would not disappear from circulation even though it was banned by legislative act. An abundance of evidence from private letters and public records, including trial records in which purveyors of birth control information and implements were acquitted, proves that the birth control trade continued throughout the period between 1873 and the 1930s. But the open, public movement to overturn the ban on birth control began with the efforts of two remarkable women, Emma Goldman and Margaret Sanger.

Goldman was a New York anarchist and feminist, whose reform efforts and public advocacy covered a wide range of subjects. Indeed, for her, birth control was only part of grander plans for the liberation of the working poor. Born in Russia in 1869, she emigrated to America in 1885, married, became involved in radical politics, and in 1889 served a year in jail for advocating revolution. She began her professional career as a nurse and midwife in the next decade. In later years a brilliant speaker, she traveled all over the country agitating for women's equality, reform of the working place, free speech, and other causes. She advocated "free love" based on voluntary commitment, not promiscuity. She was not, like some contemporary feminists, anti-male, but believed that men and women must work together to improve society. For her constant and fearless attacks upon government repression of free speech, even during wartime, she was ultimately deprived of her citizenship and later expelled from the country.

Goldman practiced midwifery among the immigrant poor of New York City and saw firsthand how women driven to desperation jumped off tables, rolled on the floor, drank poisonous concoctions, and used blunt instruments to abort their unwanted pregnancies. Goldman did not advocate abortion nor practice it, but she joined with Ben Reitman in 1908 to pass out birth control information wherever they lectured. When other birth control speakers were jailed for violating state Comstock laws, Goldman rushed to their rescue by raising funds.

Goldman favored the overthrow of existing governments and the establishment of a society without coercive institutions, but her allies in the drive for birth control were Socialists, who believed in public ownership of utilities, public welfare and health programs, and greater economic democracy within existing governments. The Socialists, with their connections to labor unions, were a viable third party for much of the period until the Second World War. Some in the Socialist Party thought that true socialist reform might make birth control unnecessary, for with genuine distribution of wealth, women could have as many children as they wanted and still support them. But Socialists did believe in the equality of women and strongly supported one of Goldman's causes—sex education for all women. Socialist women like Dr. Antoinette Konikow, another immigrant from Russia, gave speeches and wrote articles in Boston that tied sex education to birth control.

Goldman's example and the Socialist program strongly influenced Sanger. Born in 1879 to an upstate New York Irish Catholic family, she had watched her mother die from the wear and tear of childbearing. From her father, an intellectual, Margaret learned to love books and ideas, and her first job was school teaching. But she resented the drudgery of replacing her mother as her father's housekeeper and moved to Manhattan. There she fell in love with a liberal-thinking painter, Bill Sanger, married, and had children, but still chaffed at the restraints of "tame domesticity." In 1910, she and her husband attended a Socialist Party meeting, and she was never the same. With newly opened eyes, she saw that her mother's suffering was shared by millions of poor people. None of it was their fault.

Although the enthusiasm of her initial attachment to the cause of labor and the laboring classes waned after her experiences in a series of violent labor strikes during the 1910s, her participation introduced her to the leading figures in American radicalism, including Goldman, "Big Bill" Haywood, the leader of the Industrial Workers of the World, and John Reed, a Harvard-educated Communist and one of the first American journalists to travel to the Soviet Union after it was founded. Although in time she would reject the exclusively economic approach of the Socialists, she still retained the gift of making strong friendships and cultivating the brightest people around her.

In later years Sanger revealed the moment when she decided she must dedicate her life to the birth control movement. She had trained as a nurse and in 1917 was working in the tenements of New York City. There, as she told the story, she met Sadie Sachs, the wife of a truck driver. Unable to afford more than the three children she already had, Sadie performed an abortion on herself and nearly died from the infection. Sanger came calling, and in the heat of the summer carried water and food up the three flights of the tenement to the Sachses' tiny apartment to nurse Sachs through her agonizing recovery. But Sachs could not convince a doctor to fit her for a diaphragm, her husband would not use a condom, and after another pregnancy and another abortion, she died in Sanger's arms. Sanger vowed never "to go back to merely keeping such victims alive." Sanger would instead change the world for these mothers. The story, told to great effect for many years, was not literally true, for two years before she met Sachs Sanger had written a pamphlet called *Family Limitation,* discussing in detail a variety of birth control methods, and had asked Haywood to print and arrange to distribute hundreds of thousands of copies. He did, as she left for Europe to be with her husband and avoid prosecution under the Comstock laws.

In Europe, Sanger gravitated into the circle of leading theorists on women's rights, birth control, and sexuality. The most intellectually imposing of these was Havelock Ellis, and she became his devoted protégé. Ellis was already one of the world's leading psychologists, and he liberated Sanger from the remaining clutches of Victorian prudery. He convinced her that women should see their own sexual impulses as natural and worthy of fulfillment. Such sex drives could even be "transmuted" into art, literature, science, and social activism. Ellis also turned Sanger away from extreme forms of social protest like Goldman's, urging her to find gradualist and respectable ways to promote her birth control program. When she returned to the United States she was no longer the Emma Goldman–type radical, but a liberal reformer.

Still, Sanger never hid her light under a bushel. In 1916, back in the United States and separated from her husband, she went on tour in support of birth control, opened a birth control clinic, went to jail, then charmed her jailers with her moderation and her arguments. She lobbied in the New York State legislature for amendment of the Comstock laws to permit a "doctors only" exception to the ban on birth control information, held conferences of social and medical reformers at posh hotels, and pushed the agenda of the very respectable American Birth Control League that she had founded. Her marriage to Bill Sanger ended, and she remarried, to millionaire industrialist J. Noah Slee, who funded her organization. By the early 1930s, despite the ban on importation of birth control devices, Sanger and her cohorts across the country had opened fifty-five birth control clinics, and by 1938, there were over five hundred. To staff them, she turned to her new friends—the doctors.

Birth Control's Recruits: The Doctors

Why did Sanger's efforts bear fruit in a country whose laws forbade birth control discourse and practice? The success of Sanger's movement owed itself to one obvious reason. In 1925, Sanger played host to an assemblage of who's who among the medical sciences. The invitees included university sociologists and economists, as well as doctors like Dr. William Allen Pusey, head of the American Medical Association. In the 1860s, a far less confident AMA had found that Horatio Storer's anti-abortion agitation helped the AMA to establish its credentials. Then, by asserting the need to protect women against themselves, the doctors claimed what they took to be their rightful place in a paternalistic world. Now, a kindlier, gentler, and far more entrenched AMA found in advocacy of birth control a way that they could affirm the paternal role of professional medicine while conceding that women had gained a measure of independence in political activity, employment options, and sexual conduct.

The doctors heard lectures on Economic Poverty and Child Labor, Eugenics and Welfare, and Sex and Reproduction. One observer reported that "[t]hrough it all Mrs. Sanger smiled as quietly and unconcerned as though she never had envisioned anything different from this focusing of all kinds of professional competence upon the subject which has been her life work." Sanger closed the doors to noninvitees, the exact opposite of what Emma Goldman (or a younger Sanger) would have done. The issues were for the experts to decide, not for popular clamor or ordinary people. The conference attendees then resolved "that this meeting on contraception consisting of members of the American medical profession, affirms that birth control, being a very important and complicated problem requiring scientific study and guidance, [is] completely within the province of preventive medicine." The lay movement was over; the professional program had begun.

Sanger had played the doctors, sheltering the controversial birth control movement within the stronghold of expertise—the laboratories and professional societies of the doctors. But they had played her as well, for as one reporter noted, she had "placed the direction of the medical activities of the American Birth Control League in the hands of a representative medical group. Now it is up to the doctors." In effect, she had made a women-centered, woman-led movement into a men's movement. Not surprisingly, after this step, the importance of her contribution began to fade, even though she remained active.

With the doctors' support, Dr. Marie C. Stopes's scientific study, *Contraception*, was deemed an exception to the Comstock laws by a federal judge in 1931. The doctors cheered when an English court, in 938, liberalized its anti-abortion laws. According to the *United States Law Review*, "the British medical profession was deeply interested in the recent trial of Dr. Aleck William Bourne, one of London's foremost obstetricians and gynecologists, for performing an abortion on a fourteen-year-old girl who was pregnant in the consequence of a rape." Two troopers of the Royal Horse Guard had lured her into the stables and attacked her. Bourne, who had been openly critical of the restrictions on abortions in England and was looking for a test case, obtained the permission of the parents and operated, after which he turned himself in to Scotland Yard. At trial, a jury of ten men and two women took but forty minutes to acquit him, in large measure because of the instructions they received from the presiding judge.

Although the law provided that abortion was a crime except to save the life of the mother, and Dr. Bourne admitted that the mother was in no danger of losing her life through the progress of the pregnancy, the judge instructed the jury that if the doctor "believed the girl's nervous system would have been greatly affected and her health would have been seriously endangered if the child had been born, and he was unable to draw a distinction between danger to life and danger to health," the jury might acquit him. Other leading doctors agreed that Bourne's course of action was one they would have followed.

The judge had created a "constructive" or fictive life-and-death situation out of the doctor's estimation of the likelihood of lasting mental and physical distress to the mother. Through such a huge loophole, the strict requirement that the mother's life be in immediate peril passed to become a far broader category of mere "harm." The fact that the judge told the jury that such decision must be left to competent physicians gave the physicians the discretion to help patients whose desire for an abortion was not quite a matter of life and death. Later commentators, including those who opposed the judge's instructions to the jury, recognized that the case widened the category of therapeutic abortions and let private (that is, confidential) negotiations between doctors and patients define that category.

In 1936, doctors joined birth control advocates in supporting federal Judge Augustus Hand's opinion that doctors might import birth control devices from Japan. In *United States v. One Package*, Hand contended that if Congress had available to it in 1873 evidence about the dangers of pregnancy relative to the safety of contraception, it would not have passed the Comstock law. When doctors acted "for the purpose of saving life or promoting the well being of their patients," the laws should not interfere. The doctors' contribution to Hand's thinking was significant, just as their predecessors' opposition to birth control and abortion had been crucial to the passage of the Comstock Act in 1873.

Hand had turned the federal court into a miniature legislature, in outward appearance an example of "substantive due process" (using the Bill of Rights or the Fourteenth Amendment to overturn legislative regulatory acts), a doctrine that many liberal legal reformers in the 1930s rejected. And with reason: in the early twentieth century, conservative judges routinely voided progressive acts concerning workplace safety, wages, child labor, and working hours on substantive due process grounds. Hand, fully aware of the earlier cases and the liberals' views, never mentioned substantive due process.

For a decade after the exclusive New York City conference of 1925 called for medical study of birth control, state and national medical associations dithered over the birth control question. Catholic doctors opposed birth control; conservative doctors worried that it would promote immorality. Finally, at the 1935 AMA annual meeting, the doctors fought it out. Some, following the 1925 resolution, wanted the AMA to press legislatures to allow doctors to obtain supplies and give out information "necessary to conserve health or life itself [of women]." From 1931 to 1935, resolutions of this sort had been presented and tabled, as a large minority of the doctors objected to any revisions of the laws against birth control. The new head of the AMA, James McLester, supported the resolution, however, and a committee was formed to act. Two years later, over the objections of its Roman Catholic members, the AMA abandoned its official opposition to birth control.

In his 1935 address to the AMA, McLester explained his reasons for supporting doctors' right to counsel patients on birth control. He hailed from Alabama, hard hit by the crash of cotton prices, and he knew firsthand how much poor rural women suffered from the burden of too many mouths to feed. McLester saw the connection between people living "near or below the threshold of nuitritive safety" and the absence of birth control information.

The year after McLester gave his talk to the AMA, author James Agee and photographer Walker Evans visited central Alabama tenant farmers. Their words and pictures, published in 1941 as *Let Us Now Praise Famous Men*, documented the relation between poverty and family size. Agee imagined what the parents must be thinking, surrounded by all the children barely fed and clothed: "[H]ow was it that we were caught? Why is it things always seem to go against us?" In 1937, a young Ph.D.

candidate from the University of North Carolina, Margaret Jarman Hagood, spent a year among poor farmers, and concluded, "Sex education of the daughters, which is given to daughters just before or at the time they begin to menstruate, is usually limited to meager information about menstruation and babies being born. From then on the weight of sex education is admonitions not to 'get in trouble' with boys." Without more detailed birth control information, including the availability of birth control devices, most of these young women would end up "in trouble."

Birth Control, Abortion, and Eugenics

McLester connected birth control to the health of the mother and her child—fewer children meant that parents could protect "the health of the race." This phrase was not a platitude. The pairing of birth control and racism reflected the underside of Sanger's program. European neo-Malthusianism saw birth control as a way of lifting the economic burden from the poor. The English founder of the newer "Eugenics" movement, Francis Galton, was a geologist and statistician of note before he began writing about genetics and inherited traits. He soon became a leader of the effort to improve the human species by selective breeding, but he did not argue for forced sterilization of any group. Nevertheless, his somewhat naive and even hopeful faith in voluntary breeding programs among the superior classes, widely shared by the beginning of the twentieth century among upper-class intellectuals in Europe and the United States, appealed as well to those who feared the spread of supposedly inferior races and the reproduction of "dysgenic" traits among individuals.

Other advocates of genetic engineering saw birth control methods in a different light. Their agenda was less scientific than social and cultural and went back to the nineteenth-century origins of Anglo-Saxonism. They associated "good blood" not with proof of genius but with certain cultural traits, which some ethnic groups supposedly had and others lacked. In effect, they made cultural diffusion—nurture—a substitute for nature. Even otherwise liberal social scientists like Edward Ross were concerned about the decline in population—that is, the declining birthrate—among the cultural "better sort." As he wrote in the *American Journal of Sociology* in 1907, "this exaggerated individualism, that avoids marriage or else dodges its natural consequences [that is, procreation] forebodes the extinction of the class, the people, or the race that adopts it.... [T]he one-child or two-child ideal growingly in favor with the middle class would, if popularized, hurry us to extinction. In such families prodigious pains are taken to keep breath in defective or sickly children. Instead of being weeded out in infancy by natural process, the weaklings are kept alive by lavish care, and the national vitality is lowered." Theodore Roosevelt was similarly concerned about what Ross had called "Race Suicide." In 1907, on a western tour, he lavished praise on "civilized" peoples who had large families. "No race suicide here," Roosevelt's supporters echoed.

The eugenicists' conflation of the cultural with the natural had become a staple in mass circulation magazines by the end of the 1920s and was already reflected in the actions of some state governments. In 1907, Indiana introduced the first law for the sterilization of habitual criminals. By 1917, fourteen more states had passed such laws. Included among the "defectives" were epileptics, mentally ill persons, and persons who scored low on the newly introduced "I.Q." tests. The assumption behind the program was that such traits were inheritable. As Dorothy Dunbar Bromley reported in *Harper's* in December 1929, "To meet this problem, twenty-three states have active eugenic laws providing for the sterilization of individuals so degenerate mentally or physically that their progeny would become a burden to the community." This did not satisfy her, however. "In the remaining states ... defectives continue to spawn, and their offspring frequently became a menace to the community." In a technique familiar to all alarmists, Bromley adduced a sea of horrors from a single shipwreck: the murder of "a three-year-old child perpetrated by two boys of seven and eight, the sons of a man who had formerly been an inmate of an insane asylum." The case, reported in the newspapers, convinced her that the man "obviously should have been sterilized before he was released."

On some occasions, state courts prevented sterilization of the institutionalized on the grounds that general sterilization laws gave too much power to legislatures, who in turn passed on too much discretion to asylum and prison directors. But in the leading case of the 1920s,

Buck v. Bell (1927), the majority of the United States Supreme Court allowed Virginia authorities, following an act passed in the state to sterilize imbeciles, to operate on Carrie Buck, a supposedly mentally ill woman who had mentally ill parents and had produced a mentally deficient child. In fact, the woman was not mentally ill but had been institutionalized by her family to hide the fact that a relative had raped her. What was more, the child proved, in time, to have an above-average intelligence. Nevertheless, the Supreme Court, by an 8 to 1 vote, upheld the rulings of the state courts, and the sterilization proceeded. Justice Oliver Wendell Holmes Jr.'s caustic remark that three generations of imbeciles are enough, though factually incorrect, was widely cheered in the American eugenics movement. Without any fanfare, the state also sterilized Carrie's sister, Dorris.

To the eugenicists' long-term plan for the improvement of the race, the Great Depression added the specter of a neo-Malthusian crisis. As Henry Pratt Fairchild read the danger in 1932, "The simple fact is that there is no species of living organism in nature whose capacity to increase is not sufficient to over flow the earth in a very brief period if there is nothing to stop it. . . . Man is no exception to the principle of excess fecundity." Abortion was, when performed by doctors in sanitary conditions, "doubtless a great improvement over nature's method of killing a newborn," but "only through the measures commonly called birth control or, in a narrow sense, contraception, can the control of population be reduced to that minimum of suffering, inconvenience and self denial" that rational man so desired and needed. In the very next article in the *Nation* that January in 1932, C. V. Drysdale warned of the seething discontent of Asian nations like India, China, and Japan, as their population burst national boundaries. When their population density reached critical levels, they could be expected to seek new lands for their excess men and women. This was the other, not so polite side of neo-Malthusianism, in which birth control would have to be ruthlessly applied to non-western peoples rather than rationally adopted if civilization as western nations knew it was to survive.

Advocates of some form of eugenic engineering had long pointed to Sanger as an ideological ally and to birth control as a useful tool in their program. Had not her long-time mentor Havelock Ellis complained that it was silly for governments to attempt social improvement programs when they allowed "the weak, the incompetent, and the defective" to breed at will? Thus, when Sanger held her first birth control conference in New York, in 1921, a commentator in the *Nation* saw birth control as one way to avoid the proliferation of "diseased and unhealthy children." Sanger herself repeatedly argued that some people should not have children. Epileptics, the feebleminded, and other genetic "defectives" should be encouraged to use birth control.

But she never advocated race engineering or the other portions of what she derided as "that strange argument" that inferior people should be induced to agree to sterilization. In a rebuttal to her critics, published in the *North American Review* in May 1929, she agreed with President Hoover: "[T]he ideal to which we should strive is that there shall be no child in America that has not been born under proper conditions; that does not live in hygienic surroundings . . . that does not have prompt and efficient medical attention and inspection . . . that has not the birthright of a sound mind and a sound body." In other words, Sanger straddled the eugenics question—society should provide for all its newborns, but all the newborns should exhibit the best bloodlines. She pressed college graduates to have more children, but in her autobiography, published in 1938, she mocked the eugenicists for their own small families. As far as she was concerned, they never did explain who was "fit" and who was "unfit" to have children.

In the end, she wanted "American mothers . . . to choose the time and conditions best suited for fulfillment of the maternal function." That is what she had argued in her book *Motherhood in Bondage* (1928). For all the concessions she would make to the doctors and the legislators over who could disseminate birth control information, when push came to shove, it was up to the prospective mother to decide how to use that information. Her stance thus not only cut the ground from under the so-called active eugenicists, it once more gave women control of their reproductive fates.

The accumulation of biological data suggesting that dysfunctional traits in individuals were not inheritable, the use to which Hitler and his dutiful subordinates in Nazi Germany would put eugenic ideas— mass murder of Slavs, Jews, Romanian gypsies, homosexuals, suspected deviants, political dissidents, communists, and socialists—and the opposition of the Roman Catholic church eventually doomed negative eugenics to the discard pile of historical ideas, although echoes of the old canon are still heard in the writings of a wide variety of modern race theorists. But the decline of pseudo-scientific eugenics did not of itself alter the states' sterilization laws. These, based on rationales that preceded the rise of the Nazis, continued to function, and inmates of asylums, correctional facilities, and hospitals were still sterilized to prevent their reproducing undesirable traits.

Abortion Prosecuted and Defended:
The 1930s and the 1940s

Ironically, as birth control, supposedly the alternative to abortion, emerged as a respectable public cause, economic crisis drove many American women to seek abortions and authorities to warn of a new abortion epidemic. Dr. Frederick Taussig judged in his influential *Abortion—Spontaneous and Induced* (1936), "Economic distress is at the root of the largest number of induced abortions." The cause of the distress was the Great Depression of 1929–1939, when the birthrate dipped to its lowest levels in the history of the United States as families adjusted for their diminishing income. Abortions contributed to the declining birthrate.

Social scientists' and doctors' estimates of the numbers of abortions varied widely, from 200,000 to a 1,000,000 a year. Taussig's figure of 680,000 per year for 1935 was the most widely quoted. Dr. George Kosmak, who wanted the medical profession to "purge its own ranks of the commercially minded criminal abortionist," estimated in 1937 that over 500,000 illegal abortions took place every year. From 1930 to 1931, the number of illegal abortions that one New Orleans hospital saw rose 166 percent. Social class and race did not matter in the increase, and a study of Protestant, Jewish, and Catholic working women in New York City showed that they had roughly the same abortion rate, though the Jewish and Catholic women sought abortions later in their reproductive life than the Protestant women.

Opponents of birth control like Monsignor John A. Ryan warned that the rising numbers of abortions were a direct result of the rise of birth control. In the magazine *Catholic Action* he predicted that the declining birthrate would inevitably lead to "national decadence with the ultimate result of either national extinction or conquest by an alien nation or alien race." Following his lead, churches still set aside days of prayer for larger families. Advocates of women's rights, such as Genevieve Parkhurst, also saw the connection between the growing legitimacy of birth control and the surge of abortions, but regarded that linkage in a different light: "[T]his question reaches down to the very foundations of human liberty—the right of all human beings, as free men and women, to be the masters of their own bodies and souls." In an essay for *Harper's* in January 1941, she declared that the attempt to dictate to women how many children to have was one of the "acute symptoms of totalitarianism." She compared American military and religious leaders' demand that women have more children to *Mein Kampf*, Hitler's battle plan for taking over the world. For in it, Hitler saw women as breeding stock for the master race—the same sort of proposal, albeit phrased in less racist terms, that she found in the admonitions of the anti–birth control experts.

In the meantime, Sanger sorted through bundles of mail from women who wanted her to help them find a safe abortion. Sanger publically condemned abortion, though in private she believed that "women should be free to terminate pregnancies where it is not de-sired." Denouncing abortion publically was one price she paid for the respectability of the birth control movement.

Ryan, Parkhurst, and Sanger knew that just as the ill-fated 1920s experiment in the prohibition of the distilling and selling of alcoholic beverages led to a thriving black market in distilled beverages and widespread disregard for the law, so those who wanted abortions would find those who performed abortions outside the law. Some of the lat-ter prospered from their practices. Many abortionists in the 1930s and after were men, such as California physicians Simon Parker of Long Beach and John Folsom of Oakland. They were not full-time abortion-ists but performed abortions when requested to do so by their patients. Physicians such as Norman Powers of Seattle wanted the money that performing abortions would bring to their tottering practices. Other doctors, such as Portland, Oregon's Alys Griff and Josephine Gabler of Chicago, specialized in abortion, and performed tens of thousands of abortions in their downtown offices. The vast majority of the patients were married and came through referrals from other doctors. Fees ranged between thirty-five and three hundred dollars, but on average were below seventy-five dollars.

Griff and Gabler performed abortions in part as a service to other women in need, in part for the money. Women doctors were not uncommon but rarely had prosperous practices. More typical of the career female abortionist was Ruth Barnett, of Portland, Oregon. The daughter of a storekeeper whose pioneer family followed a prairie schooner across the country to Oregon, she apprenticed with Griff and then with a series of male doctors. For much of the period 1929–1953, she practiced abortion openly, in a well-appointed office downtown, with a receptionist and nurses. Her services were known to doctors, who referred patients, and the police, who looked the other way. Indeed, many of her patients were known to the police, and a few were related to the police and other city officials. She was clean, efficient, and safe—a valued member of an underground and criminal profession allowed to flourish. Her daughter estimated that over the course of her career, Ruth Barnett made millions of dollars and treated hundreds of thousands of patients.

When Barnett was finally convicted, in 1952, prosecutors attacked her for her lavish lifestyle and the money she charged her desperate clients. In truth, her abortion practice gave Barnett a good living and high visibility, but she charged very little, less than forty dollars on average for the entire procedure, and little in comparison to what regular doctors charged for other medical services. Barnett saw herself as a savior of women in trouble, not a ruthless parasite living on other women's misfortune. Before she went to jail, Barnett worried, "God almighty, what would my women do without me?" As another abortionist arrested in the 1951 Portland raids told reporters, "Many of these girls who get into difficulty beat a path to my door for help ... I felt it was my duty to help these girls. I believe in every community there must be someone to do the work that I have done."

Oregon had a strict legal ban on abortions, except when the mother's life was in danger, but that did not deter Barnett and the other Portland abortionists. As one student note in the *Columbia Law Review* in the mid-1930s conceded, "The [anti-abortion] statutes seem never to have been satisfactorily enforced." "Satisfactorily" in this law note was a relative word—it meant that law enforcement and anti-abortion advocates were not satisfied. They continued to argue that legalized abortion would undermine the morals of the community and would cause drastic decline in population. The Roman Catholic church agreed. Pope Pius XI, in a 1930 encyclical on Christian marriage widely read here, maintained that the purpose of marriage must be procreation and that the "unborn child" had a soul that abortion destroyed.

Doctors who opposed abortion, such as Kosmak, added that abortions caused sterility and thus endangered the reproductive prowess of women "at the most fertile period of their lives." Somewhat illogically, Kosmak used the high rate of death from abortions—over 17 percent of all women's mortality during pregnancy and delivery, according to a New York report—to argue against expanding the therapeutic exception to the criminal laws against abortions. (Had the women been able to gain expert help, to go to hospitals or have accredited physicians perform the procedure, the very steps that Kosmak condemned, the mortality figures would have dropped.) Yet, even if doctors performed some therapeutic abortions under lenient state laws, the laws still had a chilling effect on the doctors, who well knew that thousands of women victimized by botched abortions every year perished for want of expert medical assistance.

Although the mainstream doctors of the AMA had finally taken notice of the medical reasons for abortions, they would not expand the list of exceptions to include illegitimacy or economic exegency—the very motives that induced most women to seek abortions in the depression years. As A. J. Rongy, a maverick immigrant doctor and amateur sociologist wrote in 1937: "Abortion cannot be wished out of existence. No amount of neglect, no campaign of deliberate oversight, no enforced avoidance can conceal the fact that hundreds of thousands of American women resort to abortion, and will continue to do so unless some remedy for their predicament is supplied." By classifying abortion as a social and economic necessity, rather than a medical necessity, Rongy switched the polarities of the morality of abortion from condemnation of immoral women to condemnation of a lax medical profession: "Despite the fearsome toll of women maimed, crippled, and killed by illegal surgery—some fifteen thousand women a year"—the doctors did nothing.

As Rongy knew, the AMA, despite its tepid support for birth control, had labored mightily in the same years to prevent a comprehensive, nationally directed government program to aid pregnant women and newborn babies. The AMA admitted that some areas of the country, particularly the rural South and Midwest, had a critical shortage of doctors and maternity hospitals. Nor could the AMA doubt that infant mortality figures in the United States were worse than in any other industrialized country. What was more, the AMA leaders knew that during the Depression the cost of adequate neonatal care and medical treatment for newborns had become too great for most poor families to pay. Yet the AMA continued to argue that such government programs would deny private obstetricians, gynecologists, and pediatricians, as well as general practitioners, their income. The AMA was first and foremost a special interest lobby, and only secondarily a proponent of medical and professional progress.

The only law to aid prospective mothers and newborns that the New Deal administration could get past the lobbying of the AMA was a provision in the Social Security Act of 1935, amended in 1939, that provided block grants to states to upgrade medical facilities for soon-to-be mothers and newborn children. The provisions of the act favored those regions with few or no such facilities, and gave aid as well to medical schools and hospitals within those areas. In effect, it supported the medical profession more than the patients and so gained the approval of the AMA.

Yet the AMA did regard the patient-doctor relationship as crucial to the autonomy of the profession, and pressed states to pass "doctors acts" allowing therapeutic abortions (and giving more authority to the doctors to determine what operations might legally be performed). The results were meager: by 1939 only three states—Colorado, Maryland, and New Mexico—along with the District of Columbia, allowed abortions to preserve the health of the mother. Mississippi's poorly drafted (and thus unclear) law lent itself to that interpretation. Six states—Florida, Louisiana, Massachusetts, New Hampshire, Pennsylvania, and New Jersey—did not explicitly provide for doctors' discretion in performing the operation. The other states, using a variety of terms, permitted doctors to intervene to save the life of the mother, but gave no guidelines for doctors faced with that decision.

Just as the law was an impenetrable hedgerow of overlapping and vaguely worded provisions that gave little security to doctor or patient, so enforcement of the law against abortion was sporadic and quixotic. In many cases, police either looked the other way or accepted bribes to protect abortionists the same way that the police protected other "rackets." Abortion racketeers took advantage of the gaps in enforcement to corrupt or blackmail doctors. From 1934 to 1936, when he was caught, Reg Rankin operated a chain of abortion clinics in California, Oregon, and Nevada by paying off medical investigators to destroy evidence and threatening patients into remaining silent when cases came to court. In 1935, the medical examiner of New York, Dr. Charles D. Norris, remarked to a *Forum* writer that he had been called to testify only once against an abortionist in thirty-one years in office. A survey published in the *Nation* four years later revealed that only three doctors and a handful of midwives had been convicted for performing abortions in New York City over the previous twenty years.

Then, without warning, police might take an interest in the crime of abortion. For example, in 1936, intensive police work uncovered an abortion "insurance" plan in New Jersey, in which women paid dues and carried membership cards entitling them to regular examination and illegal operations, if needed. Raids in 1941, 1942, and 1947 on the offices of Chicago's Dr. Gabler and Ada Martin, who bought the clinic when Gabler retired, targeted not only the abortionists but the patients, the police coming away with boxes of file cards on which the clinic had listed the names and addresses of patients.

When abortionists were indicted, the newspapers and prosecutors had a field day. Reporters sensationalized the arrests and trials—they were good for circulation—in the process painting the female abortionist as a traitor to her sex. In the Martin case, the Chicago newspapers trumpeted that the crackdown had brought an organized crime ring to its knees, as though a single abortion clinic ranked with the Capone crime syndicate. In the Barnett case, the media cast the defendant as an unwomanly woman and a witch.

At trial, prosecutors produced the patients whose records the police had seized, and the patients told a very different story to the juries than they had told to the abortionists. They alleged that they had suffered mental and physical abuse at the hands of the defendants.

By showing the abortionists' instruments to the jury and describing the methods the abortionists used, prosecutors likened the procedure to a rape. To counter these tactics, defense attorneys had to undermine the credibility of the witnesses, and painted the former patients as fallen women of little virtue, easily pressured into lying by the police threats of exposure and imprisonment.

But the show trials of notorious abortionists were exceptional. A deeper trend flowed the other way, as courts and legislatures conceded to doctors the right to determine whether a pregnancy constituted a danger to a patient's health. From 1945 to 1960, doctors in almost all of the states persuaded legislatures to allow doctors to counsel patients on birth control and to perform therapeutic abortions when in their discretion the operation was necessary to save the life of the woman, the woman had been the victim of a rape, or the mental and physical health of the woman were at stake. A *Southern California Law Review* survey in 1950 found that only Louisiana and Wisconsin held out against "doctors acts." Most courts, as Dr. Russell Fisher reported to a conference at Johns Hopkins Medical School in 1953, "have held that if a physician procures an abortion, he is entitled to the presumption of correct judgment and the belief that he acts in good faith; in other words, if it be called in question, the state must prove that it was not therapeutic."

Still, a doctor had to be an astute interpreter of law to make sense of the bewildering variety of formulations of the various states' "doctors acts." In 1950 there were few actual cases on the books, and so little judicial interpretation of the statutes. As it had one hundred years before, the leading case came from Massachusetts. In *Commonwealth v. Wheeler* (1943), the court found that an "unlawful abortion" under the state law did not include an abortion, in the words of Lloyd Bulloch, a legal commentator, "performed by a physician in good faith believing it necessary to save the life of the woman or to prevent serious impairment of her mental or physical health, providing that his judgment corresponds with the general opinion of competent practitioners in the community in which he practices." Massachusetts had a strict law that allowed only life-saving abortions, but its courts, as did the English court in *Dr. Bourne's Case,* allowed the doctor's judgment great latitude. In addition, the comparison of the defendant's conduct to a community standard of medical practice in like cases almost made the act of abortion into a tort (civil harm) case, like a medical malpractice suit brought by an individual, rather than a criminal prosecution brought by the state. The Massachusetts court's reasoning, if not the precedent itself, appeared in other state cases, as well as in one from the District of Columbia. In all of these, the court put the burden of proving a doctor's judgment wrong on the prosecution, a reversal of the late-nineteenth-century courts' view that the abortionist had to prove the abortion was necessary to save the life of the mother.

But neither law enforcement officers nor the climate of opinion in the 1950s fostered any confidence among doctors performing abortions. The conferees at a 1952 meeting on abortion knew about the prosecutor who called a doctor after an abortion and told him, "You better watch your step! Any more of this, and you'll find yourself in hot water." Courts might, like South Carolina's in 1948, absolve an abortionist for acting before the fetus was quickened, but there was always a danger that a prosecutor might seek an indictment for attempted abortion. What was more, as Alan Guttmacher, one of the country's leading advocates of a liberal definition of therapeutic abortion, told the same conference, the number of doctors willing to perform abortions of any kind was shrinking.

Hospitals had imposed ever more stringent rules on staff and attending physicians who performed abortions, including consultation with other doctors, approval of the heads of services, and review by medical directors of the hospital or by special abortion committees. These committees acted as a brake on the doctors rather than a protection to women, and under the committee system the number of abortions further declined. The first of the special committees to review abortion cases was introduced in Detroit at the end of the 1930s, and the idea quickly spread. When Chicago's Mt. Sinai Hospital inaugurated its committee in 1955, the number of abortions there fell from fifteen to three per year. A similar drop was recorded when other major hospitals in Los Angeles and New York City adopted the committee approval system.

Abortion and the Cold War: The 1950s

It was not only the stiff regulations that the abortion review committees imposed that reduced the number of abortions in hospitals. Strongly flowing cultural currents in the 1950s, including the drive for conformity, the celebration of traditional family values, in particular procreation, and the connection that anxious political commentators made between abortion and communism (in some sense a successor to the connection that conservatives a hundred years before made between abortion and free love) caused women who faced an unwanted pregnancy to forgo abortions or to have illegal abortions rather than reveal their embarrassment to friends, family, and reputable physicians or local hospital staffs.

Shifts in family values affected the number of abortions, as marriages made in the 1940s and 1950s proved far more stable than those in earlier or later eras. The divorce rate did not rise from the 10 to 15 percent range until the mid-1960s, when it skyrocketed toward its present level of 50 percent. Men and women married early in their twenties, a drop from prewar levels that did not change until the 1970s, when again the age of first marriages rose sharply. Birthrates also rose, from prewar lows of barely two children to almost three, and did not sink until the 1960s.

The so-called baby boom era reflected a profound if relatively short-lived revision of cultural values within families and in the way they were viewed in mass media. The latter pictured the ideal family spending time together—the word most commonly used was "togetherness." With the spread of television viewing, bringing the whole world visually and immediately into every home, the emphasis on home life, and home improvement in the "do-it yourself" movement, afforded middle-class Americans a sense of security in a world that seemed to be spinning out of control. On the television, weekly shows such as *Father Knows Best* and *Leave It to Beaver* featured all-wise and all-knowing parents who could reassure their children when they faced the travails of growing up. In the relative prosperity of the 1950s, people could afford to have more children and still invest in them. Teenage car ownership and college attendance rates rose, as parents subsidized an extended "adolescence."

Focus on the family also relieved the terrors of atomic warfare and the Cold War in the late 1940s and 1950s. Polls and responses to questionnaires demonstrated that people saw the family as a refuge, and children as a hedge against ill fortune. Women agreed that they must postpone or even pass up a career to raise the children. As one wrote in response to a 1955 survey, "My husband works very hard in his business and has many hobbies and friends. The care and problems of children seem to overwhelm him." She had to carry the burden. The new family style reintroduced the concept of "separate spheres" so influential in the early nineteenth century, in which the ideal woman's roles revolved about domestic concerns.

For the Cold War wife, remaining childless was considered selfish, and the FBI's long-serving director, J. Edgar Hoover—echoing Theodore Roosevelt's pronouncements fifty years before—told mothers that their childrearing contributed to the war on communism. Popular magazines approvingly explored the phenomenon of the "maternal instinct," and the cult of motherhood spread to Hollywood, where actresses like Lana Turner and Joan Crawford (in fact two notoriously unsuccessful mothers) were portrayed as model caregivers to their daughters. Maureen O'Hara, interviewed during her first pregnancy, revealed, "Today I know the completeness of being a woman, a warm human being," when before her pregnancy she felt "empty." The most watched program on television in the 1950s was Lucille Ball's on-air announcement that she and husband, costar Desi Arnaz, were having a child

One mother who observed this cultural phenomenon found it appalling. Born in Peoria to a middle-class Jewish family, Betty Friedan graduated Smith College for women in 1942, moved to New York City, and began a career in journalism. She married in 1947, had children, and continued writing for magazines in the city, but found the limitations on her career frustrating. By the end of the 1950s, the mother of three children, living in the suburbs of New York City, she saw women's domestic subordination everywhere and recounted its toll: women who forsook promising careers to enter joyless marriages; women who limited themselves to endless rounds of stultifying chores; women who asked but had no answer to the question, "Is this all?"

Out of her own experiences and ten years of interviews, starting with other Smith graduates, she formulated her critique of the "feminine mystique," with its dominant canons of togetherness and domesticity. According to Friedan's research, wives and mothers made uneasy by their silken chains to husbands and children would find few answers to their dilemma in popular analytic schemes. In psychology, Sigmund Freud's psychoanalysis was in vogue, but Freudian theory and its clones subordinated women to men, and psychologists influenced by Freudian theories told women that their dissatisfaction must lie in sexual malfunctions. They must lose their innate desire to compete with men and find happiness in being more feminine, that is, in being a more desirable object to men. Friedan similarly chastized sociologists who wrote about "adjustment" and bid women find ways to conform to "norms" and "role orientations" within the family. Even higher education drew her fire. The purpose of education of women, according to college presidents, was fitting women to society's demands.

The ideals of togetherness and conformity, the impact of the Cold War, and the influence of the feminine mystique in the 1950s and early 1960s rendered "illegitimate pregnancy" dirty words. "Getting caught" was the young women's slang for becoming pregnant. The term had a moralistic tinge, as though women were paying for their sinfulness. Unmarried motherhood was not an option for good girls. But neither was abortion. One contemporary writer demanded that the word be stricken from dictionaries. Interviewed in the 1990s, women who matured in these years recalled that "nice girls" did not talk about abortion. As one woman who had an abortion reported, when she told her mother about it, "she was completely silent for about five minutes. Then she went to bed for a few weeks. She never mentioned it again." Women recalled that they felt "soiled, and filthy" after an illicit abortion.

Years later, women who got "caught" recalled the agony of facing an abortion. One respondent confessed that she had become pregnant after a brief affair but could not get a doctor to agree that she was entitled to a therapeutic abortion. Alone and fearing that she could not take care of another child, she waited until her two small children had gone to bed, then "used a knitting needle, and I probed and poked and tried to guide it into the right spot, but nothing seemed to happen that night, so I thought I'd failed. When I woke up the next morning there was blood all over the bed. So then I went to the hospital and this Jewish doctor took care of me, gave me a D & C [dilation and curettage—

a technique for abortion]." Even the near-death event was shameful. "You know," she told the interviewer twenty years after the fact, "I've told almost no one about this because I felt it was such an idiotic thing to have done."

———

Griswold v. Connecticut and the Emergence of the Concept of Privacy

Again, birth control agitation came to the rescue of abortion rights, keeping alive the hope of its defenders that abortion might one day be legal. In 1961, the National Council of Churches of Christ approved the use of birth control devices. Reverend James Pike, an Episcopal bishop, called family planning a "positive duty" for married couples who could not support a child. The number of birth control clinics continued to grow. Only one state, Connecticut, still banned the use of contraceptive devices of all kinds, doctors' and clinics' dissemination of information on contraception, and public sale of contraceptive devices, under its nearly one-hundred-year-old Comstock law.

The Planned Parenthood League of Connecticut's (PPLC) legal battle against the ban became the focus of the birth control forces throughout the country. The battle, beginning in the 1920s, had divided the state into religious and political factions, and split the major parties along ethnic and economic lines. From the early 1930s, the PPLC had fought on the legislative and the judicial fronts against the ban. In the legislature, supportive assemblymen repeatedly introduced bills to allow doctors to disseminate birth control information and married couples to make use of the information in the privacy of their own homes. Opponents countered, alternatively, that the law against contraception was not enforced or (assuming it was enforced) that the law was good for public morals. The bid to revise the state's ban on use of contraception gained larger and larger majorities in the lower house, but could not obtain a majority in the state's senate.

Catholic opposition not only expressed itself in letters from lay officials to members of the legislature, testimony before legislative committees, and audiences with the bishop of Hartford, it fell on

Catholic doctors and laymen. For example, when doctors with staff privileges in the Catholic hospitals of Hartford signed their names to a newspaper advertisement backing repeal of the contraception ban, the hospitals, under orders from the diocese, terminated the doctors' services. Dissent from the official Catholic line on birth control was not permitted, even in the private sphere. One volunteer for the PPLC's initiative to unseat anti–birth control legislators reported to its leadership that she had found her husband's reputation would be jeopardized by the church's lawyers if she continued her efforts. In tears, she pleaded that she could not go on.

The Catholic legislators explained their opposition to birth control as opposition to abortion. "I think these bills can well be a step toward legalizing abortion," one announced in 1951. Another explained, "We are not trying to impose our religious views on others, but we feel the use of the sex function solely for pleasure [and not for procreation] ... is an unnatural practice." Such principles were "unchangeable." During the assembly debate that year on the proposal to let doctors give out birth control information, one opponent insisted that with repeal of the old law, "the subjugation of man to passion and artificial sensuousness" would be complete. The theme of virtuous Adam seduced by Eve's artful sensuousness was as old as the Bible, and accurately reflected the views of the legislators who passed the 1879 Connecticut act, but in its 1951 context, the attack on women's sensuality gained new meaning. It perfectly fit the Cold War ideal of women's place as mothers of the next generation of anti-communists.

Stymied in the legislature, the PPLC sought a court ruling that the state law violated the life and liberty guaranty of the Due Process Clause of the Fourteenth Amendment. When the PPLC's birth control clinics were closed at the end of the 1930s, the birth control advocates sought a doctor who would allow himself to be named as a defendant in a case to challenge the statute. Wilder Tileston was a Yale University Medical School professor and private practitioner who lent his name to the case. The women he examined and counseled were real, but the PPLC used the names Jane Doe, Mary Roe, and Sarah Hoe to protect the women's reputations. Predictably, the Connecticut courts refused to do by opinion what the legislature refused to do by enactment. The statute stood.

In 1943, the U.S. Supreme Court agreed to hear an appeal from the Connecticut Supreme Court's decision in *Tileston v. Ullman.* (Abraham Ullman was the attorney general of Connecticut. He was not a great fan of the law, but his job was to defend the state, and he did.) The opinion for the Court by Chief Justice Harlan Fiske Stone found that the clinic's doctor, Tileston, had no constitutional grounds for opposing the Connecticut laws, for he had no justiciable interest that the law had violated. In technical terms, he had no "standing" to bring the suit. He had wanted a declaratory judgment voiding the law, but without an actual "case or controversy" before them, as the Constitution required in Article III, the justices could not get to the merits of his or the PPLC's claims. Had the PPLC's lawyers claimed that the rights of the patients under the Fourteenth Amendment were violated by the state, or that Tileston's own liberty was at stake—that is, that he might be jailed as a result of his participation in the clinic's operations–the High Court might have reached a decision on the merits. But the original pleadings before the Connecticut courts had not made these claims, so they could not be raised before the U.S. Supreme Court.

The leaders of the PPLC were disappointed. Later one of them would say that the entire project "is practically dead," but Morris Ernst, the New York lawyer who had taken the case to the Supreme Court, remained optimistic. The problem lay in the original arguments made to the Connecticut courts and the absence of a defendant whose life and liberty was at risk under the statute. In 1953 a new PPLC director, Estelle Griswold, came to the same conclusion. She convinced her board to join her in a campaign—to reach out to a broader segment of the state's women, and at the same time to convince someone to risk reputation and career by acting as point in the attack on the laws. "For thirty-seven years the upper upper and upper middle classes have been our support, but it is only the mass of people that can swing the vote," she told her board. In addition, doctors had to be persuaded to come out into the open in support of their own and their patients' rights. The Planned Parenthood Federation of America, headquartered in New York, and the American Civil Liberties Union (ACLU), a longtime friend of free speech, liked the new approach, and offered their aid.

Throughout the 1950s, the dead season of women's reform movements, the PPLC labored to build its electoral consensus and find suitable candidates for a court challenge to the laws forbidding use of contraceptives. In 1958, Lee Buxton, a Yale Medical School professor and private practitioner, as well as a longtime friend of the PPLC, found for it two plaintiffs. Both were married women whose medical conditions counter-indicated pregnancy. By law, he could not advise them and they could not practice birth control by unnatural means. To protect their identities, the PPLC filed their suit in the names of Roe and Doe, and the legal combat began again.

Fowler Harper, a Yale Law School professor whose career featured advocacy of many liberal causes, and Catherine Roraback, counsel for PPLC, wrote the brief for the PPLC, stressing the law's denial of Dr. Buxton's liberty and property interests in violation of the Due Process Clause of the Fourteenth Amendment, as well as the liberty interests of his patients. In New York City, Morris Ernst and Harriet Pilpel of the PPFA assisted. The state, confident that the issues had been settled by *Tileston* and that any doctor who wanted to counsel his patients or provide birth control devices for them privately could do so without fear of prosecution, merely cited *Tileston* and the refusal of the state legislature to amend the law.

When, predictably, the cases were dismissed in the Connecticut courts and the legislature again refused to act, the PPLC stepped up the pressure. Even though times had changed in Connecticut, and liberal Roman Catholics called for an end to the church's political campaign against birth control—it pit Catholic against Protestant and made the church into a political actor instead of a guardian of private conscience—the church's hierarchy continued to lobby against repeal.

But Harper had found a moral counterargument for repeal of the statute to balance the church's long-standing claim that marriage had its sacred foundation in procreation. He argued, as much against the Roman Catholic church hierarchy as against the state, that the law violated "the right to engage in normal marital relations," which meant the right of married people in their own bedrooms to exercise "a personal freedom or privilege to procreate or not procreate as the individuals may desire or as medical factors may dictate." Harper had introduced the privacy issue. "When the long arm of the law reaches into the bedroom and regulates the most sacred relations between a man and wife, it is going too far." If the right of privacy could not be found in the actual language of the Fourteenth Amendment, it must be somewhere in the Constitution, Harper proposed, for it was basic to any scheme of ordered liberty. The ACLU amicus (friend of the court) brief stressed the privacy issue as well.

In May 1960, the U.S. Supreme Court agreed to hear *Poe et al. v. Ullman* and *Buxton v. Ullman.* (Poe was one of Buxton's patients.) States have, in general, sovereign immunity against suits, so they are filed against an official of the state by name. If the suit challenging a state statute is successful, it does not matter that the official is named, for the state is ordered to void the statute. No one on the High Court expressed much solicitude for the Connecticut law, but was it unconstitutional and did the plaintiffs now have the standing that they lacked in *Tileston?* When the justices met in conference to discuss the briefs and the oral arguments of counsel for the PPLC and the state, they did not talk about the long history of state intrusion into the lives of women and men, or the wisdom of passing laws and then not enforcing them, or the great shifts in sexual attitudes from 1879, when the Connecticut law was passed, to 1961. Instead, they dwelt on technical legal issues like standing and substantive due process.

For the PPLC and the thousands of married couples whose interests it espoused, judge-made doctrines such as standing were obstacles to getting a court to hear the merits of their cause, and constitutional terms such as due process were arcane formulas, categories of the law that palely, if at all, captured the reality of the long struggle for birth control rooted in the personal experience and individual necessity of women and men. But for the Supreme Court's justices, procedural classifications such as standing and constitutional texts such as the Fourteenth Amendment had a reality of their own apart from the experience of ordinary people bringing their cases to the courts.

Indeed, in one sense, the justices' view was far broader than that of the lay petitioners before the Court. The judges saw in the briefs of counsel the doctrines in their long span of development, a rich context full of subtle twists and turns over time. The justices had the task, as women seeking birth control information and their legal counsel did not, of directing the flow of law, of making precedent that would

{ *Roe v. Wade* }

influence the filing of thousands of cases to come. For the bench, the consistency of the law and the limitations on what courts could do were more important issues than the theoretical or potential harms that some laws might work on women and men.

Justice Felix Frankfurter, a liberal Democratic appointee of Franklin Delano Roosevelt who had become more conservative once seated on the Court, strongly believed in deference to the legislative branch. This, and the absence of evidence (in Harper's brief at least, as well as in the facts of the case) that anyone had been prosecuted under the law, caused him to vote to dismiss the case.

A similar thought that the case seemed contrived, if not collusive, occurred to Chief Justice Earl Warren and his law clerk that year, John Hart Ely. Warren, a California Republican whom President Eisenhower named to the Court and who led the Court's liberal wing in a series of civil liberties, free speech, and procedural rights cases, was especially concerned that the Court's intervention represented a resurgence of the doctrine of substantive due process. He preferred not to set the Court up as a super-legislature reviewing all state statutes. Moreover, he wanted to see a real prosecution and trial in Connecticut under the law before the U.S. Supreme Court decided the constitutionality of the Connecticut statute.

Hugo Black, a former Alabama senator and another Roosevelt appointee, whose view of the Bill of Rights was literal but not broad, saw nothing in the Constitution that forbade Connecticut from regulating the use of contraceptive devices. But the same literalism caused him to balk at the state's restrictions on Dr. Buxton's freedom of speech, including his counseling of married people in the use of birth control methods. He was not sure of how he would vote.

Justices Tom C. Clark and Charles E. Whittaker agreed with Frankfurter: there was no case or controversy for the Court to decide. Had the PPLC opened a clinic and the state prosecuted the patients and the doctors in it under the statute, then a case could be brought. They would affirm the Connecticut holding.

Justice William Brennan of New Jersey, an Eisenhower appointee who had become one of the most liberal men on the Court and Warren's alter ego, was hesitant to agree with such a facile dismissal of the privacy claim. Brennan later called the Constitution a marvelous instrument for social change, but here he went along with Frankfurter's opinion dismissing the suit for want of a real controversy. In laymen's terms this made no sense—controversy over the birth control laws had roiled Connecticut politics for thirty years. But Frankfurter's argument had recast the suit in more precise legal terms: because no one had been prosecuted under the law or was likely to be prosecuted, the plaintiffs should have no fear. The law was a "harmless, empty shadow."

The other justices found the privacy argument novel but compelling and the case anything but a shadow. They dissented from the majority. Justice John Marshall Harlan, ordinarily cautious when it came to invalidating state laws, authored a deeply moving opinion based on the sanctity of marital relations urging the Court to strike down the law. In his dissent from the majority, he wrote, "The intimacy of husband and wife is necessarily an essential and accepted feature of the institution of marriage, an institution which the State not only must allow, but which always and in every age it has fostered and protected." Thus it was marriage, not women's rights as individuals, that he saw protected by the concept of privacy.

Justice William O. Douglas, a Roosevelt appointee who had authored some of the most liberal and courageous opinions defending individual freedoms during the era of the Red Scare early in the 1950s, agreed, but his brief dissent went beyond mere defense of the institution of marriage. Privacy itself was protected by the "emanations" of a number of constitutional provisions, for "privacy" was a requirement of every "free society." Potter Stewart, a Republican appointee to the Court who thought that the plaintiffs need not go to jail for the law to have bite, agreed, as at last did Black, the latter two men without writing a dissenting opinion of their own.

If the High Court wanted a clinic and arrests under the law, the PPLC would provide both. On November 1, 1961, Griswold and Buxton opened a birth control clinic for New Haven's married women, and then arranged for the town's police to arrest the staff and any willing patient. At the police station, Griswold, Buxton, and a number of the patients gave statements about the clinic's purpose and activities. At trial, the magistrate, himself unsympathetic to the law, had no choice but to find the defendants guilty. When appeal to the state supreme court resulted in confirmation of the convictions, the PPLC once again applied to the United States Supreme Court for relief. Harper was terminally ill, but his colleague on the Yale Law School faculty, Thomas Emerson, agreed to frame the final brief and argue it before the Court. At its core, now, was the right of privacy, based in part on a law review article by law professor Norman Redlich that influenced Harper and Emerson to move privacy to the center of the appeal.

But how would the Court find space in the Constitution for privacy? Emerson's brief waffled: "[W]hether one derives the right of privacy from a composite of the Third, Fourth, and Fifth Amendments, from the Ninth Amendment [Redlich's notion] or from the 'liberty' clause of the Fourteenth Amendment, such a constitutional right has been specifically recognized by this court." The First Amendment, protecting private conversations as well as publications, was also relevant in this "composite." With the morality of family life that privacy protected as the core of the PPLC argument, it gained adherents in new quarters. For example, the Catholic Council on Civil Liberties filed a supporting amicus brief that attached personal freedom to privacy and rested both on marriage and the family. Cardinal Richard Cushing of Boston agreed. He supported a bill in Massachusetts to repeal that state's anti–birth control provisions.

Now it was up to the justices of the U.S. Supreme Court to revisit its holding in the two earlier Connecticut birth control cases. The composition of the Court had changed, and that made it easier for the Court to reverse itself. Arthur Goldberg, a liberal labor lawyer, had replaced the ailing Felix Frankfurter. Goldberg strongly agreed that privacy was a right the Ninth Amendment included. Warren, with the trial record from the Connecticut courts before him, could no longer doubt that there was a real controversy. He would still have preferred the Connecticut legislature to repeal the law and was troubled that a decision striking down the law based on an abstract right of privacy might also strike down anti-abortion laws, but he thought that the statute was overly vague—the narrowest possible grounds for voiding it. Black was equally hesitant to write privacy into the Constitution, but unlike Warren, did not lean toward finding the state law unconstitutional.

Douglas returned to the arguments he had made in *Poe*, and this time Justice Tom Clark found them persuasive. With Clark, Harlan—now ailing but still strongly opposed to the birth control law—found the intrusion on married couples' rights intolerable. Brennan joined them—the right to privacy was paramount. But Potter Stewart had second thoughts, and reversed his view in *Poe* that the statute must go. Then, he was willing to base reversal on the Fourteenth Amendment. A reversal based instead on the right to privacy was not so appealing to him. But Charles Whittaker's replacement on the Court, Byron R. White, a deputy attorney general under President John Kennedy, joined the majority. His vote, along with Goldberg's, ensured that the Connecticut law would fall.

Warren, voting with the majority, exercised his privilege as chief justice to assign the majority opinion to Douglas, who, as was his custom, wrote quickly and powerfully. His first-draft opinion explicitly renounced a substantive due process basis for the Court's opinion. The Court was not a "super-legislature" telling states how to regulate business, medicine, or social life. But at stake here was the "most intimate of all relations"—marriage. Although he would revise this draft following suggestions from Brennan, the thrust of it remained the same: privacy rights living in the "penumbras" of the "emanations" of a combination of the provisions of the Bill of Rights and the Fourteenth Amendment protected the married couple from the intrusion of the state.

To find authority for the right to privacy, Douglas cited two old cases, neither concerning marriage or conception. *Pierce v. Society of Sisters* (1923) held that the state of Oregon could not pass a law compelling every school-age child in the state to attend public schools. *Meyer v. Nebraska* (1923) struck down a 1919 state law forbidding the teaching of languages other than English to children who had not passed the eighth grade. The purpose of the law was to bar the teaching of German, the language of the country's recent European enemy, in the schools. Neither decision mentioned privacy, but courts often reason by analogy, and Douglas likened the "kind of confidential relation" in them to that of the "rights of husband and wife."

Douglas found zones of privacy in the penumbras of other constitutional provisions—including the Third Amendment's prohibition on quartering soldiers in private homes in time of peace, the Fourth and Fifth Amendments' protections against illegal invasions of homes and papers, and the Ninth Amendment. What was more, these rights must be found in the Constitution because they were "older" than the Bill of Rights, the political parties, and the school system. They must therefore have been assumed by the framers of the Constitution to be part of a system of "protected freedoms."

Goldberg signed on to the Douglas opinion, as did Harlan and White, but it did not have the fifth vote necessary to make it the opinion of the Court. Instead, Warren and Brennan joined Goldberg's concurring opinion, resting privacy squarely on the Ninth Amendment. In effect, he began where the final paragraph in Douglas's opinion closed. Goldberg wrote: "The language and history of the Ninth Amendment reveal that the Framers of the Constitution believed that there are additional fundamental rights, protected from government infringement, which exist alongside those . . . specifically mentioned in the first eight constitutional amendments." Privacy, so vital a concern during and after the American Revolution, must have been one of those, in the words of the Ninth Amendment, "retained by the people."

Goldberg cited James Madison's words to bolster the argument, though Justice Black, who dissented, found no such commitment to privacy in Madison's words. The right to privacy on which the Court relied, in his opinion, was too vague, too broad, and would have dangerous consequences, opening the door to the Court's sanction of private sexual misconduct, such as homosexuality, that Black abhorred. It was the breadth of the Court's holding that disturbed him, for it smacked of the "natural law due process philosophy which many later opinions repudiated and which I cannot accept." The Court had no business substituting the personal morality of the bench for the legislation of a duly elected body, a view that had led Black, a leading liberal in the 1940s, to reject many of the liberal judicial innovations of the Warren Court.

Stewart, in dissent, found the law "uncommonly silly" and "obviously unenforceable." Moreover, "as a matter of social policy" he agreed that every individual should have legal access to birth control information. But he found nothing in the Constitution that would sustain voiding the law. Moreover, he expressed that same concern that Black had for the breadth of the privacy right. "The Court does not say how far the new constitutional right of privacy announced today extends," and he hoped that "even after today a State can constitutionally still punish at least some offenses which are not committed in public."

Harlan agreed that the privacy right was too broad, but he still thought that the statute violated the due process clause of the Fourteenth Amendment because it violated basic liberties. He was not bothered by Black's condemnation of the dangerous consequence of the new substantive due process. The rest of his concurrence was a summary of his earlier, longer opinion in *Poe*.

White concurred as well, as little bothered by the imputation of reviving substantive due process analysis as Harlan, but for White that was a departure of sorts. In his short tenure on the Court he had already berated his colleagues for reintroducing substantive due process in knocking down state criminal laws against drug use. Thus, like Harlan, for White it was the subject matter of the Connecticut law—its interference with marriage—not the far broader idea of privacy that made the law untenable. Throughout his long career on the Court, White would show reverence for the values of family life. Privacy and childrearing were among these. Connecticut's ban on the use of contraceptives so endangered fundamental constitutional rights that the state had to show its law was "closely related to a compelling state interest," not merely that it was "reasonably related to a legitimate government interest."

In the latter test of the constitutionality of state laws, the Court presumes that the law is constitutional if it bears a rational relation to a legitimate function of government. Those challenging it bear the burden of showing that the law violates the Constitution. In "strict scrutiny" the state must show that a law is both necessary to the welfare of all its people and well tailored to achieve that objective. For White, Connecticut's intrusion into married people's bedrooms to ensure that they did not use birth control information or devices failed to meet both tests of "strict scrutiny." But he did not need to apply this higher standard. He could invalidate the law on the absence of any rational relationship between the substance of the statute and the state's claim that the purpose of the law was to deter married people from practicing illicit sexual relationships like homosexuality, adultery, and incest. Plainly, the means by which the state sought these goals in the birth control information ban did not gain them. How could a ban on birth control information deter homosexuals or adulterers from engaging in private sexual congress?

Near the end of the oral argument in *Griswold,* when Emerson was using his rebuttal time, Justice Black asked a question that was on more than one of the justices' minds, to judge from Warren's and Stewart's later remarks. "Would your argument . . . relating to privacy, invalidate all laws that punish people for bringing about abortions?" Emerson was aware that birth control advocates had disassociated birth control from abortion. "No, I think that it would not cover the abortion laws . . . that conduct does not occur in the privacy of the home. . . . [T]here is [in anti-abortion legislation] no violation of the sanctity of the home." On its face this made no sense, for the laws in many states made it a criminal offense for the mother or the family to attempt or complete an abortion in the privacy of the home. Indeed, a great many abortions that women performed upon themselves did and could only take place in the privacy of the home, lest someone inform the police. Not content with Emerson's distinction, Justice White attacked the subject from another direction. "Well, apart from that, Mr. Emerson, I take it abortion involves killing a life in being, doesn't it? Isn't that rather a different problem from contraception?" This was part of the rationale for Cardinal Cushing and other Catholic clerics' retreat from their political campaign against birth control, although they still argued that Catholic couples were conscience bound not to practice artificial methods of contraception.

Emerson, worried that his attack on the Connecticut law could be undone in the blink of an eye by the introduction of the abortion issue, eagerly conceded White's point. But Black was not finished. "Are you saying that all abortions involve killing or murder?" Following the logical implications of this argument would have banned all therapeutic abortions, for if the fetus was fully alive from the moment of conception its protection under the states' criminal laws would be absolute and its claims to medical care would be as compelling as the mother's. Emerson, caught in a trap not of his own making, bumbled, "Well, I don't know whether you could indeed characterize it that way, but it involves taking what has begun to be a life." This was the issue that would inspire the most virulent controversy in the years after *Roe*, but the privacy right–based attack on the birth control laws, added to the therapeutic exception that some states already offered to their anti-abortion laws, had opened the door to discussion of the right to an abortion.

CHAPTER 3

From Repression to Reform, the Road to *Roe*, 1960–1970

The struggle for married couples' freedom to use contraceptive devices was over, but more important for advocates of women's rights, the argument that prevailed in the High Court, whether based on the penumbras of a group of the amendments or on the rights reserved to the people in the Ninth Amendment, opened a door for assertion of other, as yet unnamed, rights. Ill with heart disease, Margaret Sanger nevertheless celebrated the *Griswold* decision. For her, privacy had always been the central issue.

The right to reproduce was also the right to choose not to reproduce, and women had found a convenient and relatively inexpensive way to exercise this right before *Griswold* was decided. It was called "the pill," a chemical contraceptive device developed in the 1950s that went into commercial production in 1960 and soon was relied on by over one-fifth of all American women. Its pedigree went back to the 1930s, when Clarence Gamble, heir to the Proctor and Gamble fortune, began to sponsor research on an easy-to-use and cheap birth control device that people could employ at home, safely, without having to go to doctors for help. Like Sanger, he saw birth control in moral terms and was soon a pillar of the Pennsylvania Birth Control Federation. Gamble also invested in the delivery of reliable existing birth control devices to poorer sections of the country and sponsored birth control clinics.

In the meantime, Sanger convinced her friend Sarah McCormick, widow of the heir to the International Harvester Company fortune, to invest in the project. McCormick funds underwrote research into synthetic hormones that inhibited ovulation. Dr. John Rock, a physician, and Gregory Pincus, an experimental biologist, worked with pharmaceutical firms to develop the first of many pills that could be taken daily in relative safety by women in their homes to prevent conception.

Rock, a devout Catholic, hoped that the organic composition of the pill, mirroring a woman's own hormones and mimicking the natural ovarian cycle, would make it acceptable to the Roman Catholic church as a form of natural conception. His *The Time Has Come* (1963) urged Catholics to recognize the need for birth control choices, and Boston's Cardinal Cushing endorsed Rock's arguments. But Pope Paul VI's encyclical "Humanae Vitae" (1968) repeated the church's official ban on all forms of artificial contraception. If the church's stance did not stop Catholic women from using the pill (estimates placed the number of Catholic women who regularly used the pill at well over 50 percent), the side effects of the first versions of the pill detered many women from continuing to use it. And church leaders from many denominations decried the pill as an invitation to promiscuity.

The pill was not the only medical advance that betokened the liberation of women from unwanted pregnancies in the 1960s. Improved intrauterine devices, safer condoms, and more effective spermicides did not quite match the pill's efficiency, but they had fewer side effects. Together, these contraceptive devices seemed to provide an answer to the Malthusian nightmare of uncontrolled population increase among the poor. A presidential commission in 1959 concluded that information on contraceptive devices like the pill should be supplied to third world nations on demand, but President Dwight Eisenhower's administration, influenced by Roman Catholic pressure, backed away from any federal aid to the project. In 1961, the birth control movement successfully lobbied President John F. Kennedy to add birth control studies to the agenda of the federally funded National Institutes of Health. Federal family planning would go from these small beginnings to a standing national policy.

From the Sexual Revolution to the Women's Movement

The pill and the other birth control devices seemed to give women the freedom to engage in sexual activity if they chose without fear of unwanted pregnancy. Pundits called the pill the fomenter of a "sexual revolution." In fact, the social and cultural setting was already ripe for changes in sexual behavior, and the availability of the pill merely accelerated these changes. Still, the pill gave women a choice that they did not have before, which in turn made choice a central concept in an emerging culture of women-centered consciousness.

The path from the restrictive feminine mystique to the new sense of autonomy was neither linear nor sought by every woman—or man— however. Some feminist scholars have questioned whether the revolution lay in women's choices or men's manipulation of those choices. African-American writers like Amiri Baraka and community leaders like Whitney Young regarded the distribution of the pill in the African-American community as an attack upon African-American procreation, and in the 1960s local NAACP branches denounced the pill as an instrument of "genocide." In reply, African-American congresswoman Shirley Chisholm snorted, "[T]o label family planning and legal abortion programs 'genocide' is male rhetoric, for male ears. It falls flat to women listeners and to thoughtful male ones," but black women as a group did not place the same emphasis on birth control as middle-class whites.

Even as more and more women tried the pill (polls suggest that the numbers escalated rapidly from 1960 to 1970, finally including more than 80 percent of women), advertisers, large employers, educators, and political figures refused to abandon the 1950s' domestic ideal of winsome children, a happy husband, and a house in the suburbs. Thus, in one sense, the success of the birth control movement was not a liberation for women, much less a revolution, but another link in a long chain connecting women to the productive/reproductive cycle. Ironically, the arrival of the pill meant that women no longer had the excuse, used so effectively by the feminists of earlier years, that women's autonomy could be achieved only outside of marriage. Indeed, the sexual urges that the pill's use unleashed could become an opiate as dulling to women's fulfillment as the Victorian ideal of domesticity. As Betty Friedan had written in 1963, "Instead of fulfilling the promise of infinite orgiastic bliss, sex in the America of the feminine mystique is becoming a strangely joyless national compulsion." For men, on the other hand, the sexual revolution seemed to be a license to prey on women, and feminists protested by gluing together the pages of *Playboy* on the newsstands and picketing the Miss America pageant in Atlantic City, New Jersey. In 1970, feminists Deirdre English and Barbara

Ehrenreich appropriately titled an essay, "Sexual Liberation: The Shortest Revolution."

Friedan's book *The Feminine Mystique* was a best-seller in 1963 and after (selling over a million copies by 1970) because it touched a raw nerve among its readers. Working women, middle-class homemakers, and women in the professions recognized themselves in the many women that Friedan had interviewed. One of the authors of the present book recalls how her working mother (a school secretary) and her mother's friends interrupted their Thursday-night mah-jongg game to discuss the book, revealing to each other for the first time how frustrated they were submerged in household, husband, and children. Young women of the next generation recalled that sampling *The Feminine Mystique* turned them into feminists. Thirty years later, Friedan recalled that women called her out of the blue after reading the book and told her, "It changed my whole life. . . . I decided to go back to school. . . . I decided I would be more than a secretary. . . . I told my husband, you're not the only one around here that counts. I'm a person, too."

Yet even as Friedan's book topped the nonfiction best-seller charts, the "feminine mystique" itself was falling out of favor with women, if not with men. After over two decades of declining age at marriage, low divorce rates, and high birthrates, Americans' reproductive statistics sharply reversed course. The children of the baby boomers had come of age, but they did not repeat their parents' domestic strategies. The new generation, a record 63.5 million, eventually married and had children (only 16 percent remained childless), but the age of marriage rose from an average of twenty to over twenty-seven, and the average number of children in families declined from over two to only one and a half.

Diminished economic prospects—increased unemployment and double-digit inflation—deterred some young people from marrying and having children immediately. By the end of the 1960s, nearly 40 percent of all women held jobs outside the home. Many of these paid far less than the same jobs held by men, and a good portion of the women's jobs were menial positions, but employment meant that the frustrations of being female were no longer swallowed up in the silences of the home. Women began to agitate for equal treatment in the workplace, an activity that brought women together outside the home and empowered them to explore the roots of their frustration. Small groups of women met to "raise their consciousness." In the process, they gained an identity other than homemaker and mother, and that in turn changed the structures and expectations of family life. Women who had long before abandoned hopes of a career began to return to college or professional schools. Husbands recognized the shift. Polls in 1970 showed that husbands of women who worked outside the home were almost 50 percent more likely to approve of equality for women than those whose wives were homemakers only.

The general disillusionment with the Cold War ideology and increasing political turbulence during the Vietnam War era changed the way that women viewed the ideals of conformity and togetherness. In the new cultural environment of protest, the pro-natalism of the 1950s waned. Women's magazines began to question the "myth of motherhood" and publish articles extolling the "career woman." New studies (from the same institutes and universities that had in the 1950s charted the course for domesticity) now announced that having children decreased women's sense of contentment. The National Association of Non-Parents committed itself to the task of helping people find social space for activities that did not involve children. The association collapsed in the early 1980s, but some of its purposes appealed as well to couples who delayed having children, and the average age of first conception among these two-career families moved well into the thirties, where it remains today.

In 1964, a fundamental alteration of federal employment and education law recognized and furthered changes in the way that women viewed themselves. The provisions of the Civil Rights Act of 1964 prohibited discrimination based on sex, race, color, religion, or national origin. Although the reference in Title VII to sex was added to the bill in Congress to degrade and defeat it, the new law put the federal government on record in favor of legal equality for women in the workplace, schools, and the public sphere. Federal law forbade an employer to refuse to hire or to discharge an individual, to segregate an individual in the workplace, to deny entrance to training programs, or to refuse to give a job referral because of that individual's sex. Similar language applied the new rule to labor unions. The only exception was a bona fide occupational qualification reasonably applicable to the job or union. Women's entry into and full participation in state-run and secular educational institutions, including college and graduate programs, came under the same federal scrutiny. The statute allowed employers to use merit or seniority systems to make distinctions in salary but explicitly barred employers giving "preferential treatment" to anyone based on their sex.

The law also created an Office of Equal Employment Opportunity that had the power to investigate claims of sexual discrimination using federal, state, and local agencies and to compel testimony from individuals. The EEOC (the Equal Employment Opportunity Commission), empowered to administer the statute, could refer complaints directly to the attorney general's office, but more often it acted as a mediator in employment disputes women had with private businesses or with state offices. The EEOC could also certify a complaint to a federal district (trial) court, and could act as a plaintiff's counsel in such cases. Courts could order reinstatement of individuals fired for wrongful reasons, restitution of back pay, and other forms of relief. Within a year of its creation, the EEOC had encouraged many women to bring suits for discrimination. Over one-third of its case load in the first years of its existence was sex related.

In 1967, as the effects of the Title VII litigation mounted, President Lyndon Johnson finally added the term "sex" to executive orders forbidding discrimination in federal offices. More indirectly, Johnson's Great Society initiative in 1965 also empowered women. Federal commitment to family planning, welfare, jobs, and educational aid reached down to the lower half of society. Whatever the limitations of that initiative, and there were many, it did result in government commitment to reform for women on a scale that dwarfed all previous programs.

Despite the portions of the civil rights law that mandated greater women's participation in the world of men, Johnson's administration, mired in the war in Vietnam, did little to focus on women's issues. Although she had been invited to the White House the year before, by 1965 Friedan professed herself fed up with "more talk." She put aside the unfinished manuscript of a sequel to her best-seller and began to organize an association to lobby government for women's legal and political rights. As one early ally suggested, it was to be "like an NAACP for women." The allusion to the NAACP was apt, for the civil rights movement had attracted many idealistic young women. The two organizations crossed racial lines. Both sought the help of men and women.

But the comparison was not entirely accurate, as women who participated in the civil rights movement discovered. In 1966, Susan Brownmiller, a journalist and college graduate, joined white and black civil rights workers in the South, marching, registering voters, and desegregating public facilities. The experience was enlightening in more ways than one. Not only did women like Brownmiller see that protest brought change, they learned that men in the movement treated women in the movement as second-class citizens. When women who were members of the Student Nonviolent Coordinating Committee in the South or Students for a Democratic Society in the North raised issues of women's equality or women's rights—for example, the need to put more women in public leadership positions—they were met with ridicule and threats. At one Washington, D.C., anti-war rally in 1968, women reading feminist statements to the largely male crowd of demonstrators had to be protected against their audience.

Thus Friedan wanted an organization that women led and that had as its agenda women's issues. At the bottom of these was "a sex role revolution for men and women which will restructure all institutions: childrearing, education, marriage, the family, the architecture of the home, the practice of medicine, work, politics, the economy, religion, psychological theory, human sexuality, morality, and the very evolution of the [human] race." In 1966, Friedan called a conference to "take action to bring women into full participation in the mainstream of American society now." The last word in her address to the conferees became the name of the organization: the National Organization for Women (NOW).

In NOW's program, the "liberation" of women from unfair treatment in private life was tied to the equality of women in the public sphere. NOW lobbied for day-care centers for working women and for election of women candidates to Congress. NOW helped form a "woman's political caucus" and pushed for the Equal Rights Amendment to the Constitution. Friedan and others in NOW demanded enforcement of the provisions of the 1964 Civil Rights Act that guaranteed equality in pay, job security, and education for women. NOW's leadership also saw opposition to the war in Vietnam as a women's issue. The organization relied on traditional political and legal techniques—lobbying, holding parades and picketing, drafting legislation, and bringing lawsuits—to further its goals.

Like Friedan, NOW members tended to be women with professional training who almost invariably had prior work experience or came from colleges and graduate schools. But feminists were not satisfied with Friedan's conventionality and personal style of leadership. She and NOW's board were attacked for personal ambition—"going on power trips." These critics demanded that the women's movement reject the cult of personal leadership. Other challenges to her leadership of NOW came from those who saw sexual orientation as the most important statement a woman could make and discrimination against lesbianism as the most important obstacle true womanhood faced. Friedan derogated these opponents as "man-haters," but this was too harsh a judgment. The differences of opinion simply reflected deep cleavages in the rank and file of the organization.

As bitterly as some of the feminists castigated one another, there was no doubt that the women's liberation movement had come of age when, on August 26, 1970, thousands of women, veterans of the movement and newcomers to it, lesbians and straights, literary radicals and Socialists, linked hands and marched down Fifth Avenue in New York City. As Friedan recalled, history seemed to beckon them on. "The mounted police were trying to make us march on the sidewalk, but I saw how many we were. There was no way we were about to walk down Fifth Avenue in a little, thin line. I waved my arms over my head and yelled, *'Take the street!'* . . . What a moment that was. Suddenly there we were, holding hands, marching in great long swinging lines from sidewalk to sidewalk, down fifth Avenue. . . . People leaned out of office windows and cheered. Passersby left the sidewalks to join us."

The purpose of the march was to change New York's abortion laws, but the project did not begin with NOW, or even with women. When the woman marched down Fifth Avenue, the effort to "reform" abortion laws was already under way.

Abortion Reform and Its Limits

In an address to the founding meeting of the National Association for the Repeal of Abortion Laws (NARAL) in 1969, Friedan had proclaimed that the women's movement must strive for women's reproductive autonomy—in other words, women's power to choose when and if to have children. Thus one of the foremost goals of the women's movement was the repeal of the anti-abortion laws. But the women's movement came to the abortion reform issue late, after it had been dominated by men for thirty years. And the men did not want total repeal (or "abortion on demand" as one judge was later to write), they wanted to expand the exception for therapeutic abortion in existing restrictions——an exception that would be applied to women through the male-dominated medical profession.

The roots of the reform effort lay in the 1930s, with doctors' attempts to expand the definition of therapeutic abortion. Indeed, obstetrician Alan Guttmacher and his psychiatrist brother Manfred, both of whom had grown up in that earlier movement, led in the reform efforts of the 1950s and 1960s. It was Manfred who took Alan Guttmacher to a meeting of the American Law Institute on May 21, 1959, to hear discussion of a provision of the ALI's Model Penal Code that would have revised all the states' abortion laws. A tentative draft of the abortion reform provisions written by Professor Louis B. Schwartz of the University of Pennsylvania Law School was approved, and in 1962 it became part of the Model Penal Code.

The American Law Institute, founded in 1923 by a group of elite law professors, practitioners, and judges, had immense influence upon private law (that is, contracts, property, and the like) and significant impact on public law. The founding director, William Draper Lewis, had another agenda—reform of the law—and frequently the Restatements of the Law that handpicked ALI drafting committees prepared actually reformed law in a liberal direction. Sometimes the extent of that liberality had to be concealed to get the changes past the far more conservative general membership of the ALI. The Model Penal Code was one of these subtly liberal documents and included reforms of many kinds. But it was only a code in form—states could accept any or all of it, or reject it.

Neither the ALI nor the Model Penal Code was especially sensitive to the special needs of women. In the abortion law revision, the work that then ALI director and law professor Herbert Wechsler had assigned to Schwartz, one thus saw the old pattern of a paternal male organization ameliorating the dangers that women faced from backstairs abortion providers but not dealing with the question of women's right to an abortion. Indeed, the proposed reform went in the opposite direction. It provided that abortion should be allowed if two doctors certified that the mother's mental and physical health were at stake, if the child was likely to be deformed, or if the pregnancy was the result of rape or incest, but not simply because the woman wished to have the procedure done in a safe environment.

Schwartz himself was not happy with the limitations of his proposal. "It does not legalize abortion in a variety of cases where individual hardship might seem to call for a dispensation from the general rule. . . . We cannot regard with equanimity a legal pattern which condemns thousands of women to needless death at the hands of criminal abortionists." Yet Schwartz did not regard abortion as a woman's right, and his enumeration of the categories of allowable abortions included in the Model Code had a certain patronizing tone, for example, abortion "where the child will be one of multiple illegitimate offspring of a woman who has already demonstrated her incapacity to rear children decently." There is a whiff of the population control language of the first half of the century in his apology for the restrictions, though in all fairness to him, his proposal was about as much as the conservative lawyers and judges in the ALI would allow to pass. In any case, the decision would not be in the woman's hands.

The ALI leadership did not use Schwartz's logic to gain approval for the reform. Instead, Wechsler argued that reform was necessary because the state laws were regularly flouted by doctors of otherwise high reputation. In 1962, forty-two states still restricted abortion to cases when it was necessary to save the life of the mother, but rarely did a state define what saving the life of the mother entailed. Only the eight others and the District of Columbia provided additional exceptions for "health," "to prevent serious bodily injury," or for the "safety" of the mother. A law so vague and varied, and so often disregarded, brought all law into disrespect. The motive for the change was not, thus, a growing sense of women's privacy rights, or autonomy, much less women's wishes, but the need to protect the effectiveness of the criminal justice system.

As Zad Leavy, a California lawyer who worked for reform of that state's abortion law, and Jerome Kummer, a professor at the UCLA School of Medicine, wrote in the *American Bar Association Journal* in support of the reform, the old laws "drove large numbers of desperate women into the hands of the very person from whom the law seeks to shield them, the unskilled criminal abortionist." Alan Guttmacher agreed with Leavy. As Guttmacher observed in 1962, during the ALI discussions of the proposal, "In many legitimate institutions, physicians often have to disguise the true indication for therapeutic abortion to make the operation sound legal. I am sure many a psychiatric patient who merits legal termination [of the pregnancy] is made to sound far more suicidal than she truly is." Monroe Trout, a doctor who taught law and medicine, made the connection between Leavy's and Kummer's arguments and Guttmacher's observations. As Trout wrote in the *Temple Law Quarterly* in 1964, the law had to fit "changing mores," and it was doctors such as Trout, Kummer, and Guttmacher who were best positioned to interpret those changing mores to the legislators and the judges. As Kummer remarked in 1963 at a California conference on abortion reform, the reformers were not trying to give women the right to an abortion outside of the scope allowed by the doctors.

But the pro-reform doctors who actually practiced in the big-city hospitals were not motivated by abstract theories of law or general principles of sociology. The exact opposite was true—it was the particular immediacy of the danger to their patients that moved these physicians. The illegality of abortion for other than dire medical emergencies still spawned hundreds of thousands of medical emergencies— the kind that women created when they attempted to end their own pregnancies. For example, in St. Louis, Missouri, where abortion was illegal, a group of doctors and midwives were drawn together because of their experiences with dying women. They narrated these to one another as in a litany of horrors, an inverse of the Hippocratic oath, forced on doctors by anti-abortion laws. The healers had seen the effects of abdominal and uterine abscesses so putrid that they could be smelled from yards away; corroded tissue lining cervix surfaces; distended and hemorrhaging blood vessels; burned and punctured holes in rectums and vaginas. "Help me, I'm dying," the patients said, and the doctors sewed and patched and watched as their patients died. In consequence, doctors like Melvin Schwartz, a future president of the city's medical society, secretly referred women seeking abortions to doctors or nurses who would do a safe and sanitary job. In Chicago, the women who assisted the doctors formed their own collective, "Jane," and comforted the patients they helped gain abortions by reminding them of their worth as people.

The cases that particularly troubled doctors in the early 1960s were those of women who had taken some form of the drug thalidomide, which caused fetal deformities, and those who had been exposed to rubella, or German measles, early in their pregnancies. Thalidomide, developed by German chemists as a headache remedy, was not approved for use in the United States by the FDA, but some pregnant women had taken it by mistake. One of these was Sherri Finkbine, a Phoenix mother of four who hosted a local television show called *Romper Room*. In July 1962, she discovered that she had taken a drug containing thalidomide. Despite her doctor's strong support for the abortion on the grounds that the fetus was likely to be deformed, she and her husband were not able to convince a judge to allow them to use Arizona hospital facilities for the procedure. Local newspapers were already carrying the story when the Finkbines boarded a plane for Sweden, where therapeutic abortions of this kind were legal. The fetus was indeed deformed, and she returned home to tell her story to the women's magazine *Redbook*. Fifty-two percent of the women the Gallup poll contacted thought that Finkbine had acted morally. The Vatican Radio condemned her.

The rubella epidemic of the spring of 1965 put even more mothers at risk, but under existing state laws the fear of disease-induced damage to a fetus, and the shortened agonized life of the infant born with such damage, was not grounds for an abortion. Even so, California newspapers reported that city hospitals were quietly performing abortions on women who had caught rubella. The confusion between law and practice, and the distance between the doctors and the legislators so evident in the 1950s, was widening into a chasm.

Some young state legislators saw this yawning gap and determined to close it. They introduced reform bills that incorporated significant elements of the Model Penal Code's provisions. For example, in California, young assemblyman Anthony Beilenson's proposed reform bill would have expanded the scope of medical discretion, although even he conceded that it would have made no more than a 2–3 percent difference in the number of abortions allowed. Despite his repeated efforts in the mid-1960s to get his bill out of committee, he could not get a floor vote. As the rubella epidemic swept through the state, popular magazines published articles on the agony of women whose newborns were likely to be affected, and major television networks covered the medical crisis, but Beilenson's bill still languished. He agreed to amend his bill to give even more discretion to the hospitals, and still made no progress. In New York, Morris Ernst and Harriet Pilpel of the PPFA labored mightily to sway opinion in favor of abortion law reforms, but as their coworker, law professor Cyril Means, concluded, "There is not a chance of a snowball in hell" that the state legislature would act.

Not so surprisingly, in light of the changes in American families and the rise of the women's movement in the late 1960s, popular opinion on abortion reform raced ahead of the legislators. The Gallup poll in January 1966, when all efforts to reform abortion through legislative action were stalled, reported that 77 percent of respondents thought abortion should be legal when the mother's health was in danger, a significant difference from state laws that required imminent mortal peril. Fifty-four percent thought that the likelihood of a deformed child was sufficient. The Finkbine case fit this category. Each day brought a few more leading Protestant clergymen, such as the Episcopal leader Lester Kinsolving; professors, such as UCLA public health expert Ruth Roemer; and doctors, such as Keith Russell, one of California's leading obstetricians, on board the organized reform effort. The recruitment of corporate sponsors like Joseph Sunnen, a contraceptive foam manufacturer, enabled reform associations to publicize their arguments. Reform lobbying groups such as the Association for the Study of Abortion gained access to the media and testified before committees of legislators, but as little came of the reformers' pleas for revision of the criminal codes in 1966 as in the preceding years.

Reform advocates agreed that the same approach the PPLC had taken in Connecticut—simultaneous applications to the legislatures and the courts—might work where reliance on the lawmakers alone failed. A few state courts had found ways to read statutory provisions limiting abortion to permit abortions. California courts, among the most liberal in the country, led the way. In *People v. Abarbanel* (1965) the state's supreme court held that the abortion was not criminal if the doctor performing it believed, in good faith, that the mother would have committed suicide. The state did not look behind the doctor's discretion, allowing the kind of necessary duplicity that Guttmacher found expedient and still deplored.

In the same year that the court handed down *Abarbanel,* a number of California doctors openly violated the abortion law to help pregnant women who had contracted rubella. J. Paul Shively was one of these, and in 1966, he faced discipline from the state Board of Medical Examiners for his actions. To his defense came all of the leading pro-reform doctors, including Lee Buxton. They signed on to an amicus brief that Leavy submitted. The brief based Shively's right (not privilege, not discretion, but right) to perform the abortions not just on the mental health exception in the law, but on the privacy right that *Griswold* had just established. "It is a palpable invasion of the right of privacy guaranteed by the Due Process Clause of the Fourteenth Amendment for the state to inject itself into the sanctity of the marital relationship and dictate that the advice of the physician may not be followed."

Leavy had taken the step that Emerson, in oral argument, had avoided—bringing abortion under the umbrella of privacy that birth control rights had opened. "Both [the Connecticut non-use of contraceptives and the California abortion] statutes invade the intimate realm of marital privacy," Leavy concluded. Such intrusion, after *Griswold,* was "constitutionally repugnant." The California courts found that Shively and other doctors who followed his lead could not be punished by the Board of Examiners but based their ruling on narrow procedural grounds. They did not deal with Leavy's privacy argument.

Meanwhile, in a few of the state legislatures reform efforts began to bear fruit. In 1967, reform bills were docketed in twenty-five states. In three of these, Colorado, North Carolina, and California, the bills became law. These ALI Model Penal Code–type bills, sponsored by leading doctors and medical societies, were not based on broadening conceptions of women's rights. Instead, in all three acts, teams of doctors under the supervision of hospital authorities were to make decisions on the appropriateness of women's applications for abortion. Statistics from the three states showed that the number of abortions under the new laws rose only slightly.

In 1968, another state joined the reform column. In Georgia, a reform coalition that had narrowly lost its bid in 1967 restyled itself Georgia Citizens for Hospital Abortions. Led by some of the same liberal lawyers and ministers and doctors who supported integration in the state, it eschewed all imputations of advancing women's liberation. The new bill entailed a four-month residency requirement, effectually limiting access to abortions to residents of Georgia, and allowed abortions in only a few well-equipped hospitals. Then it passed, with little debate. Maryland followed suit with a bill modeled on the ALI proposal, now a decade old. Reform efforts in New Mexico, Hawaii, and Illinois fell just short of success.

Leavy's argument that doctors should be able to perform abortions when they thought it appropriate medical practice, as distinct from a woman's right to choose them, had become a staple in suits that doctors filed against existing laws, but two young men, Roy Lucas and William Baird, assayed another approach to reform based on the federal Constitution. Their efforts, along with the two lead cases before *Roe,* the trials of Dr. Leon Belous in California from 1967 to 1969 and of Dr. Milan Vuitch in Washington, D.C., in 1969, would alter the legal landscape significantly.

Lucas finished law school in 1967 and worked for a year in Alabama, where he recoiled at the effects of the traditional anti-abortion law. In 1968 he published in a law review a paper he had written as a law student, arguing that the federal courts and the federal Constitution provided an arena where women might win broader abortion rights. The article was guilty of a little hyperbole and some historical sleight of hand, but even these had a tactical purpose. For Lucas wanted to raise the panic factor from the outset: as many as two million illegal and dangerous abortions a year, compared to only eight or nine thousand legal and therefore safe ones. Such persistent flouting of the law grew not from immorality but social and economic necessity and "the currents of modern thought." He reported that the ALI and the American Medical Association agreed that change in the law must come, and it had already occurred in other countries. But the poor young American woman seeking a safe abortion could not fly to Japan or Sweden, and the mother who could not afford another child or who had contracted rubella or taken thalidomide could not get a therapeutic abortion in most states.

Although Lucas's arguments for reform of abortion law seemed to be couched in terms of the old paradigm in which the doctor's rights were more important than the pregnant woman's, and his treatment of the "women's interests" was brief and not especially incisive, at least compared to a much more expansive section on the doctor's rights to counsel and treat their patients, he was inching in a different direction than Leavy. He argued that the cause of the criminalization of abortion in the nineteenth century was not the desire of doctors to protect hapless women, but "the interests of community elders in compelling uniform adherence to specified moral norms." He believed that these norms were religiously inspired and found them echoed in the arguments of modern opponents of abortion rights that the fetus was alive at conception—a human being in prospect—and its interests could only be protected by the state.

But Lucas ruled these views out of order, for they "presuppose a framework of subjective religious assumptions about the nature of man, the acceptability of a given theological system and the meaning of life and death." Indeed, "to the extent that a religious purpose has entered into the retention of strict abortion laws, a technical violation of the establishment clause would appear present." Lucas was a minister's son and had grown up with similar arguments. Now he opposed them with polish and aplomb, for he knew that "in theological circles abortion is hardly a subject for light philosophical speculation—on the contrary, it typically evokes at the outset emotional charges of 'murder' and 'immorality' which generally are not conducive to a full investigation of underlying issues."

Instead of the misplaced fulminations of the clergy on the law, Lucas bid those interested in abortion look closely at recent Supreme Court decisions on the sanctity of the marital relationship. By insisting on a state-imposed criminal sanction against abortion rather than a private, conscience-based decision by individuals, the anti–abortion rights clergy wanted to do just what the Constitution, and after *Griswold* the U.S. Supreme Court, said the state could not do. Lucas's contribution to the debate was to insist that a woman's right to decide not to remain pregnant was a fundamental constitutional right, like the freedom to speak, associate, and be safe from racial discrimination, rights the Court had already protected. It was, he concluded, a short step from *Griswold* to a judicially imposed end to state laws forcing women to continue to bear children against their will.

Lucas recognized that there were arguments on the other side that the courts could and would balance in the scales against the doctors' and mothers' rights. But, he asserted, the fetus, a collection of living cells that would become a person in time, had no such claim to the protection of the courts. Nor did the states' claims that the anti-abortion laws deterred sexual incontinence have any evidentiary weight. Strict laws only drove women to seek illegal abortions. Moreoever, the laws as written, including reform laws, worked a special hardship upon the poor, who could not afford to move from state to state to seek one with liberal laws or a sympathetic hospital abortion committee. Residence requirements posed similar obstacles and displayed the same undesirable vagueness and variation as the therapeutic exceptions to the ban.

Better than reform through the legislatures was a suit in federal courts based on the constitutional right to have an abortion. With funding from Morris Dees, a brilliant and courageous Alabama civil rights lawyer, Lucas founded a think tank, the James Madison Constitutional Law Institute, devoted to abortion law repeal, and intruded himself into every state case involving prosecution of abortion providers.

But Lucas was not the only freelance abortion reformer. A year before Lucas started organizing, William Baird, a Long Island medical student and crusader for birth control, managed to get himself arrested for passing out contraceptive foam samples in violation of Massachusetts law at a Boston University talk. His case wound its way through the state courts to the First Circuit Court of Appeals, which reversed his conviction on the grounds that the state law did not reasonably relate to any compelling state purpose. In 1972, the U.S. Supreme Court in *Baird v. Eisenstadt* affirmed, in the effect extending *Griswold* to the unmarried woman. Not surprisingly, Baird was a vocal opponent of anti-abortion laws, claiming that they violated the same right of privacy as bans on birth control.

Leavy's brief, Lucas's ideas, and Baird's persistence did not bring change in the legislatures, but they helped inch the courts toward a kinder reception of doctors' extension of the medical discretion allowable in the laws. In the cases of Drs. Leon Belous and Milan Vuitch, the courts did not speak of women's rights but doctors' rights and the vagueness of the anti-abortion laws. In short, these cases appeared to end in victory for reform rather than repeal. But the language the courts used to strike down the laws allowed advocates of repeal to claim the cases as precedent for repeal rather than reform.

Belous was indicted in California for giving a patient the name of an abortionist. He replied that he thought the young woman might take her own life if he did not intervene (the standard loophole in the law), but the state did not feel that the facts warranted his action. He had practiced obstetrics and gynecology in the state for thirty-five years and had pushed the old statute to its limits again and again. Now he had gone too far. But when he was tried in January 1967 for his actions, his many patients came to his aid, and his counsel argued that his actions were protected by *Griswold*. Unpersuaded, the trial court noted that the student to whom he had given the telephone number was unmarried, and so not covered by *Griswold*.

California reform advocates, with Leavy in the lead, decided to make Belous's case a test of the new law, although he had been indicted under the older, stricter statute. By a 4 to 3 vote, the California Supreme Court agreed with Leavy that the new statute was too vague. That was enough to strike down the new law and free Belous, but the majority of the court went further. In dictum (a statement not necessary to dispose of the case, but expressing the opinion of the judges) the majority announced that although the state had a right to regulate matters such as abortion, on balance the privacy rights of the young woman and the doctor whose exchange of information had led to the charges were more important than the state's interest in potential life. Courts often employed such balancing tests in freedom of speech cases (balancing the state's need to keep order against the defendant's rights), and the extension of such a test to the abortion laws was logical but unprecedented. Labeled a landmark ruling by the local press, the opinion did not disclose where in the Constitution the right to an abortion might be found, nor argue that the legislature should rethink their abortions laws' overall impact on women.

In the same year that the California high court was dismissing the case against Belous, a federal trial court for the District of Columbia was hearing the prosecution of Vuitch under a 1901 District of Columbia ordinance. Vuitch was a full-time abortionist whose reputation was widely known, but Judge Gerhard Gesell threw out the prosecution. Criminal laws had to be drawn narrowly and precisely, and the terms "mother's life or health" in the ordinance were too vague. But, like the majority in *Belous*, Gesell did not stop with the vagueness of the ordinance. In dictum, he cited recent U.S. Supreme Court decisions that extended "woman's liberty and right of privacy" to "sex matters" and "may well include the right to remove an unwanted child at least in early stages of pregnancy."

Along with *Belous* the Vuitch case encouraged pro–abortion rights lawyers and doctors to bring test cases against the states' anti-abortion laws. Citation of the two cases could be no more than persuasive in courts outside California and the District, but in another twist of the story, the two cases accelerated the adoption of reform statutes as state legislatures realized that courts might overturn existing abortion laws. In 1970 states whose opposition to reform had seemed immovable a year before passed reform bills. Moreover, new voices were heard in state legislatures—the voices of women assembly members—and in places as far apart as Alaska, Hawaii, and New York, women, including Roman Catholic women, were pressing for abortion repeal.

But the majority of the legislators were men. To be sure, not all were gripped by longing for the good old days before the Nineteenth Amendment (granting women the right to vote), and in fact, polls in the 1960s showed that men as a group had more liberal views on abortion rights than women. But what motivated so many of them to accept reform of the abortion laws when for so long they had been unimpressed by arguments for reform? The limitations that the reform laws still imposed on women's bodies suggest that the male converts to reform could fit it into the older legal worldview or paradigm of women's role in society, sexuality, marriage, and childbearing. Abortion at will—the act that confuted the traditional ideal of womanhood—was still unobtainable. The reform laws that expanded the therapeutic exception did not call into question maternal values, and abortions under the exception would still be managed by trustworthy physicians.

In the 1960s pieces of the old paternalistic legal paradigm were falling away, and new information undercutting the old worldview's basic assumptions about women's place in a male-dominated society flooded into the mass media, the legislative halls, and the courtrooms. The declining size of families and the increasing use of birth control methods, the growing numbers of women in the workplace doing jobs once reserved for men, the growing volume of women's protest, and the increasing organization of women's protest groups, all tore at the bland, constricting ideal of domestic womanhood that undergirded the Victorian legal regime. With this breakdown of the paradigm of "feminine mystique" in mind, one can see that the reform abortion legislation in the last years of the 1960s presented itself to many legislators not as a step away from the old paradigm, but as a last-gasp measure to stem the onrushing tide of change. Given that the new laws actually enlarged the authority of the doctors, support for reform by some male lawmakers who had no sympathy for women's rights generally can be explained as an attempt to accommodate women's demands within the older legal ideology.

If the adoption of ALI Model Penal Code–based legislation and the handful of judges' opinions stopped far short of suggesting that a new paradigm, a new way of thinking about women and the law, was necessary to accommodate women's new roles in the family and the workplace, such an ideology was already forming in the minds of feminists. It had two interlocking parts. The first was the paramountcy of choice—individual autonomy. If choice, rather than hierarchy, was the model for law, women's special needs would no longer be ignored. The second was the appropriateness of intimate speech and private experiences in legal proceedings. Only then could ordinary women's voices change the law.

In the hands of movement leaders like Friedan, this new worldview of women and the law had abortion at its center and worked out from that center a rationale for the legitimacy of women's reproductive autonomy. Just as narrations of abortion experiences had the power to bond women to one another in consciousness-raising and liberation groups, so the logic of freedom of abortion provided a foundation for rethinking women's relations to men, to power, and to their own experience.

The right to an abortion was thus an issue that the leaders of the women's movement hoped would empower women in a way that few other women's issues could. The search for equality with men raised important questions for women's liberation, but the struggle for freedom of abortion differed from goals like equal pay for equal jobs. Abortion was an experience that only women could have, and as the leaders of the women's movement explained, abortion rights must thus be explained in the language of the legitimacy of differences rather than mere facial equality.

In 1966, the first woman to organize a group to lobby for repeal of abortion laws, Patricia Maginnis, had immediate experience of abortion. A Roman Catholic from a large, poor family, she had performed two abortions on herself. She understood in an intimate way the importance of choice. As she created her California Association to Repeal Abortion Laws, she realized that reform was not what women wanted. They wanted repeal. At the NOW convention of 1967, Friedan agreed with Maginnis. Friedan pushed the organization to adopt a plank opposing all abortion restrictions. Only then did mainstream reform groups like the ACLU adopt a proposal for abortion on demand before quickening and new organizations like the National Association for the Repeal of Abortion Laws (NARAL) gain credibility for their efforts.

If, as feminist leader Judy Gabree reported in 1969, she still had to "pretend to be crazy and suicidal" to get a therapeutic abortion, women were no longer ashamed to talk about the agony of that experience in public. Gabree narrated her travail to over three hundred women at an "abortion speak out" sponsored by the "Redstockings," one of the New York City women's liberation groups, in 1969. A year before, as Brownmiller recalled, she herself truly committed to women's liberation in similar fashion. At a gathering of women, she admitted that she had three abortions. "Saying 'I've had three illegal abortions' aloud was my feminist baptism, my swift immersion in the power of sisterhood. A medical procedure I'd been forced to secure alone, shrouded in silence, was not 'a personal problem' any more than the matter of my gender in the newsroom [where she worked] was 'a personal problem.'"

Motivated by such realizations in the winter of 1970, three hundred women led by a group of feminist lawyers brought suit in the federal District Court for the Southern District of New York against that state's anti-abortion laws. Judge Edward Weinfeld was assigned the suit, captioned *Abramowicz v. Lefkowitz* (Abraham Lefkowitz was the state's attorney general). The state's law was one of the strictest in the nation, permitting therapeutic abortions only when the mother's life was in imminent danger, but a group of Roman Catholic physicians, "Friends of the Fetus," with the church's hierarchy in support, asked to intervene on the side of the state's law. Thus the fight over abortion rights mirrored that over birth control.

The plaintiffs gathered at the Washington Square Methodist Church under a banner that read: "Women of the world unite; you have nothing to lose but your coat hangers" (one of the traditional tools for self-abortion). There they began to give depositions. These sworn statements of relevant facts were ordinarily taken in private, and Judge Weinfeld had so ordered, but the women wanted a public airing as well as a legal hearing of their experiences. The press filled the pews as women prepared to reveal their hitherto secret agony. The lawyer for the Catholic doctors was outraged at what he denounced as a travesty of proper procedure; depositions were always taken in private. Both sides went to Weinfeld, and he agreed that the depositions must be moved to the courtroom, but the press could stay (without cameras). For two weeks, woman after woman revealed the agony of hidden pregnancies and secret abortions. Brownmiller appeared, retelling how her desperation grew as she sought someone to help her.

Journalist Gloria Steinem, a feminist but not yet an open supporter of the movement, covered the event for a magazine. She changed her mind about abortion and law when one of the women in the gallery quipped, "I bet every woman here has had an abortion." Steinem had pushed hers to the back of her memory, but the sudden realization that she belonged to the movement she would later call a revelation. In the piece she wrote for *New York Magazine* on the gathering, she asserted, "Nobody wants to reform the abortion laws . . . they want to replace them. Completely." Claudia Dreifus, another freelance journalist, agreed: "Abortion. It's a hard thing to talk about. Not because abortion is murder, as the Friends of the Fetus had suggested, but because admitting to an illegal operation was admitting to being a criminal." Just as bad, she continued, it forced good women to go "into an underground existence. . . . endless searches for one humane doctor who might be cooperative" and risk his or her own freedom to help.

Dreifus later recalled how stunned and relieved the plaintiffs were when suddenly the New York State legislature repealed the law and replaced it with one of the most liberal in the country. It included a provision that made abortion legal during the first two trimesters of the pregnancy. With *Abramowicz* hanging over its head, the state legislature finally acted. But the battle inside the statehouse in Albany was a foretaste of the bitter and uncompromising politics of abortion rights to come. New York had a far more active reform tradition than most states, but as the New York State Assembly debates on the reform bill from 1968 to 1970 demonstrated, abortion crisscrossed older lines of liberal-conservative division. The law was introduced by Constance Cook, a member of NOW. Earl Brydges, a devout Catholic and long-time speaker of the senate, had not let any abortion law reform come to a vote for three years. Without warning, on March 18, 1970, he relented, and the debate consumed five hours. He was gambling that the liberality of the bill—with no restrictions on the abortion at all—would lead to its defeat in a floor vote. To his shock, it won, thirty-one to twenty-six, with a large majority of the Democrats, many from Catholic districts, supporting it. Brydges slumped back in his seat, tears overflowing his eyes.

Democratic Senator Albert Lewis from Brooklyn remembered why he voted for the bill: not long before it came to the floor he had stood in a hospital emergency room and watched the sixteen-year-old daughter of one of his constituents die from a botched illegal operation. As she lay delirious and fading in the arms of her tearful mother, police detectives badgered her to name the abortionist. Lewis chased them out of the room to let her die in peace. He knew that she had hidden the pregnancy from her mother to avoid shaming both of them, and under existing law, she could not go to the hospital or a doctor for help.

Aroused by the defeat in the senate, the Roman Catholic hierarchy dispatched nuns and priests to explain the church's position to the legislators. Worried that the senate's bill went too far too fast, abortion rights advocates in the assembly amended their version of the bill to allow state regulation after twenty-four weeks of pregnancy. After the first round of voting, the tally stood seventy-four in favor, seventy-four against. George Michaels, a Jewish assemblyman from upstate Auburn, New York, another heavily Democratic and Catholic district, had quietly voted "no"—the vote that the majority of his constituents would have preferred and his local party bosses demanded. But he had agonized about it, and just before the voting ended, he made a rambling, tearful address to his colleagues that he could not live with his conscience if his vote sank the reform bill. He switched from "no" to "yes." He predicted that his vote would be his swan song in politics, for his anti–abortion rights constituents would never reelect him. His prediction proved right.

The New York statute obviated the need for the lawsuit, but in Connecticut, women inspired by the New York movement filed their own suit, *Abele v. Markle.* Catherine Roraback, PPLC counsel in *Griswold,* led the plaintiff's team. The organizers made the decision to seek women as named plaintiffs and reached out to a wide variety of women's groups. "We'd always start out with a personal story," Ann Hill, one of the group, recalled, a step linking the two parts of the new paradigm—the centrality of women's private experiences and the importance of telling the story in women's own words. In Connecticut, as in New York, abortion rights advocacy spurred women to speak to the law in their own voices, based on their personal knowledge.

Women in the legal profession understood the importance of this step. As Kathryn G. Millman wrote in a note for the *Case Western Reserve Law Review* in 1970, these women had concluded it was time "to dig America out of the sand" on women's law questions. The place to start was abortion law. Millman tracked the abortion laws to their social and cultural roots in "a Victorian trend to legislate moral behavior." That trend had little insight into and less sympathy for women's attitudes, needs, or rights. Millman believed she could see the future: Hawaii's new law allowed abortion on demand before quickening. But Hawaii was ahead of the curve; "whether women have a constitutional right to plan their families in any chosen manner and whether the fruits of their sexual relations are no concern of the state are questions which remain [in 1970] unanswered in the courts." The first full test of the new paradigm of choice would come when the state laws were challenged in a federal court, and that challenge was already under way in two states: Texas and Georgia.

Searching for *Roe*

Texas's anti-abortion law went back to the days of Horatio Storer, in 1857, when doctors campaigned against all abortions, and subsequent amendments had only made it more unyielding. The only exception on the books in 1970 was an abortion to save the life of the mother. Under the law, Norma McCorvey was not entitled to a legal abortion. When they met, Linda Coffee and Sarah Weddington told McCorvey that it was unlikely a court would be able to hear the case in time for her to have an abortion. This would place an obstacle in the path of any decision whatsoever in a case like hers. Courts require that parties to litigation have a stake in the outcome of the case, and most pregnancies would have come to term before a case against the abortion laws could be prepared, filed, and argued—leaving aside the time that the judges customarily take to render an opinion. McCorvey had thus to be willing to forgo the abortion in order to win the legal right to one.

Weddington sympathized, for she had secretly had an abortion herself. As she revealed in her autobiography, she and her boyfriend, later husband, had driven across the Texas border to Nogales and spent all her savings, four hundred dollars, on a clean and safe abortion. She was already in law school, but the shame of a minister's daughter having to sneak about to get an abortion was indelibly burned in her memory. Although she did not meet them until years later, the experience bonded her to Maginnis, Brownmiller, Steinem, and the millions of other women who had secret abortions, as well as to McCorvey. Soon after law school, Weddington joined a consciousness-raising group that was looking for a way to make the personal (to borrow a phrase from Carol Harnisch, one of the leaders of the women's movement) into the political. They all resented having to get credit cards in their husbands' names, the lack of job opportunities for professional women, and the insulting treatment that women received under prevailing domestic law. In effect, they sought a way to challenge the old paradigm of women's legal place. What better way than through a lawsuit? And what more appropriate lawsuit than one that focused on a problem only women could have? Other members of Weddington's group gave information about contraception and abortion to those who requested it, referred students to the doctors who performed abortions to save the lives of mothers, and helped set up clinics to advise women on the dangers that sexually transmitted diseases and drugs like thalidomide could cause, knowing that the clinics were also providing abortion counseling.

Coffee and Weddington had graduated in the same class. Coffee clerked for Judge Sarah Hughes on the federal district court but found the only law firm job open to her was with a small bankruptcy practice. Weddington did not get an offer from a firm but found work with a law professor on an American Bar Foundation project. For a time, Weddington remained in Austin, the seat of Texas politics, and there joined in the effort to pass repeal legislation. Coffee was busy handling bankruptcies. For both, mistreatment at the hands of the male Texas legal establishment was a continuing reminder of the second-class status of women. Coffee joined NOW and the Women's Equity Action League. She thought of herself as the only feminist lawyer in Dallas. In the fall of 1969 the two women began to spend time on the telephone talking about seeking the right plaintiff or plaintiffs for a suit against the abortion law.

One such plaintiff approached Coffee in late fall 1969, during one of her many talks to feminist groups. Marsha and David King were a married couple and revealed that they were afraid of another pregnancy for medical reasons. Marsha was willing to offer herself as a plaintiff out of "moral conviction," according to Coffee, and Marsha had already become active in the effort to repeal the statute. She became Mary Doe and her husband John Doe—there was no need to expose them to more public opprobrium than necessary to file a suit.

That same month Coffee heard about McCorvey, and after two short meetings with McCorvey, arranged the get-together with Weddington.

Near the end of the interview at the pizzeria, McCorvey offered the two counsellors an option that neither wanted: "Would it matter if I said the pregnancy was the result of a rape?" Weddington replied: Did you report it? Were there witnesses? Weddington did not challenge McCorvey's story outright. (In fact, years later McCorvey admitted that she had not been raped.) Instead, Weddington told her new client that the Texas law made no exception for rape. Would McCorvey's interests (as opposed to the interests of all women electing an abortion) have been better served if Weddington had added the rape information to her brief? What if such an assertion would have brought McCorvey's veracity, and thus her life history of abuse and petty crime, before the court? Weddington prudently omitted McCorvey's spur of the moment assertion from her pleadings.

Weddington knew that this was to be a constitutional suit, not a criminal defense, and constitutional adjudication does not turn on the reputation of the named plaintiff. In 1896, the Supreme Court of the United States did not care that Homer A. Plessy could pass for white when it denied him the right to sit in a Louisiana whites-only train compartment. Nor did his unblemished personal reputation deter them from pronouncing that "separate but equal" accommodations satisfied the Fourteenth Amendment requirement that states provide all citizens with equal protection of the law. A half century later, the High Court did not inquire into Linda Brown's grades at the segregated Monroe Elementary School she attended in Topeka, Kansas, when it determined that separate but equal could never be truly equal, in *Brown v. Board of Education* (1954). Better thus to let Norma McCorvey become every woman, for her personal history mattered less than the rights her suit would vindicate for all who found themselves in her predicament.

Eight weeks passed before the lawyers filed suit on behalf of Roe and the Does, a short time to prepare such a complex suit, but McCorvey was growing frightened that she would deliver before she had her day in court, and Coffee and Weddington did not want to lose their plaintiff. In a way, they were caught between a rock and a hard place. Would the court hear a suit without knowing the identity of the plaintiff, without which condition McCorvey would bolt? Would the suit be moot (that is, have no justiciable issue at stake) when "Roe" was no longer pregnant? McCorvey was hard to find in those weeks, adding to the two lawyers' worries. Both women had to steal time for the suit from their regular jobs. They had no political action group, institute, or corporate sponsor to pay researchers; they went to the library themselves in the evenings and on weekends. When they did file suit, help would come from the ACLU and the PPFA in New York, from Tom Emerson in New Haven, and a host of others. For now, they had to go it alone.

Under Texas law anyone either administering or attempting to administer drugs or use mechanical means to procure an abortion on a pregnant woman, or furnishing the means for an abortion, was liable for two to five years in prison if the fetus was destroyed as a result. If the abortion was performed without the mother's consent, the punishment was doubled. If an abortion did not result, the provider or abettor was still guilty of a finable offense. If the mother died in the attempt, the charge was murder. If the attempt took place during the birth process and the child died, the penalty was a prison term of five years to life. Abortions to save the life of the mother after medical advice were exempt from the statute. The law did not criminalize a mother's attempt to abort herself or to seek an abortion. Thus McCorvey's complaint was not that she would be punished for seeking the abortion or attempting one, but that the law prevented her from getting a safe abortion, by a reputable doctor, in a hospital. It was her right to the abortion, just as it was Marsha King's right to an abortion should she become pregnant, that was at stake.

But Roe's and Doe's rights to an abortion (particularly if McCorvey had already delivered her child and King was not pregnant) were speculative and prospective. The state could argue that they had nothing to fear from the statute because it did not penalize the woman who sought an abortion. Coffee and Weddington would benefit if a third plaintiff—a doctor who had performed abortions—could be found. True, the doctor's claim to counsel and aid patients as he or she saw fit, according to the best medical standards of the day, was the impetus behind the reform statutes and were, to some extent, safeguarded by the vagueness of the laws in most states. Thus, nothing in such a doctor's right to practice medicine without fear of criminal indictment mandated repeal of criminal abortions statutes. But a doctor who was already under indictment under the Texas statute would present an obvious "case or controversy" on the model of Lee Buxton in *Griswold v. Connecticut,* and a court could not reject such a case as speculative.

1970: Year of Decisions

On March 5, 1970, the day that Coffee was typing the papers to file with the clerk of the Northern District of Texas federal court the next day, a federal court in Wisconsin decided a "doctors suit." Sidney G. Babbitz was a Milwaukee doctor who wanted the federal court to block his prosecution under the Wisconsin anti-abortion laws. Wisconsin had refused to amend its laws, despite repeated efforts by abortion reformers. His arguments did not rest upon the new women's rights paradigm and so did not preempt *Roe,* but the federal court found the state's anti-abortion law unconstitutional.

The Wisconsin court reasoned that the privacy right that *Griswold* applied to the use of birth control devices "compels our conclusion that the state may not . . . deprive a woman of her private decision whether to bear her unquickened child." By making a distinction based on the early nineteenth-century concept of quickening, the court deferred not to the premodern civil or religious reliance on "quickening" but to modern medical standards of viability. The court recognized the state's interest in the prospective life of the fetus but balanced that against the woman's right and found the latter compelling. In Michigan and South Dakota, federal trial court judges agreed with attorneys for doctors that the state laws were unconstitutionally vague. Doctors could not predict when their intervention in a pregnancy would be deemed a crime. The Seventh Circuit Court of Appeals overturned an Illinois trial court's refusal to enjoin the state from prosecuting.

But Coffee and Weddington wanted more for Roe than a declaration of a doctor's rights. The three-page filing for Roe asked for a declaratory judgment that the Texas law was an unconstitutional violation of the plaintiff's rights under the First, Fourth, Fifth, Ninth, and Fourteenth Amendments, an argument based on *Griswold.* A five-page complaint added the case John and Mary "Doe." Coffee also sought injunctive relief—an order from the court barring Texas from enforcing the statute against her clients. Coffee averred that Roe could not gain relief under Texas law and could not afford to travel to another jurisdiction. Texas law denied Roe's right to decide whether to remain pregnant or terminate the pregnancy, and "the fundamental right of all women to choose whether to bear children," an argument grounded in the new paradigm of women's rights. Roe had a "right to privacy," which included her relations with a doctor who performed the abortion, and a "right to life" protected by the Due Process Clause of the Fourteenth Amendment. The complaint for the Does added that a married couple had the right to marital happiness. The state could not force them to bring a pregnancy to term.

Six weeks later, under prodding from Weddington, now in contact with the ACLU and other pro–abortion rights legal groups, Coffee amended her submission to the court to add the phrase "and all others similarly situated." The addition made the suit a "class action" under provisions of the Federal Rules of Civil Procedure facilitating such actions. These were already commonplace in civil rights suits.

It was not clear, however, how far a class action would reach. The federal court system is a hierarchy, with district (trial) courts, sometimes two or three to a state, at the bottom, and (at the time of *Roe*) ten geographically contiguous circuits, over which a number of appeals court judges preside, forming a middle level of review. At the top sits the U.S. Supreme Court. The circuit courts hear appeals from the district courts when a point of law is at issue or the appeal is based on some error by the lower-court judges. The nature of the federal courts' hierarchy, with district and then circuit courts, means that a victory in a district court affects people in that district. If a ruling is upheld (or review of it denied) by the circuit court of appeals, the district court's ruling applies in the entire circuit. When circuit court holdings on an issue vary, the U.S. Supreme Court will often hear the cases to establish a uniform rule. Thus in seeking to certify *Roe* as a class action, Coffee and Weddington were already looking ahead to review in the Fifth Circuit Court of Appeals and the U.S. Supreme Court.

On March 19, lawyers Fred Bruner and Roy Merrill Jr. of Dallas asked permission to intervene in the suit on behalf of their client,

Dr. James Hallford. He had been indicted for performing an abortion on a woman who had contracted rubella. There was no provision for this in the Texas law. Under the Federal Rules of Civil Procedure, intervention in a suit—the adding of another plaintiff—was relatively easy. Although Hallford was a well-known abortionist and undoubtedly knew he ran the risk of prosecution, Bruner, an experienced former prosecutor himself, argued that Hallford could not determine whether his actions crossed over the line into the criminal because the Texas statute was vague. It permitted the physician to act if the mother's life was at stake but did not define the danger. Thus Hallford had acted in good faith when he performed abortions. Using this argument, Hallford's counsel convinced the state criminal court judge sitting in Hallford's case to delay docketing the case until a federal court ruled on their challenge to the statute. If they lost, the case would come back to the state for prosecution. On March 23, the federal court granted leave for Hallford to join Roe and the Does. Now Coffee and Weddington had a doctor whose liberty and professional practice were at stake in the outcome of the suit.

Henry Wade, the Dallas County district attorney, was the respondent in all the suits. A longtime Democrat, he was famous for his prosecution of Jack Ruby in the Lee Harvey Oswald murder case. He had no fondness for feminist causes but was not eager to prosecute abortion cases and had not brought many over the past few years. He seemed oblivious to the fact that abortion rights advocates were setting up abortion counseling clinics throughout the country, that legislatures in some states, such as New York, were debating repeal of their criminal abortion statutes, that the ACLU was preparing a test case in New York to argue that abortion laws were unconstitutional on their face, and that abortion rights forces were putting a referendum on the ballot in states such as Washington. In March 1970, surrounded by evidence that abortion laws were everywhere under attack, Wade did not see abortion as important one way or another. Still, he was the county's prosecutor, and he did not like to lose a suit.

To *Roe* and its companion cases Wade assigned John Tolle, a World War II veteran who had attended Notre Dame and then Southern Methodist University Law School. In a later interview Tolle recalled that his Roman Catholic affiliation did not affect his approach to the case and that he did not recall any Roman Catholic anti-abortion campaign before *Roe,* but he also was well known for his wry sense of humor—so that his disclaimer ought perhaps be taken with a grain of salt.

On March 23, 1970, he filed his answer with the Northern District of Texas federal (trial) court, and built his defense of the statute solidly on the religious objection to abortion: the fetus was alive at conception, and the state had a duty to protect that life. Tolle did not discuss the privacy issue—a surprising lapse—and he was confident that the statute would survive the challenge, an equally surprising attitude given the *Belous* and *Vuitch* dicta. But his discussions with doctors, his religious convictions, and his reading in the anti-abortion literature had convinced him that the fetal-life argument was sufficient to repel the challenge of *Roe.*

In modern legal pleading, counsel are allowed to argue in the alternative, that is, they may base their case on a wide variety of arguments that may contradict or ignore one another. Thus, Tolle also wrote that the statute did not apply to Roe because it did not penalize the pregnant woman directly, nor to the Does because Mary Doe was not pregnant. (He would have filed a similar motion to dismiss Roe, but he did not know if she was still pregnant.) In legal terms, there was no actual case or controversy, and neither Roe nor the Does had "standing" to sue. To counter the Brunner brief for Hallford, Tolle asserted that the state law was quite precise, not vague at all.

Jay Floyd, an assistant attorney general for the State of Texas, also prepared a brief to defend the constitutionality of the abortion laws. His boss, Robert Flowers, and Flowers's boss, state attorney general Crawford Martin, were more interested in abortion cases than Wade, for Martin thought that abortion was murder (Tolle's argument) and instructed his subordinates to treat it as such in their briefs. Floyd was a compulsive worker and prepared carefully, but he and Flowers could not make Martin's argument in straightforward fashion because the statute did not call abortion murder nor punish it as murder. Thus they fell back on the standing question that Tolle had outlined in his alternative pleading.

Lawyers know that sometimes the most important element in victory or defeat is the particular judge that one gets in a case. This certainly proved true in the abortion cases of 1970. *Roe* originally went to

Judge Sarah Hughes, sitting in Dallas, a feisty and outspoken liberal and feminist septuagenarian appointed to the court by Lyndon Johnson after a long career in reform politics. She brought together counsel and told them that the cases would be "consolidated" (heard together). Because Coffee and Weddington had sought federal injunctive relief against the state, Chief Circuit Judge John R. Brown of the Fifth Circuit (Florida, Georgia, Alabama, Mississippi, Arkansas, Louisiana, and Texas) assigned the cases to a three-judge panel, under sections 2281 and 2284 of United States Code title 28. The judges were Hughes, William M. Taylor, a quieter and more conservative Democrat, but committed to liberal causes such as desegregation, and Irving Goldberg, a mercurial and brilliant legal scholar whose decisions on the court marked him as a leading liberal jurist.

Oral argument on the case opened on May 23, 1970, the courtroom overflowing with reporters from local and national papers and friends of Coffee and Weddington from all over Texas. Coffee spoke first, addressing the key technical question of why a federal court should hear a challenge to the state law. Why not go into the elective branch of the state and get the law changed? Or seek a remedy in the state's own courts? As is so often the case, the question of jurisdiction (where one should file the case; what court can hear it) turns on the last stage of litigation—the remedy or "relief" that the plaintiff seeks. Coffee told the panel that the declaratory judgment she sought could come only from them, for it rested upon federal constitutional guarantees. What is more, the injunctive relief—the order from the court to the state not to enforce its own law—could only come from a federal court.

An injunction is a command by a court to a party before it or (if not actually there in court) to a party in the court's jurisdiction to do or to refrain from doing something. The origin of the injunction was the English king's chancellor's power to force people to do right by one another in court. This was called equity. In equity proceedings, the person who did not obey the chancellor's command might be jailed or otherwise punished. Under the Federal Rules of Civil Procedure as drafted in 1938, all federal judges have the powers of the king's chancellors. In the 1960s and 1970s federal courts used injunctions to provide relief in a wide variety of cases, from complex civil rights suits to simple nuisance cases. But here Coffee and Weddington may have made a mistake. They had named Wade, not the attorney general of Texas, as the respondent. Goldberg asked Coffee and Weddington how far the injunction, if granted, would reach? Would it be enough if the court simply enjoined the district attorney named in the suit, Henry Wade, of Dallas County? Did not the plaintiffs want statewide relief? "We goofed," Weddington admitted.

The panel was not eager to provide injunctive relief in an ongoing state criminal matter for a variety of reasons. The United States Constitution created a federal rather than a unified national system of governance. Congress has told the federal courts to defer to the laws of the states where the federal courts sit, unless the issue turned on a federal constitutional issue. Federal judges have not always followed this mandate, but they certainly understand it. There was no need to tell the panel that where state laws conflicted with the federal Constitution, the latter was the "supreme law of the land." The Supremacy Clause of the federal Constitution in Article VI made the laws of the United States and the provisions of the Constitution the ultimate source of authority in controversies with states, and federal courts were charged with interpretation of the Constitution. Yet this constitutional mandate only had the weight of the paper on which it was written in the South of the 1950s and 1960s, where state governments both openly and covertly nullified congressional law and federal court orders in civil rights cases. Texas was one of the states that had resisted federal desegregation orders.

So the panel nudged Coffee—why not remand the case to the state courts, with instructions to broaden the basis of medical exceptions? Would that not succor Dr. Hallford and permit women like Mary Doe, for whom pregnancy currently posed a health risk, to get an abortion? Coffee replied that Texas had seen plenty of cases like Hallford's and the Does' and not rethought its abortion laws.

Then how was the federal court to explain its intervention, if it did intervene? Coffee avoided the Ninth Amendment privacy argument, feeling it too novel and too vague, but when she tried to base the right to privacy upon First Amendment freedom of speech between doctor and patient, Judge Goldberg grew impatient. He pressed her on the Ninth Amendment. Would it not serve, as it had in *Griswold,* as a basis for a sweeping right to reproductive privacy? Coffee retraced her steps:

yes, it could; indeed, Ninth Amendment rights deserved the same protection that courts had given First Amendment rights. "In other words," she improvised, "they involve fundamental human freedoms, which I think recent cases have indicated are beginning to be given the same priority treatment that First Amendment rights have always been afforded." Goldberg seemed to agree: "You think sixty-three years of unconstitutionality should have worn everyone's constitutional patience. Is that what you're saying?"

Weddington did not match Coffee as a legal researcher, but was a far more effective public speaker, and the gallery seemed to sit up straighter and listen harder when she began to weigh the mother's rights against those the state asserted belonged to the fetus. Life was an "ongoing process"—it should not be tagged to impregnation, any more than to the creation of the sperm in the man or the egg in the ovaries. Goldberg interrupted: did it matter to Weddington's case if the mother was married or not? Did it matter if the procedure was performed in a hospital or a clinic or a doctor's office—in short, what was the rationale for the state's requirements? Goldberg was clearly leading Weddington to challenge not only the state's discretion but the doctor's discretion. But there lay dragons: the court wanted to know if invalidation of the laws would lead to a general increase in promiscuity or to an insupportable financial burden on states funding abortions for the poor.

Weddington was quick on the uptake. The state's requirements did not bear any rational relation to the mother's needs or to the state's goals of protecting the mother from her own moral weakness. Thus any interpretation of the law failed the rational relation test—the lowest level of constitutional scrutiny. Promiscuity was not deterred by the existing law, and the state would save money on welfare payments by paying for abortions. There may have been a hint of both racialist and class innuendo in the court's reference to "promiscuity"—but Weddington either did not see it or did not wish to raise the issue. Perhaps she sensed, correctly, that Goldberg had already made up his mind in favor of Roe.

Brunner spoke next. He explained what needed little explanation to anyone who knew about women's travails in trying to obtain an abortion. The Texas law drove women to seek unsafe abortions. The law's vagueness only added to the problem. Moreover, Brunner suggested that the old law was unrealistic—it did not fit modern medicine, modern sexual customs, or the needs of a modern state. Merrill added that the statute, as written, reversed the doctrine of innocent until proven guilty. In the Texas abortion law the burden was on the defendant doctor to prove that the abortion he performed fit the exception in the statute.

Flowers and Floyd wanted to lead off with the moral argument that abortion was tantamount to murder, but the law, a relic of the 1850s, did not speak for the fetus, or the law would have made criminals of pregnant women who attempted to perform an abortion on themselves or allowed another to attempt the abortion. Instead, the law was meant to protect pregnant women from abortionists. Floyd could only repeat what he had written in his brief—there was no case or controversy because the Does and Roe did not have anything to fear from the statute. The judges' questions hinted their sense that Roe did have something to fear, since the law made it a crime for a licensed Texas doctor in a Texas hospital to provide her with an abortion. As well, Hallford had standing, for his was a palpable case or controversy.

Floyd was thrown back on the argument that he wanted to make in the first place: "There have been many, many arguments advanced as to when an embryo becomes a human being. There have been religious groups that have joined in the controversy, and it's my understanding, and I'm not setting forth the Catholic faith"—that is, he was setting forth the Roman Catholic position, but not basing the argument on the authority of the Roman Catholic church. Goldberg interrupted Floyd in mid-sentence: did the state wish to say that life began at conception? Yes, Floyd answered. In that case, would not an abortion at any stage of the pregnancy, for any reason whatsoever, be taking a life? No—the mother's life was still a valid exception. How so, if the fetus had life at conception? The judge persisted. Well, that was the law, Floyd replied. Goldberg then wanted to know how the state decided when a pregnancy so endangered a woman's life that the exception to the statute would apply. Floyd declined to give what he called a medical opinion. Judge Hughes intervened: what legal authority did Floyd have for this line of reasoning? *Belous*, Floyd replied. But *Belous* had rejected the notion that life began at conception, Goldberg retorted. Well, Floyd replied, stumbling out of the frying pan into the fire, at least *Belous* did not claim an absolute privacy right. Goldberg rejoined, "But apparently everybody wants to use it."

Tolle finished the state's oral presentation with an argument that had lurked in the shadows from the start. What business had the federal government interfering with the state's protection of its own citizens, that is, pregnant women and unborn children, from abortionists? Even if the court found the statute ill-suited to that purpose, controversial issues like this belonged not in federal courts, whose judges were appointed and had lifetime tenure, but in popularly elected state legislatures. Let the legislature balance the rights of the pregnant woman against the rights of the unborn child. Tolle's balancing test was hardly novel. Judge Hand had used it to allow delivery of birth control devices to doctors in *One Package*. For some of the justices who decided it, a balancing test was at the heart of *Griswold*.

But Tolle was not really asking the court to apply a balancing test. He was asking the court to defer to the legislature so it could apply a balancing test. Deference to legislatures was another part of the birth control story; for Justice Frankfurter it was the reason not to overturn the Connecticut birth control statute in *Poe v. Ullman*. But that was before the High Court finally decided *Griswold* and found that privacy was protected, even from state legislatures, by the federal Constitution. Thus Tolle was trying to turn the clock back on the past decade's U.S. Supreme Court's jurisprudence on privacy.

The panel's decision, handed down June 17, 1970, was unanimous. Roe had a justiciable constitutional right. Hallford had standing to "raise the rights of his patients . . . as well as rights of his own." The Does could not show an actual case or controversy, and their suit was dismissed, but an actual case or controversy existed for Roe and Hallford. The court would not abstain, as the state urged, because the federal court was duty bound to determine the Ninth Amendment claim of the plaintiffs. (State courts can and do decide cases before them on federal constitutional grounds. The court in *Roe* was suggesting, albeit gently, that the state courts were unlikely to find the Ninth Amendment a persuasive grounds to overturn the state law.)

So much for standing and jurisdiction. The nub of the substantive holding that followed was "the Texas abortion laws must be declared unconstitutional because they deprive single women and married couples of their right, secured by the Ninth Amendment, to choose whether to have children." The court was willing to listen to the state argue for its interest in the potential life of the fetus, but did not find that argument outweighed the rights of the pregnant woman.

In support of his opinion for the panel, Judge Goldberg cited an article that former U.S. Supreme Court Justice Tom Clark had published in the *Loyola Law Review* the year before. Turning what would be Tolle's argument on its head, Clark reasoned: "Abortion falls within that sensitive area of privacy . . . one of the basic values of this privacy is birth control. . . . If an individual may prevent contraception, why can he not nullify that conception when prevention has failed?" Law review pieces, even those authored by sitting or former justices of the High Court, may have great weight, but they are not precedent. The court in *Roe* used Clark's article not because it was definitive, but because what Clark said helped the court to articulate its response to Floyd and Tolle's moral argument.

In the case of Hallford, the court found that the Texas law was indeed overbroad and vague. It failed "to provide Dr. Hallford and physicians of his class with proper notice of what acts in their daily practice and consultation will subject them to criminal liability." In particular, it did not say how "likely" death of the mother must be for a physician to act. Thus the act violated the Due Process Clause of the Fourteenth Amendment.

The court did not issue the desired injunction, however. One may ask, how can there be a right that is vindicated by a court without a remedy? Apparently, the court wanted and expected that Texas would simply cease to enforce its law, or at least decided that a federal court was not in a position to monitor Texas's compliance, although federal courts were doing just that in civil rights and employment discrimination cases, albeit with mixed results. Still, one can sympathize with the court's reluctance to set itself up as a super-administrator of Texas's criminal law enforcement.

Weddington and Coffee had taken a giant step toward validating the women's legal paradigm, however, for the court made choice into a constitutional doctrine. Freedom to choose was, for the present, deemed "a fundamental right." But the job was not done. Coffee,

Weddington, and their supporters were not content. They would appeal the court's dismissal of the Does' case and the refusal to grant injunctive relief. The state would appeal as well, seeking to reverse the declaratory judgment.

For McCorvey, Marsha King, and Dr. Hallford, the fruits of victory remained elusive. McCorvey was six months pregnant when the panel ruled in her favor. She had the baby, placed it for adoption, and returned to a life of waiting on tables. She would later write an autobiography, become the hero of the pro-choice forces, then switch her allegiance to the right-to-life movement. King got pregnant and had to go to Mexico for an abortion because the court did not issue the injunction. Later she had children. Dr. Hallford, still under indictment, left Texas. A victory in law is not always a victory in life.

Strong support for the Texas three judges' ruling came from another district court in the Fifth Circuit. Sitting in Atlanta, a three-judge panel handed down its opinion in *Doe v. Bolton* on July 31, 1970. The leadership of the Atlanta ACLU (the ACLU is headquartered in New York City but is in fact a loose coalition of local chapters) and the Legal Aid Society were disappointed with the restrictions the abortion reform bill passed by the Georgia legislature left in place and preferred repeal to reform in any case. A group of female lawyers turned to Margie Pitts Hames, a thirty-six-year-old mother and former law firm partner who had taken a leave to have a second child. Hames agreed that she would help recruit plaintiffs willing to challenge the newly minted Georgia "reform" abortion statute. They were looking in particular for a pregnant woman whose desire for an abortion the new law could not accommodate.

Sandra Bensing fit the bill. She was married but separated from her drifter husband, had three other children no longer living with her, and was again pregnant. Unable to get a therapeutic abortion under the law, Bensing agreed to sue the state of Georgia under the pseudonym of Mary Doe. On April 16, Hames filed *Doe v. Bolton* in the United States Court for the Northern District of Georgia, seeking declaratory and injunctive relief for married and unmarried women who sought abortions and for physicians, nurses, and social workers who helped the women find abortions. The suit named as respondent the attorney general of Georgia, Arthur K. Bolton.

Doe introduced a novelty that was a logical extension of the fetal-life argument Tolle and Floyd assayed. The *Roe* decision had convinced anti-abortion forces to formally introduce fetal rights in the pleadings. Ferdinand Buckley, a Roman Catholic Atlanta lawyer, intervened in *Doe* seeking to be appointed the guardian ad litem (literally "during the legal proceeding" or "for the purposes of the suit") for the unborn fetus. Buckley had strongly opposed the 1968 reform bill. His intervention meant that the argument that the fetus was alive from conception—an essentially religious concept—would become part of the legal record because Buckley, as counsel, would have the same status in addressing the court as Hames or the state's attorneys. In some sense, this was a device to publicize the right-to-life position rather than make a legally cognizable claim, but Buckley's intervention set a precedent in future cases as well as making a splash out of court. The court initially allowed him to intervene, then changed its mind when Hames reported that Buckley's motion was making it difficult for her client to find any hospital willing to perform the operation under the existing laws.

Hames's chief opponent before the court was Assistant State Attorney Dorothy Toth Beasley, a New Jerseyan who had moved to Georgia and worked for a time in the same firm as Hames. She switched jobs to join the criminal enforcement division of the state attorney's office in 1969, and was widely regarded as one of the most capable advocates of law enforcement there. The core of her defense of the state was that the Constitution of the United States did not confer on pregnant women the right to destroy a "living child." The fetus was never part of a woman, it was "from its earliest stage already a boy or girl, with its own organs." The supposed right to an abortion was one that "invaded" the life and liberty of the unborn child.

The Georgia court's three-judge panel of Sidney Smith, Lewis Morgan, and Albert Henderson found the logic of *Roe* persuasive. The plaintiffs had "obvious" standing because the statute applied to them. Was there a case or controversy? After all, no one was under indictment. The court opined that declaratory judgments not only were permissible under the Federal Rules of Civil Procedure, they were granted in high-visibility public law issues like the teaching of evolution in the schools (citing the recent U.S. Supreme Court in *Epperson v. Arkansas* [1968] overturning a state statute prohibiting the teaching of evolution, even though the teacher had not been indicted under the statute). The hospital board that denied Mary Doe's application for an abortion acted under the color of law. Doe could thus point to a case or controversy.

On the merits of the case: although the court rejected the proposition that a woman could use her body "any way she wishes," the court found that *Griswold*'s logic applied to the matter of abortion. The fetus might have the potential of becoming a human being, but nothing in federal law made it an independent being at conception, and therefore the woman's right to end the pregnancy outweighed any interest of the fetus or the state in forcing her to carry the pregnancy to term. The state could regulate abortions to ensure that they were safe and to put "abortion mills" out of business. But the state could not limit the reasons for which an abortion was granted.

Like the *Roe* court, the court in *Doe v. Bolton* refused to grant the injunctive relief sought, for there was no "pending state court proceeding against which the injunction . . . would operate." The Georgia panel was not going to issue a blanket injunction against prospective evils. In the interest of the health of the patients, the court would not interfere with Georgia's requirements that the woman seeking an abortion get the approval of a certified physician, ratified by two other consulting doctors, and then approved by the abortion committee at the admitting hospital. Abortion was to be legal but still not easy to obtain. Hames was delighted, but not content. She would appeal, as would the state, the former to lift the remaining restrictions on abortion, the latter to reinstate the stricter rule.

The Texas and Georgia suits buoyed the hopes of the pro–abortion rights forces. Pro-choice groups had also commenced suits for women's right to an abortion in Minnesota, Kentucky, North Carolina, Missouri, and California. But before the latter suits brought definitive results, two more cases were decided that had a chilling effect on the pro-choice movement, the first in Louisiana and the second in Ohio. These, *Rosen v. Louisiana* and *Steinberg v. Brown,* were parallel in some ways to *Roe* and *Doe.* If the repeal advocates could win these, the opposition to repeal in the state legislatures might fall away, and abortion law return to its status before the 1820s. But divided courts in both cases rejected the arguments that had won in Texas and Georgia.

In Louisiana, Isadore A. Rosen, a doctor, challenged the constitutionality of a provision of the criminal code that suspended or revoked the licenses of physicians who participated in abortions when the mother's life was not in danger from the pregnancy. Rosen was facing disqualification, and he wanted the court to enjoin the state medical board from acting. The district court panel of three judges knew all about *Babbitz* and *Roe* but did not see the Louisiana law as vague at all, if one used common sense rather than the unnecessarily confusing language of doctors. The court suspected that doctors like Rosen were not a bit confused by the statute, but simply intended to break the law.

Judge Robert Ainsworth, writing for a two to one majority on August 7, 1970, found that while a doctor might believe the statute was too restrictive, its language was plain enough. Nor was it overbroad, for it was neatly tailored to its purpose. Rosen's contention that his patients had a fundamental right to choose to have or not to have children fell before "the interests of the embryo or fetus that the pregnant woman carries." In effect, Ainsworth suggested, a pregnant woman was a kind of trustee whose womb was a carrier of life. If a woman did not want to fulfill this living trust, she had "abstinence, rhythm, contraception, and sterilization" available to her.

Ainsworth continued that the right to choose whether to bear children in *Griswold* ended with conception. A "living organism" was created when egg and sperm came together, "belonging to the species homo sapiens." He admitted that "men of intelligence and good will" had argued that such organisms were not fully alive until a "later stage," but added that others ("for example the official Roman Catholic position") found that the moment of conception is the "moment at which distinctively human life begins." The state law, amended in 1964, took the latter view—"children in the mother's womb are considered, in whatever related to themselves, as if they were already born." Although the state did not penalize killing the fetus as severely as it did killing a live infant, the state had long recognized its duty to protect the life of the fetus.

As in *Roe* and *Rosen,* much of the controversy about abortion law in America had been, and would increasingly be, concerned with competing views of religion and religion's place in American law. Colonial law had established churches, punished blasphemy, and fined men and women who did not keep the Sabbath. In the revolutionary era most states disestablished churches, but many states still had laws that regulated conduct on Sunday. The First Amendment to the Constitution barred Congress from passing any law that established a national church or discriminated against any religion, supposedly erecting a wall separating church from state, but the purpose of the wall was as much to protect the church as it was to protect the state. The precise language of the First Amendment, applied to the states in the Fourteenth Amendment, was in itself confusing, for the clause guaranteed free exercise of religion at the same time that it barred the establishment of an official religion. To this day, free exercise cases and establishment cases crisscross one another with confusing frequency. For example, by 1970, the U.S. Supreme Court had barred denominational prayers in schools but had not abolished its own invocation, "God save this honorable court."

The religious argument, soft-pedaled in *Roe,* became the centerpiece for Ainsworth, like Tolle a Roman Catholic. What was more, unlike Georgia and Texas, Louisiana had a large and politically important Roman Catholic population and a powerful Roman Catholic church with influence in state politics. True, public opinion polls had revealed what many abortion reformers already knew: 90 percent of Catholic laymen and women believed that abortion should be legal when a mother's health (not just life) was at stake, and four out of ten Catholics believed that abortion was an acceptable means to limit family size. But the Catholic hierarchy had made abortion a litmus test of theological orthodoxy, and even liberal Catholic clergymen had little wiggle room. The Roman Catholic church is not a monolith, and diversity of opinion on some issues thrives within it, but on the matter of abortion, the papacy and the American bishops agreed—no compromise. As in Connecticut during the birth control reform campaign, the hierarchy, rather than the laity, had the ear of the legislature.

Although he frequently cited Roman Catholic writings with obvious approval, it was not clear at all that Ainsworth was guilty of abusing or exceeding his discretion as a judge or acting outside of his judicial role in borrowing Roman Catholic precepts to shape the contention that "abortion . . . raises a basic issue of public interest concerning the value of the human embryo or fetus." Appointed to the federal bench by President John F. Kennedy and elevated to the Court of Appeals by President Johnson in 1966, he was regarded by other judges as a moderate, polite, and cautious jurist. In *Rosen,* he concluded that questions such as abortion rights were best left to the democratic process, rather than a court sitting as "a super legislature"—the very language that Douglas had used to avert the charge that the *Griswold* court was returning to substantive due process standards. Even Justice Clark's article had said, "It is for the legislature to determine the proper balance, i.e., that point between prevention of conception and viability of fetus which would give the state the compelling . . . interest so that it may regulate or prohibit abortion without violating the individual's constitutionally protected rights." Clark did not put that "point" at conception—he thought that it should come at quickening—but Ainsworth did not quote that portion of Clark's piece.

In dissent, Judge Fred Cassibry disputed the notion that human life came into being at conception. Cassibry was a feisty New Orleans Democratic politician before President Johnson elevated him to the bench, and he saw the case for abortion rights as a matter of simple logic. The state law did not protect the fetus, for the mother who sought or obtained an abortion was not prosecuted. Instead, the state law and the majority in *Rosen* were trying to "enforce certain views of private morality against those not sharing those views." *Griswold* told states not to impose a legislative majority's moral preferences upon individuals in certain fundamental areas. Private decisions about whether to have children were among these. *Griswold* controlled *Rosen,* or should have, for its "broad command" was to "protect the privacy and the intimacy of family life" from state intrusion.

Federal district judge Don J. Young wrote for the two to one majority in *Steinberg v. Ohio,* the opinion announced on December 18, 1970. His writing, unlike Ainsworth's, had a sharp, almost bitter tone. The plaintiffs included a physician (Dr. A. H. Steinberg), a psychiatrist, a social worker, a minister, and a married woman separated from her husband who wished to terminate a pregnancy. The judge knew that repeal forces had recruited this slate of plaintiffs to challenge the state's law from all directions. There was also an intercessor, one Homer Schroeder, a doctor who wished to be named guardian ad litem of the unborn child. No one was threatened with prosecution, so Young denied the plea for injunctive relief. Authorities were divided on whether a statute like Ohio's was too vague, but taken in its ordinary meaning, instead of the "strained construction" of the doctors, the statute seemed clear to Young.

The privacy argument failed as well. "When the meringue is sluiced away, " Young opined, the contention that *Griswold* extended to abortions vanished. *Roe* and its companion cases "have not been based on a proper legal or factual understanding." The state had a legitimate right to protect the fetus. "One of the great puzzles of the law is why its practitioners blithely argue their cases and make the decision in total disregard, if not ignorance, of the laws of nature . . . the facts of biology." Young did not see this as a religious question. *Griswold* dealt with very tentative life forms, which might or might not survive. "Once the preliminaries have ended, and a new life has begun," the very same constitutional amendments that the plaintiffs cited required the state to protect the fetus. For the mother who incautiously became pregnant and sought now to end it, Young's advice was "Those who dance must pay the piper."

Judge Ben C. Green dissented. He was outraged by the tone of the opinion and unimpressed by its logic. The court should have deferred to the doctors when they said that they could not give precision to the language of the statute rather than flippantly proposing a common-sense interpretation. After all, the purpose of the statute was to tell the doctors what they could and could not do. Judge Young's biology lesson did not impress Green either. For him, the bottom line was that the woman's right to control her own body outweighed the right of the embryo or its guardian, the state, to force a woman to remain pregnant. Even the history of the statute demonstrated that it was the pregnant woman's health, not the fetus's, that motivated the framers of the act. Moreover, the framers understood that legal life did not begin until quickening.

———

By the end of 1970, the future of abortion law was unclear. Early victories for the pro–abortion rights forces had given way to confusing and contested losses. Coffee and Weddington correctly regarded the decision in *Roe* as a monumental triumph—the first time that women's rights to control what happened to their own bodies had become a principle of constitutional law, but they could not predict how long or in what form that principle would survive.

One fact had not changed. As in the 1950s, when the fate of a pregnant woman seeking an abortion depended upon the overwhelmingly male profession of medicine, so in *Roe* the fate of women depended upon nine men who sat on the U.S. Supreme Court. Despite the vital importance of women in bringing the case to the Court, men would decide it. None had ever been pregnant or faced the dangers of childbirth. While the arguments that counsel made revolved around abstract constitutional concepts like liberty and privacy, at the core of the case, in the warp and woof of real people's lives that the language of the law in appellate courts often masked or elided, was an experience entirely foreign to the men on the bench. It required a leap of imagination, an act of empathy, for them to see that reproductive autonomy for women was uniquely a women's question, and without doubt some of them would hesitate to make such a leap. Others would be persuaded that the fetus was alive from conception and that its life must be protected by the state.

In the meantime, Coffee and Weddington set about preparing their appeal.

CHAPTER 4

The Decision in *Roe*, 1971–1973

The early years of the 1970s were heady times for women's liberation. Radicals in the movement were demanding that women be seen as an oppressed class, and used organizing and protesting techniques from the civil rights movement to press their case. Women lawyers filed suit to gain equal pay for equal work and close the loopholes in the law such as combat veterans' special privileges in employment and medical benefits that favored men over women. NOW boasted a membership of a million people, and the National Women's Political Caucus had nearly forty thousand members.

In New York City, Gloria Steinem launched the controversial women's magazine *Ms.* Unlike other magazines for women, it did not feature recipes and fashion tips. Instead, it was a forum for all segments of the movement to express opinions on public as well as private issues. The original issue in July 1972 sold out immediately, as did successive numbers. Attacked by conservatives for undermining the traditional values of home and family and by radicals for bowing to mainstream conventions, *Ms.* profoundly and permanently affected American society. It not only publicized movement activities and questioned myths of womanhood, it brought to light the extent of spousal abuse and rape. In part because of the magazine's influence, courts and communities began to take these long hidden problems seriously. Shelters for battered wives and rape crisis centers appeared all over the country. *Ms.* also altered the English language, as many women rejected the conventional Miss and Mrs. titles (reflecting marital status) and opted for Ms.

The percentage of women attending college grew faster than that of men, and higher education for more and more women served a consciousness-raising role. In 1970, women at the University of Washington won a federal lawsuit requiring equal facilities for women. A year later, the Women's Equity Action League filed 350 more suits against colleges and universities discriminating on the basis of sex. In 1972, federal law required equal facilities in all institutions that received federal funding. At the University of California, Berkeley, women marched to the president's office to demand more courses on women's history and more women on the faculty. Sarah Lawrence College would inaugurate the first full-fledged women's studies program in 1972, and female professors became role models for women who wanted a career to go along with marriage and motherhood.

Surveys that had documented the political apathy of women in the 1950s when repeated in the 1970s showed a dramatic turnaround. Women had become much more interested in politics and political issues. By the 1970s, women were voting in numbers closely approaching the numbers of men, a change from the 1950s, and as more women went to college, the gap narrowed still farther. The trend was clear— women and women's issues could no longer be ignored by state legislatures or Congress. Even President Richard Nixon, no particular friend of women's rights, sensed change in the wind. On January 8, 1971, he signed the congressional act repealing the District of Columbia's anti-abortion statute.

The most visible evidence of the rising tide of women's expectations was the House of Representatives' approval of the Equal Rights Amendment, on October 12, 1971, by an overwhelming vote of 354 to 23. The amendment, prohibiting sex discrimination by the federal government or the states, with provision for congressional enactments to enforce it, was first introduced in 1923. It languished until the Women's Caucus in Congress made it a priority in 1970 and pushed through hearings in Congress. With the growing number of women voters and the growing strength of women's lobbying groups, the Senate fell in line in 1972, voting 84 to 8 to send the amendment to the states. The most vocal critic on the Senate floor, Senator Sam Ervin of North Carolina, worried that if the amendment became law, it would destroy all the special privileges the law conferred on women, but within six years, thirty-three of the thirty-eight states needed to ratify the amendment had signified their approval.

As striking as all of these gains might seem, none was irreversible or complete. In 1972, for example, the New York Court of Appeals narrowed the state's reimbursement for abortions to those "medically indicated." Critics of the ERA argued that there was no need for special treatment of women in the law; they need only use the Equal Protection and Due Process Clauses to gain equality. Quietly, the insurance industry lobbied against the ERA, rightly fearing that it would have to change its discriminatory reimbursement scales for women (they got less in pensions and other payouts). Indefatigable and persuasive, conservative Republican lawyer and organizer Phyllis Schlafly convinced men and women that the ERA was the work of lesbians and Communists and would undermine the American way. Her Eagle Forum spread fears of unisex bathrooms and the end of alimony and child care payments, as well as the decline of the traditional family, under a legal regime featuring an ERA. The ratification of the ERA, consequently, was problematic. It would have been foolhardy for women's groups to hope that abortion rights could and would be secured through the amendment.

Thus *Roe* remained the focus of the new legal paradigm. If the U.S. Supreme Court found constitutional grounds to extend the birth control cases' logic that women's bodies belonged to the women themselves, the concept of choice would become a core value in constitutional law. If, in addition, the Court heard the intimate voice of women in the roar of legal rhetoric, the new paradigm would have a sure legal foundation on which to stand. Conversely, a reversal of the district court's ruling in *Roe* would not destroy the women's movement, but it would make all gains dependent upon an endless round of exhausting political and legal battles in every state, a course of action that the women's movement was ill prepared and ill equipped to pursue.

––––––

Appeal to the Supreme Court

Coffee and Weddington were delighted with their partial victory in Texas, but the burden on them of appealing the district court's refusal to enjoin the state was almost unbearable. Coffee was overwhelmed by the demands of her regular job, Weddington and her husband were moving to Fort Worth from Austin so that she could assume her new post as assistant city attorney. Both women were busy helping friendly legislators prepare a repeal bill for the next session of the Texas legislature and keeping up with abortion cases throughout the country. Without a staff and regular funding, their efforts on the *Roe* appeal dangled on a shoestring They both dreaded the expense of an appeal to the fifth Circuit Court of Appeals, and then to the United States Supreme Court.

To their aid, unbidden but eager to take charge of the case, came Roy Lucas. Lucas claimed to be more knowledgeable than anyone about the state of abortion laws and had already made their repeal a personal mission. Already NARAL's counsel and a member of its board, he had a hand in just about every legal assault on state anti-abortion laws. He reminded Weddington and Coffee that Congress had provided a direct appeal from three-judge panels to the Supreme Court. On August 17, 1970, Coffee filed notice with the clerk of the United States Supreme Court of their intention. to appeal (as "appellants") the panel's denial of injunctive relief. Lucas, whose interest in all the abortion rights cases had led him to visit with Weddington and Coffee that summer, prepared a thirty-three-page jurisdictional statement (a necessary preliminary to convince the court to hear the appeal) and submitted it to the High Court on October 6, 1970.

Raising the stakes, Texas's legal authorities (the "appellee") denounced the ruling. Henry Wade boasted that absent the injunction he would continue to prosecute abortionists, and the state's attorney general held a press conference to announce his intention to appeal the declaratory judgment. Floyd drafted a seven-page response to the Lucas jurisdictional statement and filed it with the High Court on November 5, 1970.

Lucas's jurisdictional statement for *Roe* cited section 1253 of title 28 of the United States Code, providing for direct appeal to the High Court, followed by a string citation (a list) of cases in which the Court had heard a direct appeal. It noted that the appellants had filed a notice that they would appeal to the Fifth Circuit, but the present petition superseded that notice.

That was the easy part. Now came the hard work, for in reality the position of the plaintiff-appellants in the suit had changed as a result of the passage of time after the district court's ruling in *Roe*. The Texas panel had dismissed John and Mary Doe's suit because she was not pregnant when the suit was brought, and there was thus no case or controversy. The statement argued that only an injunction would provide sufficiently speedy relief (that is, to allow her to get a legal abortion in the state) to protect her health in the event of an unwanted pregnancy. But permanent injunctions are rarely issued when the harm or the nuisance is only a prospective one.

The second plaintiff, Roe, was no longer pregnant, and no longer at risk from the law. This was a key problem, for given the pace with which federal courts ground out their decisions, a pregnant woman would have to carry the fetus for a year or more before all levels of the courts ruled on her case. In such a situation, no woman could sustain a suit if the High Court insisted she be pregnant from the beginning of the suit to its end. Lucas contented himself with narrating the events that led Roe to bring a suit, as if time had stopped when Weddington and Coffee filed *Roe v. Wade*. Legal time and real time are not always the same.

The third plaintiff, Dr. Hallford (along with all other similarly situated doctors in the state—these were all class action suits) was still in danger because Wade had proclaimed his intention to move ahead with criminal prosecution. In addition, Hallford would have to turn away patients like Roe because they did not fit the stringently defined exceptions to the ban on abortions. The Supreme Court had already shown itself willing to issue injunctions in state criminal cases when appellants could convince the Court that the state prosecution was in bad faith—for example, to stifle freedom of speech—in *Dumbrowski v. Pfister* (1965). But the Texas panel had explicitly distinguished *Roe* from *Dumbrowski*. There were still two outstanding indictments against Dr. Hallford when Lucas filed the jurisdictional statement, but the statement did not ask the Court to enjoin them. Instead, it asked the High Court to bar Texas from filing any new indictments against the doctor.

If, as the federal panel had found, the Texas statute on abortion was overbroad and vague, and it violated women's Ninth Amendment right to choose whether to have children, the state should not be able to move against the doctor. The statement tried to turn the lower court's refusal to issue the injunction on its head, portraying it as an opportunity for the Supreme Court to "clarify" the grounds under which plaintiffs could expect to win suits for injunctive relief. Such invitations are double-edged swords—they might induce the Court to take a case and then use it to define the reasons for not issuing injunctions. Lucas almost admitted as much when he conceded that two of the three plaintiffs were "total strangers to any pending prosecutions."

The jurisdictional statement's extensive reportage of court opinions in current abortion cases, the historical background of the anti-abortion and reform laws, and the special pleading of the lawyers drew on Lucas's extensive personal knowledge, but filled only half of the statement. The rest of the space was devoted to extensive medical evidence. Although statements like this are supposed to argue the law rather than social opinion, since the early twentieth century lawyers have put more and more contextual data into their arguments to the Court. The first such submission, the so-called Brandeis Brief in the case of *Muller v. Oregon* (1908), demonstrated the deleterious effects of long work hours on women with two pages of law and nearly one hundred pages of medical and social findings. Attorney Louis Brandeis, who pleaded the case for the women workers, later sat on the High Court and introduced sociological and medical facts into his opinions there.

In the end, however, Lucas's statement fell short of the mark in its main task—to explain how the lower court had erred in not issuing the injunction and why the High Court should order the lower court to do so. The lower court had feared that the intrusion into the state's criminal law enforcement would generate great friction, perhaps hoping that the state would take the declaration of the unconstitutionality of the law as a cue to cease its enforcement. In fact, the state had ignored the federal panel, the best reason why the High Court should hear *Roe*'s lawyers' appeal.

Still, the statement had to provide some response to the lower court's refusal to issue the injunction other than the bald assertion that it was wrong. The argument that federal-state friction was only "hypothetical" hardly worked, given the state's actual response. The contention that the issuance of such an injunction would have prevented federal-state conflict flew in the face of federal courts' experience with southern states in desegregation cases. The assertion that the High Court had to reverse the lower court in order to provide guidance to other lower courts merely assumed what it was supposed to prove, that the lower courts should be issuing injunctions against a state's enforcement of its own criminal law. The final allegation, that only the issuance of the injunction would prevent irreparable injury to the plaintiffs (the standard reason for issuing any injunction), failed in the face of facts: only Hallford was in danger of prosecution under the statute, and he was indicted for his actions before the statute was declared unconstitutional. The state could be enjoined from filing new indictments against him, but that did not relieve him from the burden of trial under the old indictments. Altogether Lucas's initial submission was an able but not a brilliant effort. One should remember that Lucas was only thirty years old, a few years out of law school. At the same time, Lucas could and did have at hand the assistance of Harriet Pilpel and the other veterans of the birth control fight.

Fortunately for the appellants, the appellee was equally overworked and understaffed. Floyd had the task of preparing a response to the jurisdictional statement. He had not distinguished himself in oral argument before the federal court in Texas, and with work on other cases piling up, his usually orderly desk was now cluttered with case files. His superior, Robert Flowers, stepped in to help, with Attorney General Crawford Martin looking over both their shoulders. Wade and Tolle were listed on the submission as well, for both men had a vested interest in the outcome of the trial.

The reply Floyd and his coworkers drafted to the jurisdictional statement identified all of the weak points in Lucas's arguments, but failed to provide a definitive case that the appellants' jurisdictional statement was inadequate on its face. They questioned whether Roe still had standing, given that the filing came eight months after the trial court's opinion was announced, and she was unlikely to be pregnant. "It can only be logically assumed that Appellant Jane Roe is not in need of an abortion at this time to terminate her pregnancy." In fact, this statement was not logically compelling and could easily have been false. There was no way for the state to know whether McCorvey was again pregnant. As the potential for pregnancy was always there and pregnancy was repeatable, McCorvey might well be facing a crisis similar to one that led her to Weddington and Coffee in the first place. The same was true for every pregnant woman who went to court to seek relief from a restrictive state abortion law.

Against Hallford's appeal for injunctive relief, the state asked the High Court to follow its own reluctance to interfere in ongoing state criminal proceedings. The problem here was that if the law under which the prosecution took place was unconstitutional, the state or the federal courts would have provided relief after Hallford was convicted (assuming that he was convicted, an unlikely event given the tiny percentage of guilty verdicts in such cases). The state's insistence on prosecuting looked petty, if not vengeful, in light of the latter considerations. And with those few arguments, the state closed its jurisdictional statement.

Weddington later recalled that she and Coffee did not know whether the High Court would take the case. On May 3, 1971, it did. The old adage that the U.S. Supreme Court follows the election returns has much truth to it, and with the debates on the ERA going on in Congress, it may seem hardly accidental that the Court agreed to hear the abortion cases. But as opponents of abortion rights denounced what they labeled as "abortion on impulse" and pro-repeal advocates filed more cases every month (in March 1971 alone women's groups filed new cases in Connecticut and Vermont), the Court must have realized that any action it took was bound to be controversial.

As sensitive as they are to political currents, courts prefer to avoid political questions on the assumption that they are better settled by legislatures. In February 1971, the Court in *Younger v. Harris* signaled a retreat from *Dumbrowski*, in part to avoid the wracking federal-state friction that had almost paralyzed the courts during the early years of civil rights litigation. In fact, four of the nine justices had voted not to hear *Roe* when the appeal was filed, reasoning that the appeal should be dismissed for want of a justiciable federal issue. After all, the lower court had covered all the bases, and issuing an injunction when no injunctive relief was warranted would have involved the High Court in the micro-management of every state's criminal justice system. But the Court's aversion to political questions had eroded in the voting reapportionment cases filed in the early 1960s, and the differences of rulings on the state abortion laws in the various federal circuits in 1970 was a substantive reason to hear the case.

Following that logic, however, nothing required the Court to limit its purview to *Roe* and *Doe*. Had it so desired and appellants come forward, the High Court could have consolidated all the cases as it did in the appeals of the school desegregation cases from Kansas, South Carolina, Virginia, the District of Columbia, and Delaware, in *Brown v. Board of Education* (1954). If it followed the latter course, by March 1971 the Court would have had to include not only *Roe, Babbitz, Rosen,* and *Steinberg,* but cases from Illinois knocking down the state statute for vagueness, and from Missouri, Minnesota, Missouri, and North Carolina upholding state statutes. Together, those cases would have presented a very different landscape to the Court than *Roe* and *Doe* alone. Weddington later surmised that the Court simply chose two states that had, respectively, the unreformed or "restrictive" version of anti-abortion law (Texas) and the reformed or "liberal" version (Georgia). Another possibility has weight: it was a strategic decision of the pro–abortion rights forces to press ahead on the Texas and Georgia cases, in which federal panels had accepted the rationale for striking down state laws, rather than to challenge panels that had upheld state laws.

In the spring of 1971, assuming that he was now in charge of the Texas litigation, Lucas invited Weddington to join the staff at the Madison Institute's New York City offices for the summer and there help prepare a full brief. When Weddington's lawyer husband arrived there for a visit in midsummer (Weddington begged him to come), he was soon put to work, for the Institute was involved in all the abortion cases, not just *Roe.* The Weddingtons joined a skeleton staff of law students and soon-to-be law students such as Brian Sullivan, who would attend Yale Law School in the fall, and David Tundermann, who had finished his second year in New Haven. Dan Schneider, a first-year law student at Cincinnati, completed the small but dedicated team. Lucas and the two Weddingtons were the only members of the bar at work on the appeal, but the Institute group had the support of law scholars and birth control associations all over the country. Unfortunately, Lucas's gruff and hurried manner had already alienated him from many in the repeal enterprise. In particular, he had angered the leaders of NARAL by seeking fees from abortion providers. He had been NARAL's legal counsel until the fray, and now found himself denied a place on its board of directors.

With Lucas flitting about trying to raise funds and the other staffers of the Institute fully occupied, Weddington found she had to prepare much of the full-dress brief for the Court. Weddington's drafts went through Lucas's hands, and sometimes he left her notes for revision. Although in the end, everyone at the Institute, law students at the University of Texas and elsewhere, the ACLU's Norman Dorsen (who had represented Dr. Vuitch in his suit), Cyril Means at New York Law school (whose law review article on abortion laws in early America would prove crucial to the brief), and Harriet Pilpel at the PPFA all contributed to the brief, Lucas put his name at the top of the list of attorneys on the final document. Dorsen's followed, and Weddington's and Coffee's trailed behind, along with the names of Brunner and Merrill, still representing Dr. Hallford. The brief went to the Court on August 17, 1971.

Though he tried, Lucas could not convince Margie Pitts Hames to give him such latitude in *Doe*. Hames had been practicing longer than Coffee and Weddington, had a legal team to help her, and had amassed sufficient financing for the long haul. But Hames's, like Lucas's team, needed more time than originally granted and gained delays from the Court through the summer of 1971, and filed the brief with the Court on the same day as *Roe*.

Just as the PPF A and other groups came to the Institute's aid, so the National Right to Life Committee, through its legal counsel Martin F. McKernan Jr., came to Lloyd's assistance as he worked on the state's brief to the High Court. McKernan visited with Floyd in Austin, Texas, in July 1971, and later arranged for Floyd to contact two Chicago lawyers preparing an amicus brief in support of the Texas law. Dennis J. Horan and Jerome A. Frazel Jr. were coordinating the submission by over two hundred physicians opposed to the abolition of abortion laws. The two would provide the medical information that Floyd incorporated in his brief, much of which, including pictures of fetuses at various stages of development, appeared in the doctors' amicus brief as well. The state filed its brief on the merits on October 15, 1971.

The formal briefs of both sides filled out the arguments in their respective jurisdictional statements. The appellants' brief was clearly a Brandeis Brief—its section on the "Relevant Background and Medical Facts" ran on for forty pages. The appellants reviewed the cases on injunctive relief to distinguish *Roe* from those cases in which the Court refused to issue the injunction. Conceding the fact that the courts had not issued injunctions in pending criminal prosecutions, here the appellants sought an injunction against future prosecutions. Hallford, the appellants' brief revealed, never asked the district court to enjoin the two prosecutions already under way against him. Nor could he (any more than Roe and the Does) have a chance of winning in the state courts. Only the federal courts' intervention would provide an "orderly, civilized" way to vindicate rights that arose from the federal Constitution.

On the declaratory judgment, the substantive ruling of the Texas panel that Floyd was challenging, the appellants simply asked the Court to follow the logic of the lower court in basing the unconstitutionality of the Texas law on the right to privacy enunciated in *Griswold*. The right to decide to carry or end a pregnancy was merely a continuation of the right to prevent a pregnancy or a conception through the use of artificial contraceptives.

The state's full-dress brief had a harder task than the Institute's: getting the High Court to reverse the declaratory ruling. It is not uncommon for the Supreme Court to revisit a lower federal court's reading of the Constitution, but convincing the Court takes work. The state's brief continued to argue that Roe and the Does lacked standing because there was no case or controversy involving them under the existing abortion laws. There was no proof that Roe was at risk "at the time" the High Court set aside to hear her appeal and no evidence in the record that Doe's health would be impaired by a pregnancy not yet realized. The state asserted that Hallford was merely trying to avoid trial on the two indictments, but it could not show anything in Brunner's or Merrill's pleadings that substantiated this claim, and Hallford's attorneys had already conceded that he wished only to avert future prosecutions.

In opposition to the appellants' argument that the right to abortion could be based upon privacy, the appellee rejoined that the right of privacy had limits. It could not cover infanticide, incest, or pandering. "Abortion on demand" should be classed with these latter socially unacceptable and criminal acts, rather than with birth control. To counter the argument that the law violated the privileged relationship between doctor and female patient, the state replied that the doctor also owed a duty to the unborn child. He or she too was the doctor's patient. Finally, the woman's right to privacy, whether in the doctor's office or the bedroom, was never absolute. It did not prevent police from conducting lawful searches of her person or her dwelling place, and it had to be balanced against the rights of her unborn child when she was pregnant.

The state's case rested squarely on the notion that the fetus was always a human being. Indeed, the state labeled the key section of its brief "the human-ness of the fetus." But the religious foundation for the fetal-life argument in Tolle's brief had been replaced by references to modern science. The state claimed that the most recent medical findings proved that the fetus was alive from conception; its cells reproduced on their own, and in time would form a uniquely human shape. It only needed "time and nutrition" to become "a developing human being." In the womb, the fetus was an "unborn child." The state presented its own miniature version of a Brandeis Brief, depicting the developmental schedule of the eyes, organs, and looks of the fetus to show how human they were from the first weeks of gestation.

The brief included twelve photographs of fetuses, utilizing recently developed intrauterine camera technology. These were provided by Horan and Frazel and appeared in the doctors' amicus brief they had compiled. The photographs accompanied text designed to show how early human features developed in fetuses. At two places in the brief the state indicated how tiny the fetus was in this first trimester, a mere quarter of an inch after four weeks, but the photos were enlarged to make the fetuses appear to be the size of small infants, a technique widely used in anti-abortion media packets. Thus the fetus in figure 2, matched with the description of the fetus at six weeks and labeled simply "Fig. 2—6 weeks," was over three inches long. The palms of the fetus in figure 3, at "9 weeks," appear to be the size of a newborn infant's, almost two inches across in the photo. There was nothing in the text of the brief to indicate that the state had enlarged the scale of the pictures by a factor of ten, not even a disclaimer that the distortion of size was necessary to show details. It might be objected that such techniques misrepresented the facts, or that they constituted tampering with evidence, but apparently no one objected at the time.

Although the state had dropped from its brief the references to religious concepts such as the vesting of the soul at conception, the implication of its scientific evidence was the same as the religious reasoning in *Rosen:* the mother was the trustee, the carryall, for the little person, and it followed, as it had in *Rosen,* that the fetus had Fifth and Fourteenth Amendment rights to life and liberty that outweighed the mother's right to privacy.

The state's introduction of what it claimed was the most recent scientific evidence on the beginning of life was strengthened by amicus briefs from well-known experts in the human sciences or medicine with an interest in the case. These submissions are not part of the formal pleadings, but they can be very persuasive. Dr. Bart Heffernan, the self-appointed intervener as guardian ad litem for the unborn child in the Illinois case, filed an amicus brief bearing the names of 232 doctors. Many were private practitioners, but the majority held some hospital or medical school post. They urged the Court to take full cognizance of the medical evidence in the state's brief and argued that as far as they were concerned, "the unborn person is also a patient." Their brief featured the same blown-up pictures of fetuses as the state's.

The "Americans United for Life"—a nonsectarian lawyers' group— filed its own amicus brief supporting the state's view of fetal life. They accurately portrayed the strong anti-abortion cast of case and statute law prevailing in the period before the reform effort. Their assertion that courts sustained common-law tort actions against persons who injured the fetus was misleading, however, for they neglected to note that the courts in the majority of those cases required that the fetus be viable when the injury took place and that child be born alive before the action could commence. The attorneys general of Arizona, Connecticut, Kentucky, Nebraska, and Utah, all of whose states had abortion laws similar to Texas's, filed in support of the appellees. Their interest in the outcome of the case was indisputable, and their brief was little more than a repetition of the Texas filing.

The appellants boasted their own array of leading doctors. Carol Ryan, a New York attorney, superintended an amicus brief from the American College of Obstetricians and Gynecologists, the American Psychiatric Association, the American Medical Women's Association, the New York Academy of Medicine, and a group of 178 distinguished physicians. Included in the latter were chaired professors of medicine and chairmen of medical school departments, leaders of state medical associations (notably Dr. Hugh Savage, chair of the Texas Medical Association's Committee to Study Abortion Laws in Texas, along with eighteen other prominent Texas doctors), veterans of the fight for abortion law reform such as Jerome Kummer of California and Alan Guttmacher of New York, in addition to three doctors from the distinguished Mayo Clinic in Rochester, Minnesota. Not included, for obvious reasons, were Drs. Rosen and Steinberg, whose cases would be affected by the outcome of the *Roe* appeal to the Supreme Court. The doctors' amicus brief echoed the arguments in the medical portion of the appellants' brief. They did not regard the early fetuses as potential patients, whatever the state might claim.

The National Abortion Action Coalition, the New Women Lawyers, and the Women's Health and Abortion Project filed briefs to remind the Court that women in and out of the liberation movement regarded abortion as the quintessential women's issue—"the right of a woman to control her own body and life" that had "become one of the most burning issues for women throughout the country." The Texas and Georgia cases "are not local but national issues . . . problems of millions of pregnant women." Over the past few years, thousands of women had joined in class action suits in many states, and *Roe* represented their efforts as well as the doctors'.

The women amici boldly pressed the new paradigm of women's legal rights, for which they claimed women lawyers were uniquely qualified to speak. The "New Women Lawyers" addressed the Court not just as mothers and potential mothers, but as female professionals with "special insight into the problems and issues." On its face, this claim of superiority of insight because of one's gender resembled the doctors' and lawgivers' pose on abortion one hundred years before. But on that occasion, men asserted that their superiority entitled them to speak for women. The New Women Lawyers did not claim to speak for men.

From their perspective, the women lawyers claimed to see what men missed about women's experience, that "despite the fact that both man and woman are responsible for any pregnancy, it is the woman who bears the disproportionate share of the de jure and de facto burden and penalties of pregnancy." In short, the laws penalizing abortion had a disparate, unequal impact on women. Pregnant women faced obstacles that men never faced. For the offense of accidently becoming pregnant, or becoming pregnant against their will, or becoming pregnant before they could care for children, the brief asserted, the laws "condemned women" to a punishment that men never faced, to "share their bodies with another organism against their will, to be child breeders and rearers against their will." Women lost jobs as teachers and nurses because school boards and hospitals did not want pregnant women to work. Men were not at risk to lose such jobs. High schools asked pregnant women to delay completion of their education until the end of their pregnancies and discriminated against young women with children. Men did not face this problem. A pregnant woman was often denied employment opportunities, on the assumption that she was supposed to be at home. Men with children were expected to find jobs outside the home and take part in public life. The unmarried woman with children faced even higher hurdles in the marketplace. Unmarried men with children did not have to clear these hurdles. The Texas and Georgia statutes denied women equal protection of the laws simply because they were women.

NOW joined the amici for the appellants. The South Bay, San Francisco, chapter joined with the California Committee to Legalize Abortion to argue that laws like Texas's imposed an involuntary servitude on women, forcing them to bear children in violation of the Thirteenth Amendment against slavery. An unwanted pregnancy in addition was dangerous to women's health and well-being. The California Committee was the first to drop the "abortion study" or "abortion reform" title and openly demand "legalized abortion."

Planned Parenthood signed on, with a brief by Harriet Pilpel. She was entitled to this valedictory after a lifetime of legal advocacy for women's rights. Pilpel preferred straight talking to legal hyperbole. After a brief refutation of the state's claim that it had a compelling interest in regulating pregnancies, following the logic of her amicus brief in *Griswold,* she offered a series of assertions of fact backed by statistics. First, abortion was still safer than childbirth, according to statistics compiled in 1970 and 1971. Second, legalized abortion ended the discrimination against poor pregnant women who could not afford to travel in search of a safe abortion. Third, legalization of abortion did not increase the total number of abortions, but merely replaced illegal and dangerous abortion with safe and legal abortion. Fourth, abortions in clinics were as safe as abortions in hospitals. Finally, the American Bar Association and the National Conference of Commissioners on Uniform State Laws had adopted a resolution in favor of early abortion on request and liberal abortion thereafter for pregnant women in mental or physical distress, as well as for women who could show that the fetus was likely to have birth defects.

In the fall of 1971, Weddington studied all of the briefs and began serious preparation for oral argument. Lucas had other ideas. His attempt to orchestrate the cases bordered on the obsessive, and his contributions to the brief had a high price tag. Lucas wanted to argue the case in front of the High Court. There are times when local counsel defer to an experienced lawyer, as the birth control forces did when they sought the aid of Fowler Harper and then Thomas Emerson. Although Lucas hardly fit that description—he had never argued a case before the High Court—throughout the fall of 1971 he badgered and belittled Weddington. Weddington had proposed to the Court that they share time. When the Court clerk informed Lucas and Weddington that oral argument was set for December 13, 1971, Lucas, without consulting Weddington, sent papers to the Court naming himself as the sole speaker. Furious, she informed the Court that she would be speaking for Roe. The Court clerk so entered her name on November 30. With Judge Sarah Hughes as her sponsor, Weddington had been admitted to the Supreme Court bar six weeks before. She was ready.

The struggle between Weddington and Lucas over who would present oral arguments to the Court may seem a petty sidebar to a landmark case, but it was more. Had the suit been about women's equality in activities that men and women shared, for example, in the marketplace or the workplace, the issue of who would actually address the justices would have been little more than a matter of pride of authorship or professional ambition, but in an abortion case the dispute between Lucas and Weddington had a far different impetus and significance.

The claim that women were uniquely positioned to speak about abortion—the claim at the heart of the new legal paradigm of women's rights—would be undermined if Lucas gave oral argument. Then it would appear that a neutral, abstract, disengendered law—the law that for so many years men had claimed only they understood and could penetrate—should decide the fate of women's reproductive lives. In this sense, admittedly speculative, one may regard the conflict between him and Weddington as a miniature of the conflict between the old and the new paradigms of women's place in the law. So long as a man led the charge for repeal, stood in front of the courts and the cameras, and explained to the world how the law worked, the paradigm of subordination of one sex to the other survived. It would be a parallel to the notion that a neutral, abstract, disengendered medical professionalism should decide when and if women could have abortions.

Weddington had no objection to sharing time with Lucas (at least until he nominated himself sole counsel), but throughout the litigation, Weddington and Coffee believed what Friedan had told the NARAL convention in 1969, that the most important voice in the abortion cases was the voice of the woman who faced the choice. Indeed, with Hames and Beasley arguing opposite sides in *Doe*, and Harriet Pilpel and others in the audience, a journalist dubbed the oral argument "ladies day" at the Court. In a more intimate way, Weddington would bring to the counsel table in front of the High Court bench an experience that Lucas could not: Weddington's own abortion. Invisible as it may have been to onlookers and as inadmissible in court, her and other women's unique experience framed the way she thought about and the way she personified the suit. As she later wrote, "I was remembering my experience in Mexico and hoping that finally the terror of illegal abortion would end. It was a moment of personal reflection as well as professional pride." The personal had become the political. Because she was a woman arguing the quintessential women's case, she recalled, "I was feeling a heavy responsibility. I owed my best effort to the women who would continue to be forced to seek illegal abortions if we lost."

Lucas's motives are not so obvious. On the one hand, by his tone one can see that he considered Weddington unprepared to argue the case, despite her participation in "moot courts," rehearsals for the oral presentation in Washington, D.C. On the other hand, that he had given his professional life thus far to the cause of repeal of abortion laws no one could doubt, no more than that his desire for repeal was sincere. He was more knowledgeable about the current state of abortion law litigation than anyone in the country. Although he did not get to address the Court that day, he was not left out of the proceedings. He sat next to Linda Coffee and Weddington at the counsel table during the oral argument.

———

Roe in the High Court

Students of the Supreme Court agree that in the nineteenth century, oral argument before the Court played a major role in the outcome of cases. Sometimes the oratory of counsel stretched on for days. Rarely did justices interrupt counsel, who included members of Congress like Daniel Webster. In those times, the Court only sat for a short time each year and had many fewer cases on its docket than it does today. Today, each side has thirty minutes to present its side of the case. Rarely does counsel go on for more than a few minutes without a question from one of the justices, and sometimes the questions take up all of the allotted time.

Justices use the questions to probe issues the lawyers have raised in their briefs, to convince themselves (and other justices) of key points, and to surreptitiously argue with other justices. Justices Felix Frankfurter and Hugo Black were notorious for disputing points of law with one another through their questions at oral argument. Some justices, notably Frankfurter, an ex–Harvard Law School professor famous for the give and take in his seminars, relish oral argument and plunge into it with glee. Some justices, for example Justice Douglas, rarely ask a question. He was noted for writing opinions or correspondence during the Court's oral arguments.

Often the tenor of the justices' questions indicates their thinking or their concerns, and participants in the oral argument later join with observers to second-guess how the justices will vote on a case based on their questions and comments. Some justices are notorious for badgering or teasing counsel or lecturing them on the weakness of their briefs. At other times a question or an answer triggers a polite guffaw or gales of laughter. Often, the questions or the direction of a line of questioning veer off into unexpected directions. Counsel have to be on their toes when this happens. To prepare, Weddington had taped index cards to the left and right of a legal file folder to cover all possible tangents on the case. She knew that rarely is a case won in oral argument, but on some occasions cases are lost through lack of preparation by counsel.

The bench that heard the first round of oral argument in *Roe* was significantly different from the roster of justices that rendered the opinion in *Griswold*. Earl Warren, John Harlan, Arthur Goldberg, and Hugo Black were gone. No one could predict with certainty how their replacements would vote in an abortion rights case, but the parties in *Roe* knew all about the new justices' backgrounds and views on other legal matters and were free to speculate about their likely stance on abortion, federalism, deference to legislatures, and privacy.

The first of the newcomers was President Johnson's 1967 nominee, Thurgood Marshall. Marshall's career in the law was inspiring. The great-grandson of a slave and the son of a dining-car waiter, he starred at Howard Law School in Washington, D.C., where he came under the towering influence of Charles Hamilton Houston. Houston taught his students that every man must be a reformer, and made the law school into a training center for civil rights litigation. Marshall went on to become chief litigator for the Legal Defense Fund of the National Association for the Advancement of Colored People and won significant victories against racial discrimination in cases like *Brown v. Board of Education*.

President John F. Kennedy nominated Marshall to the Second Circuit Court of Appeals, and over bitter protest from southern senators, Marshall was confirmed. In 1965 he stepped down from the bench to become solicitor general of the United States, the lawyer who represents the United States government in court. (The attorney general is the president's legal advisor.) Marshall was a strong defender of the civil rights and civil liberties of individuals, rejected government claims when they infringed on these liberties, and would become a stalwart opponent of the death penalty. He won confirmation to the High Court in August 30, 1967, and took his seat on October 2, 1967. Weddington could expect him to lend a sympathetic ear to the appellants' case in *Roe*.

Warren Burger was the new chief justice, appointed in May 1969 and confirmed in June 1969. Burger was a St. Paul, Minnesota, practitioner and moderate Republican who served in President Eisenhower's administration as an assistant attorney general, and later as a judge on the District of Columbia Court of Appeals. A conservative in his jurisprudence, he opposed many of the innovations that the Warren Court championed, particularly in the area of criminal justice, but he was not averse to the civil rights revolution. He preferred, whenever possible, to leave liberal reform to the legislative branch, rather than ordering it from the bench. President Nixon appointed him because of his conservative credentials and his experience as a judge.

As chief justice, Burger made real strides in improving the management of the federal court system and brought new technology to the "marble palace," the Supreme Court building in Washington, D.C. He was never adept at the politics of the Court, however, and was never regarded as its intellectual leader, as a result exercising little leverage over the other justices, even those whose views matched his own. In time, he became especially sensitive to criticism in the press and worried incessantly about the clerks and the other justices leaking what were supposed to be secret conference deliberations to the media. He was likely to be less friendly to abortion reform than his predecessor, Earl Warren.

In 1970, President Nixon appointed Burger's longtime friend Harry Blackmun to the High Court. Although the two men had gone to Sunday school together in a blue-collar neighborhood of St. Paul, and Blackmun had been best man at Burger's wedding, they had different career paths to the Court. Unlike Burger, who had gone to night school to get a law degree, Blackmun had gone to elite Harvard Law School. Burger practiced in St. Paul, the state capital, where he made strong political friends; Blackmun practiced across the Mississippi River, in Minneapolis, where his firm represented leading corporations. Blackmun had long served as counsel to the Mayo Clinic, one of the foremost diagnostic centers in the country. He worked in close accord with many of the doctors and recalled his years there as the best in his life.

In 1959 President Eisenhower named Blackmun to the Eighth Circuit Court of Appeals. At first, Blackmun seemed even more conservative than Burger, deferring to the government, particularly in the area of law enforcement. But over time he moved from the conservative to the liberal wing of the Court. As he later said in an interview, "Because I grew up in poor surroundings, I know there's another world out there that we sometimes forget about." On the Eighth Circuit Court of Appeals, he had fashioned novel remedies for prisoners abused in jails. After he got to the High Court in June 1970, he was especially sympathetic to the plight of aliens and Native Americans. The abortion cases particularly interested him, given his background in law and medicine.

Weddington was not thinking about the special interests of the justices when she arrived in D.C. to argue the case on the morning of December 13. Instead, she was excited and proud. Along with Coffee and friends from Texas, as well as Marsha and David King, and Ron, her husband, she got to the Supreme Court building an hour early. The Court would hear two cases in the morning, starting at ten A.M., and two cases in the afternoon. *Roe* was scheduled for the first slot, *Doe v. Bolton* next that morning. At the table for counsel she found a reminder of the rules of oral argument. She was to go up from the table to the podium in front of the bench when called, compute her own time, and stop on a dime when the red light at the podium lit. She noticed that the form referred to counsel as "he" and hoped that, in time, the form would become, like the law, sensitive to differences in gender.

Seven justices assembled that morning. Harlan and Black had resigned shortly before the year's session began (always the first Monday in October), both for reasons of ill health. Weddington recalled that she was impressed but not overwhelmed by the justices' preparation for the case and thought that she did a creditable job in her oral presentation. At the outset, she had to distinguish her case from *Vuitch*, which the Court had reversed (finding the D.C. ordinance broad enough to include the doctor's actions), and did so by citing the relative severity of the Texas statute (in effect distinguishing it from the D.C. law). She had also to remind the Court of the different issues each of the three appellants raised and of the Texas courts' unlikeliness to offer relief to any of them.

Then Weddington took a moment to voice the women's case in an intimate way, using the language of women's unique experience rather than the language of the law. She spoke of the burdens of pregnancy. "It disrupts her body, it disrupts her education, it disrupts her employment, and it often disrupts her entire family life and . . . because of the impact on the woman, this certainly, in as far as there are any rights which are fundamental, is a matter . . . of such fundamental and basic concern to the woman involved that she should be allowed to make the choice as to whether to continue or terminate her pregnancy." No one—none of the seven men on the bench—interrupted her as she spoke to this point. By conflating what was fundamental to women and fundamental in the Constitution, she introduced the new paradigm at the outset of her remarks.

When she had concluded this part of her statement, Justice Potter Stewart complimented her on an "eloquent policy argument," mistaking one of the core values of the new paradigm of women's place in the law, the paramountcy of intimate experience, for the sort of policy arguments routinely made in commercial and antitrust cases. But, he told her, "we cannot here be involved simply with matters of policy, as you know," and asked for the constitutional grounds on which she based her clients' claims. He heard in her statement the Due Process Clause of the Fourteenth Amendment. Was this the constitutional foundation for abortion rights? She agreed, but added the Equal Protection Clause of the Fourteenth Amendment, the Ninth Amendment, "and a variety of others." He quipped, "And anything else that might obtain." She bantered back, "Yeah, right."

Justice Byron White continued with a question whether the Texas law made any distinction between early and late abortions, and whether, consequently, Weddington made those distinctions. That is, was she asserting that women had a constitutional right to terminate a pregnancy "up to the time of birth"? She fumbled, recognizing that this was dangerous ground. The closer the abortion was to the end of the nine months, the more anti–abortion rights advocates could claim that the fetus was independently alive—in a word, human—and therefore that the state had an interest in protecting its life. But she made no compromises—for if she agreed that the state did have an interest in protecting the life of the unborn, at what point in the pregnancy would that interest arise? If the Court was willing to follow the medical arguments of the appellee, they might conclude that the life of the fetus began with its attachment to the uterine wall, and allow the state to bar abortion after that time. White's questions had driven her to assert that abortion should be available up to the moment of birth, and she cited the evidence in Cyril Means's legal-historical study to argue that before the states began to criminalize abortion, all abortions were legal (although that assertion was not precisely true).

Sensing Weddington's dilemma, Justice Douglas looked up from the letter he was writing and asked why Weddington wanted an injunction when the lower court had already delivered declaratory relief. Douglas had dissented in *Younger*, and he used his question to her to admonish the Court. Why shouldn't federal courts enjoin state prosecutions when they were improperly "used as a device to harass the person prosecuted?"

Weddington agreed and gave a pointed reason why the federal courts had to order an injunction stopping prosecution in Texas's courts. In 1969, a Dr. Thompson had been convicted of providing an abortion in Houston, Texas. He appealed to the Texas Supreme Court, and its decision had come down in November 1971. The Texas court upheld the state anti-abortion statute, ignoring the federal court's opinion already handed down in *Roe* and citing instead one of the dissenting judges in the Illinois federal case that the state had a duty to protect fetal life throughout the pregnancy. In light of such decisions by Texas's courts, it was necessary for appellants to seek federal injunctive relief for Dr. Hallford. The justices' interest was piqued (in a few minutes they would ask counsel for the state to deliver to the Court information on Dr. Thompson's case), and they now wanted to know if Texas gave rights to unborn children in "areas of trust, estates and wills." Weddington answered: not unless they are born alive, a qualification the state had left out of its brief.

Although friends later commented that her calm and polite demeanor and command of the cases had impressed everyone thus far, one point still worried Weddington—the mootness issue. Fortunately for her, it was the very first point that Jay Floyd raised in his thirty minutes, and then, under questioning, he mangled it badly. He began, "We submit to the court that their cause of action is strictly based upon conjecture." Would the Does stay married? Would she become pregnant? With Roe no longer pregnant, was not her cause moot? Surely there was no longer any case or controversy.

Justice Stewart reminded Floyd that the cases were filed as class actions, and surely "there are at any given time unmarried pregnant females in the State of Texas." If the Court must drop the case brought on behalf of all of them when any one of them, who happened to be the named plaintiff, delivered her child, then "what procedure would you suggest for any pregnant female in the State of Texas ever to get any judicial consideration of this constitutional claim?" Floyd stuttered, "I do not believe it can be done ... there are situations in which, as the Court knows, no remedy is provided." But this was exactly appellants' complaint to the Supreme Court: the constitutional right to an abortion had been established, but no remedy was offered in the lower court. One of the justices joked, "Maybe she makes her choice when she decides to live in Texas." Miffed, Floyd shot back, "There is no restriction on moving." But again, inadvertently Floyd had made a point for the appellants: Roe, and many other poor pregnant women, could not afford to leave Texas to seek a legal abortion.

Floyd had equal trouble explaining to the Court why Texas had not cross appealed, that is, why Texas had not appealed to the Supreme Court against the district court's declaratory judgment for Roe. Floyd reported that the state had appealed the lower court's ruling to the Fifth Circuit, but, despite the justices' prodding to discuss them, seemed reluctant to go to the constitutional issues. Asked directly about Dr. Thompson's case, he waffled. He did not know if it was on its way to the High Court. Asked whether he could send the Court a copy of the Texas opinion, he grudgingly promised that he would. This is the way that a party loses a case in oral argument.

Finally the Court short-circuited the procedural questions and directly asked Floyd what was Texas's interest in barring all but a few abortions. Floyd stumbled again. He claimed the state had an interest in protecting fetal life. This was what the Texas court in *Thompson* averred. But Justice Marshall wanted to know why did the state not then prosecute the mother who committed an abortion on herself? Was she not a murderess? Floyd did not know why the state only went against the doctor. Marshall persisted: and when that statute was passed, was not its purpose to protect the mother, the victim, from the abortionist? Floyd again conceded that the statute's original purpose was to protect the mother, not the fetus, and that courts had not yet granted to a fetus "full juristic rights."

Then what, Justice Marshall wanted to know, was the state's interest and when did it arise? He pressed Floyd to answer: at what stage of the pregnancy did the state take an interest in the life of the fetus, making it the victim rather than the mother? In other words, when did the state attribute life to the fetus? "In the first few weeks?" Floyd didn't follow the question, so Marshall repeated it: "In the first few weeks?" Floyd replied, "At any time, we make no distinction." Marshall was incredulous: "You make no distinctions?" Floyd offered the highly controverted biological supposition: "We say there is life from the moment of impregnation." He continued that the embryo became a fetus "seven to nine days after conception." "What about six days?" Marshall chided Floyd, who retorted, "We don't know." But the statute "[g]oes all the way back to one hour," Marshall reminded Floyd.

Though the room was quiet (the rules of oral argument specified that no one was to speak, rustle papers, or move about during the session), it was filled with unsaid thoughts. Marshall's increasingly sharp cross-examination and Floyd's hapless replies had turned a learned discourse into a farce. Floyd crumbled: "I don't [know], Mr. Justice, there are unanswerable questions in the field." As laughter broke the tension, Marshall offered Floyd quarter: "I appreciate it." Floyd surrendered: "This was an artless statement on my part." Marshall, standing astride a defeated counsel, mercifully withdrew the question. Floyd, nervous at the start, had by the end of his thirty minutes at the podium done almost irreparable damage to the state's case.

Oral argument in *Doe v. Bolton* proceeded more smoothly. Margie Pitts Hames went on the attack against the procedural requirements—residence, consent, and approval of the hospital committee—that the federal panel in Georgia had left untouched. They were "cumbersome, costly, and time consuming," effectually surrendering to the state what the legislation supposedly won for the women seeking abortions. Dorothy Toth Beasley followed and argued for the state that the central issue must be protection of fetal life. The fetus was "another person," and privacy rights ended when another person's life was at stake.

Three days later the judges convened in conference to discuss the case. The judicial conference is in a way the heart of the Supreme Court's intellectual operation. Like oral argument, it has its own written and unwritten rules. It is a private meeting customarily held twice a week during the sessions of the Court. The conference takes place in a richly paneled and thickly carpeted seminar room, the justices occupying seats at a long table. The chief justice presides. The business of the conference includes discussion of cases already argued orally, new cases, cases that might or might not be added to the docket, and ordinary administrative business.

At conference the dance of politics and personalities on the Court is in full swing from the moment the judges arrive. The trading of drafts and ideas among the justices and their clerks that precedes the conference comes to fruition as the justices move through the list of cases appealed to the Court and try to persuade one another to accept or reject cases for argument. This give and take then gives way to formal deliberations on cases already heard. The justices speak in turn, in order of descending seniority, on the cases before them. Each justice may take as much time as he or she wishes, and they are not to be interrupted, although some justices may have only a few words to say on a case and other justices may abuse the time limits and the patience of their brethren by lecturing them on minute points of law. The justices then vote in ascending order of seniority. The chief justice tallies the votes. If he or she is in the majority, he or she assigns the opinion to one of the members of the majority. If the chief justice is in the minority, the most senior justice in the majority assigns the opinion. Sometimes the conferences are raucous and contentious, but more often they are a rehearsal for the arguments that will appear in opinions for the Court, dissents, and concurrences (opinions that agree in part and disagree in part with other opinions).

At the conference Chief Justice Burger would have dismissed the pleas for relief for Dr. Hallford. He based his view on the Court's decision earlier that year in *Younger*. The Does had no standing. But Roe did and should have injunctive relief if the state law was indeed unconstitutional. Still, he was not convinced that the state law was unconstitutional on its face. Douglas, who had demurred from the majority opinion in *Younger*, disagreed. Now the state law was patently unconstitutional. What was more, all of the parties had standing. Brennan seconded Douglas. So did Stewart.

Justice White agreed on the standing issue but thought that the state had a compelling interest in protecting the potential life of the unborn child. For him the question was what form the state's interest might take. Could it regulate the doctors? Could it bar the abortion, except when the mother's health was at stake? Clearly he did not believe in abortion on request.

Marshall suggested that the state's interest might appear stronger as the pregnancy grew longer. Abortion of an infant at the moment of birth would be murder. But abortion at a very early state of the pregnancy should be permitted. Justice Blackmun also balanced the interests of the mother with those of the fetus. He had no trouble with Roe's standing and none with her constitutional claim, but there was no absolute right to reproductive autonomy. Brennan counted six votes to affirm and one to reverse the district federal panel for Roe, although Burger's equivocal remarks showed the chief justice to be either on the fence or, more likely, not wishing to vote in the minority if he did not have to. Not yet, at least.

From the notes of the deliberations, there is no evidence that the second strand of the new paradigm of women's place in the law had any impact on six of the seven men. Weddington's intimate portrait of the travails of pregnant women, and the New Women Lawyers and NOW briefs that attempted to add women's private voices to the formal, public voice of the law, did not play a role in the discussions at the conference. Thus, for the justices, instead of raising exactly the same questions of men's control over women's bodies, *Roe* and *Doe* seemed dissimilar because the Texas law was so restrictive and the Georgia law was more liberal in the exceptions it allowed. Ignoring the core values of the women's rights paradigm—choice and the primacy of women's unique experiences—Blackmun thought that the Geogia law balanced objective, neutral interests. Burger would have found the Georgia law constitutional, as would have White.

Douglas disagreed, but not because he was listening to the women's voices. Instead, he feared that the procedural requirements of the Georgia law would discriminate against those who did not have medical advice at hand, or those who could not travel to the handful of approved abortion centers the statute defined. Marshall added that in rural areas, poor black and white women would suffer under the statute—so it failed an equal protection test. Brennan supported these arguments, and knocked out in addition the state's requirement that a hospital committee approve the operation. He had still further objections to the law, but reserved them for a private conversation after the conference was over. Stewart joined Douglas, Brennan, and Marshall. Blackmun again wanted to see the High Court strike a balance between the state's claims and the needs of the poor. In *Doe,* Marshall, Brennan, and Stewart would have affirmed, Burger and White would have reversed the lower court, and Douglas and Blackmun appeared to want a fuller record of how the various portions of the law worked in practice.

When the justices returned to their chambers after the conference, Douglas was delighted with what seemed Blackmun's independence from Burger—so delighted that, assuming he would be the senior justice on the majority in *Roe,* he planned to assign the opinion to Blackmun. Blackmun had already proven himself a slow writer of opinions, the exact opposite of Douglas, but Douglas felt that he could move Blackmun along on this one.

The next day, when Burger counted himself in the majority and assigned the cases to Blackmun, Douglas was miffed. He wrote a note to the chief justice on December 18 reminding Burger that he, White, and Blackmun seemed to favor retention of the Georgia law and so were in the minority. Burger's response, characteristic of him, was not to conciliate but to strike back. He told Douglas that the votes in the two cases could not be tallied, and would depend upon the opinion that Blackmun wrote. What was more, in a slap at Douglas's desire to move along swiftly, Burger suggested that he would set the cases down for reargument after the two new justices had taken their seats. Douglas took out a yellow legal pad and wrote in longhand a short opinion in the case, but Brennan, perhaps the best politician on the Court in the twentieth century, and certainly the best manager of its many prima donnas, convinced Douglas not to circulate the draft. Better to wait for Blackmun's, however long it took to appear.

In the meantime, Brennan had some ideas of his own. Since his appearance on the Court in 1956, he and Douglas had become coworkers on a number of liberal opinions and had developed a superb rapport. He told Douglas that they should rely upon privacy as a core constitutional right and from it derive three kinds of liberty: the liberty to be free from bodily restraint; the liberty to make basic decisions like marrying and having or not having children; and the liberty to express one's own personality. It was not the doctor's right to speak freely or practice medicine that must be defended in any opinion, but the fundamental freedoms that all people had from interference by the state. Although a Roman Catholic, he insisted that particular "moral predilections" (by which Brennan, citing Justice Clark's article, meant religious beliefs) should not take the place of legal distinctions. The Court should not take a position on when fetal life began and so should tell states they could not interfere with abortions in early stages of pregnancies, other than to require doctors performing them be licensed and facilities be sanitary. Apparently Brennan had heard the voices of the women, and he told Douglas that "the decision is that of the woman and hers alone."

Sometimes the Court is ahead of public opinion, and its pronouncements help to shift people's views. In *Roe*, however, Burger's caution ran behind what appeared to be growing public sentiment in favor of choice. The January 1972 Gallup poll showed 57 percent of respondents favored leaving the decision on abortion to the pregnant woman and her physician. Fifty-four percent of the Catholics polled agreed with this view. In February, the American Bar Association adopted a resolution calling for abortion on demand in the first twenty weeks of pregnancy. Courts in Vermont and New Jersey voided state anti-abortion statutes on grounds of vagueness and unconstitutionality. By August, the Gallup poll reported that 64 percent of Americans would leave the decision to have an abortion to the pregnant woman and her doctor. Fifty-six percent of Roman Catholics polled agreed.

But the opposition was not quiescent. The Roman Catholic hierarchy in Connecticut still had the clout to limit abortion reform in that state, and the Catholic Knights of Columbus drew over ten thousand marchers to a "right to life rally" in protest against New York's liberal rules on abortion in April. When pro–abortion rights groups led by NARAL gathered to counter-march, they were assaulted with cries of "murderer, murderer." NOW members reported being afraid to voice their views publically, for fear of physical attack. Roman Catholic members of the president's Commission on Population Growth dissented from its March report in favor of abortion law reform, and President Nixon, himself in the midst of a reelection campaign in which Roman Catholic support in the Northeast was vital, wrote to Cardinal Terence Cooke of New York that unrestricted abortion "seems to me impossible to reconcile with either our religious traditions or our Western heritage." Cooke released the text of the letter to the press.

New York became the focus of the growing anti-abortion campaign, for its law permitting choice in the first twenty-four weeks of the pregnancy was the most liberal in the country. Borrowing from the shock tactics of some radicals in the women's liberation movement, one opponent of the New York law displayed a fetus in a jar to the assembly. It voted seventy-nine to sixty-eight to reverse the liberal laws, but Governor Nelson Rockefeller vetoed the bill, citing what he denounced as the illicit force brought to bear on legislators by pressure groups.

Blackmun, usually genial and polite to a fault, was feeling the pressure of drafting the majority's decision. He tried to master every detail of the medical data available on pregnancy and fetal development. When clerks brought the wrong file or left a window open overnight, he exploded in sudden anger, then hid himself away in a corner of the justices' library and ordered that no one bother him. In May, Blackmun showed a draft of his memo for the Court to one of his clerks. The clerk recalled that he was surprised that the memo lacked focus; worse, it did not get to the constitutional issue—that is, to the legal basis on which a woman's claim to an abortion might rest. Despite the clerk's voiced misgivings, Blackmun circulated the memo on May 18.

Blackmun first dealt with the threshold questions of the standing of the parties. They passed muster. When he turned to the merits, he found the Texas statute insufficiently clear to the doctors, and therefore unconstitutionally vague. In other words, he ignored the opinion of the lower court in *Roe*. There was no mention of women's rights, of privacy, or of the Ninth Amendment, save to say that there was no reason to go into those matters because the statute failed for vagueness.

Blackmun had admitted that he did not relish the task, and the opinion showed his distaste for it. None of the justices who had voted to affirm were impressed. Stewart decided to write a concurrence. Brennan quickly sent a note to Blackmun's chambers: Brennan would "prefer a disposition of the core constitutional question." Invalidation solely on the ground of vagueness was not what Brennan had in mind, and his displeasure was obvious. It was not clear that he would sign on to Blackmun's opinion. Douglas sent a similar note the next day. It may have been that Burger anticipated this outcome when he assigned the opinion to Blackmun, for Burger was not sure how far the privacy argument would stretch, and declined to rest any decision on it.

Blackmun did a fuller job with his memo on *Doe* a week later. He proposed to strike down all of the Georgia statute, including the portions that the Georgia district court panel had left in place. All that would remain would be the willingness of the attending physician to perform the operation. His draft opinion conceded "the woman's interest in making the fundamental personal decision whether or not to bear an unwanted child," but the legality of any given abortion still rested on the doctor's choice, not the pregnant woman's. In that sense it was a throwback to the old paradigm of women's legal subordination. Nevertheless, Blackmun knew it would invalidate almost all of the states' laws on abortion. At the same time, he now revealed that he had limited his *Roe* opinion to the vagueness issue in the hope of uniting the Court. After some caucusing of their own, Brennan, Douglas, Marshall, and Stewart agreed to sign on and agitate for a stronger opinion later.

When the Court had assembled to hear oral arguments in December 1971, two of the justices' seats had been vacant. In the midst of the deliberations on *Roe* two new justices were added to bring the Court up to full strength. Because they had not heard the oral arguments in December 1971, Blackmun, who wanted more time to write his opinions, moved that the cases be reargued, and in June 1972 Chief Justice Burger ordered a second round of oral arguments. These were scheduled for October 11, 1972. Burger felt that the states should take primary responsibility for defining crimes and enforcing criminal law and saw the abortion cases as criminal matters more than constitutional ones. Some scholars believe that Burger leaned toward reversing the lower courts' declaratory judgments, certainly refusing to order injunctive relief, and hoped that the new appointees, like him conservative in temperament, would join in his views.

On January 7, 1972, Louis Powell, a Virginia private practitioner, joined the Court. He had reluctantly consented to serve. A member of the social and legal elite in segregated Richmond, he was nevertheless a moderate in his personal views on race. He objected to the state's so-called massive resistance to court-ordered desegregation in the

1950s, and helped defeat it. A true gentleman in his manners and his treatment of others, he was honored in the profession when he joined the Court in the fall of 1971, and soon he was much liked by all his comrades, whatever their politics. In his opinions, he was a middle-of-the-road jurist, not opposed to change in the law but also appalled at what he saw as the country's slide into sexual permissiveness, and said so publicly in the summer of 1972.

The second new justice was William Rehnquist. He was a more consistent and ideologically committed conservative than Powell. He had served as a law clerk to Supreme Court Justice Robert H. Jackson in the 1952 term and wrote a memo for the justice on *Brown v. Board of Education* urging that the Court not reject the older separate but equal doctrine in favor of desegregation of the public schools. From his clerkship he moved to a practice in Phoenix, Arizona, where his conservatism and Republican Party affiliation led him to support stronger government powers to enforce criminal law and fight communism, and to oppose governmentally imposed racial equality and voting rights for minorities. He served in the Department of Justice in the first Nixon administration, advocating widespread wiretapping of suspected criminals without prior court orders and preventive detention of suspected criminals without arraignment. He opposed the right to counsel and other Fourth, Fifth, and Sixth Amendment decisions of the Warren Court. On the Supreme Court, he early indicated his distrust of liberal federal programs. He was not likely to favor abortion rights for women.

Powell and Rehnquist agreed with Blackmun and Burger that the cases should be reargued. White felt even more strongly. At a May 1972 conference, he read part of a draft opinion in favor of reversing the Texas panel's ruling in *Roe,* arguing that the only reason for an abortion was saving the life of the mother. Even Blackmun was surprised by White's vehemence. But in the end only Douglas dissented from the order for a rehearing. In the meantime, Stewart had become so incensed at the way Burger had delayed the majority opinion that he took the extraordinary step of leaking his thoughts to the press. In the summer recess, Blackmun withdrew from the clamor of the Court to work at the medical library at the Mayo Clinic. There is no doubt that he had noticed the names of three of its leading doctors in the College of Obstetricians' amicus brief, and he was looking for a way to bring the Court together on the conflicting scientific evidence in the two sides' briefs.

With reargument set for October 11, 1972, and Weddington again preparing for oral presentation, Lucas once more begged her to step aside and let him argue the case. She did not reply, and this time she wrote the supplemental brief herself. It was easier now, with favorable court decisions in Vermont, New Jersey, Kansas, Connecticut, and Maryland. Hames filed for *Doe*. Both women cited the recently reported *Baird v. Eisenstadt*, in which the Court finally extended to unmarried women the right of privacy granted in *Griswold*. Floyd and Beasley declined to submit additional briefs.

Reargument began with Weddington reporting that Texas was still prosecuting doctors for performing abortions and women still had to travel out of the state to find a legal and safe abortion. Over 1,600 Texas women had traveled to New York State alone to take advantage of its more liberal laws. The figures proved that the issue was not mooted by the end of Roe's pregnancy, for she represented a class of women who faced her anguish. Weddington quoted Pilpel's data to prove that the legalization of abortion saved women's lives and health and did not increase the number of out of wedlock pregnancies, one outcome forecast by abortion rights opponents. Weddington also cited the language of federal district courts other than Texas's in support of her proposition that the constitutional rights of women trumped the varied and insubstantial interests that some states raised about protecting fetal life. For example, courts in New York had denied that a fetus had constitutional rights.

Yet here she saw the shadow on the wall, for she knew that Texas would claim its duty to protect the life of the fetus prevented the state from broadening abortion rights for mothers. Treading water, she conceded under pressure from Justice White that if the Court found that fetuses had constitutional rights, the state should balance these against the constitutional rights of the mother. That was just what he wanted to hear, for unbeknownst to her, he had already decided that the fetus was alive from conception and did have constitutional rights. He persisted: did she not agree that the stage of the pregnancy made some difference? She admitted that New York had set twenty-four weeks as the limit for abortion on request, a different stance from the all-or-nothing position she had taken in oral argument in December 1971.

Blackmun now asked how the Hippocratic oath all doctors swore when they were licensed to practice medicine—that they would do no harm to a patient—affected her case. She cited the distinguished panel of doctors who had joined in the College of Obstetrics brief. Well, then, did Weddington think it odd that the Court had just halted all capital punishment and she was asking it to impose a kind of capital punishment on the fetus? She maintained that the fetus was not a person under the Constitution, nor had it ever been accorded status under the Fourteenth Amendment, which referred only to persons. But she conceded to Justice Stewart that if the Court conferred the rights of personhood on the fetus, "I would have a very difficult case."

Robert Flowers, Floyd's superior, had replaced Floyd for the appellee. He admitted in a later interview that he had prepared little in writing for the oral argument. Attorney General Martin had lost the election, and Flowers, Floyd, and the rest of the senior staff of Martin's office were looking for jobs in the private sector. Martin was suffering from severe health problems and, although he joined his two attorneys at the counsel table, was on his way to the Johns Hopkins University Hospital for eye surgery. Flowers recalled that he and Floyd had to walk that morning through throngs of pro–abortion rights marchers. Their morale, already low, hit bottom before Flowers walked to the podium in front of the bench.

But he rose to the occasion. He had two points to make—that Texas had a compelling interest in the life of the fetus from conception, and that the balance between that interest and the mother's right to privacy "could be best decided by a legislature." Was it then a medical question only? Justice White asked. No, Flowers answered, for he knew that the great majority of doctors wanted to be free to practice without state intervention on this subject. Well then, White continued, was there a case anywhere in which the fetus was accorded Fourteenth Amendment rights to life and liberty? No, Flowers conceded, he'd have to go back to the framers of the Constitution. But the Fourteenth Amendment came long after the framers of the Constitution were dead, and the Fourteenth Amendment said "persons." Was the fetus a person? If it were not, would Flowers and Texas have a case? Flowers conceded the logical impasse. If "the fetus is a mass of protoplasm similar to a tumor, then of course the State has no compelling interest whatsoever."

For him the fetus was not a mass, however, it was a potential life. Flowers quoted the research that Texas law professor Joseph Witherspoon had done on the early cases in answer to Cyril Means's article, including the words of William Blackstone, the famous late-eighteenth-century English jurist, to prove that personhood existed "even before the child is born." Justice White interrupted, also thinking of Means's article on the history of abortion: "Is it not true that in Blackstone's time abortion was not a felony?" True again, Flowers conceded, but in the "general attitude of the time" the unborn were regarded as potential life. Then why, Justice Stewart asked, did the state not accuse abortionists of manslaughter rather than the lesser offense of performing the abortion? Following his own reasoning, Stewart wanted to know if the Texas law erred on the side of allowing too many abortions? Why should the life of the innocent unborn child be sacrificed at all, ever? Would not every abortion be a murder? That was the argument that the anti–abortion rights demonstrators were increasingly making in the streets. If the Court gave such logic full credit, the New York law and other liberal abortion laws were unconstitutional, which meant that they should not be left to the state legislatures, as Flowers had originally proposed, but should all be struck down.

Flowers could save his Fourteenth Amendment argument by dropping his plea for deference to state legislatures, but then he must prove that the fetus was an unborn person. Unfortunately, he did not have sufficient command of the medical literature to satisfy Justice Marshall's concerns on this point. He could not fall back upon the law, for "the theory in the law books," as the Court told Flowers, was that injuries to the fetus could be grounds for legal action only if the child was born alive. When he sat down, Flowers had the impression that he had been hammered by a Court uninterested in his argument, lectured to and hectored rather than heard.

But Weddington and Roe were not off the hook. In her rebuttal, she found herself pressed into a corner. Would the state's statute be unconstitutional if it banned abortions after some portion of the pregnancy? Was abortion always legal? Weddington replied in a way that showed the Court she understood their quandary:

> In this case, this court is faced with a situation where there have been 14 three-judge courts that have ruled on the constitutionality of abortion statutes. Nine courts have favored the women, five have gone against her, 25 judges have favored the women, 17 have gone against her; nine circuit judges have favored the woman, 5 have gone against her; 16 district court judges have favored the woman, 10 have gone against her. No one is more keenly aware of the gravity of the issues or the moral implications of this case, that it is a case that must be decided on the Constitution. We do not disagree that there is a progression of fetal development. It is the conclusion to be drawn from that upon which we disagree . . . we are not here to advocate abortion. We do not ask this Court to rule that abortion is good, or desirable in any particular situation. We are here to advocate that the decision as to whether or not a particular woman will continue to carry or will terminate a pregnancy is a decision that should be made by that individual.

Despite Weddington's feeling that the reargument had not gone well, her closing remarks proved that she had come a long way intellectually and professionally. Weddington's plea smoothly fused the new paradigm of women's choice with a much older legal ideal of individual rights. She asked the Court to accord pregnant women what men had gained in a revolution from an imperial power, the struggle for democratic government, a civil war against slavery, and the civil rights movement: the right to be free from invidious government intervention in the most fundamental and intimate decisions of their lives.

———

The Opinion of the Court

The Court had heard reargument, which in fact had added little light, and Blackmun had his summer of medical research, but he still did not have an opinion drafted. The rest of the Court was ready, however. At

{ *Roe v. Wade* }

conference, Chief Justice Burger conceded that the Texas statute had to go but thought that *Doe,* reargued in the afternoon of October 11, was a tougher sell, for the state had a right to regulate abortion, and the fetus's life was entitled to protection at some point. Douglas was content with Blackmun's draft of the previous May, in which Douglas and Brennan had a role. Stewart seemed content with Blackmun's previous position. White stood by his earlier pose as well—he would defer to state legislatures, at least insofar as they regulated later-term abortions. Marshall found confusing the fact that Texas would not prosecute a woman who aborted herself and at the same time claimed to base on its statute on the need to protect fetal life.

Blackmun claimed to be ready, but his thinking was still muddled. He would not rest the right to an early-term abortion upon the Ninth Amendment at all, but the Fourteenth, would make *Doe* the lead case, and wanted to get all his research on the history of abortion into his opinion. Powell had also made up his mind—he would affirm the Texas and Georgia federal panels. But he would not do so on the basis of the vagueness of the state laws. *Roe* should lead, and women's rights should be a key. Blackmun okayed the shift—Powell had convinced him, and Blackmun was still eager to bring the Court together behind his opinion. But Rehnquist would not join him. He signified that he stood with White.

Powell's remarks and his stance may have been more important in Blackmun's thinking than all of Brennan's politics and Douglas's bluster, for Powell had the power of personal conviction, and more than enough of it to go around. Later he recalled that the cases seemed simple to him: "The concept of liberty was the underlying principle of the abortion case," the concept that Weddington had stressed in the waning moments of oral argument. The choice of an abortion was a personal decision, an intimate one, and "terribly important" to the pregnant woman. A story made the rounds that Powell had intervened to help a young man at his Richmond firm avoid a prosecution for helping an older woman obtain an illegal abortion. From that experience, so rumor said, Powell concluded that anti-abortion laws only drove women into the arms of illegal and dangerous abortionists.

But Blackmun still needed another five weeks to circulate a new draft, in the form of a memorandum to the Court. On November 22, he shared it with the other justices. The memorandum on *Roe* had ballooned to forty-eight pages, thirty-one more than its predecessor, the procedural questions now taking backseat to the medical and historical ones. From his research into the latter, he proposed the division of a pregnancy into trimesters. In the first of these, a woman only needed the consent of her doctor. In the latter two, the state's interest in the potential life allowed it to impose increasingly stiff regulations on abortions. Throughout the opinion he was wedded to the old paradigm that put women's bodies in the hands of male doctors; indeed, his summer research in a medical library on the opinions of doctors had only served to embed the old ideology more deeply in his mind. Hallford's plea for an injunction was dismissed and the Does', for prospective relief, rejected.

Blackmun still wanted a united Court and was gratified that Douglas, Powell, and Stewart commended the opinions. White and Rehnquist were cordial and revealed that they would probably concur in part and dissent in part. Burger said nothing, and Brennan's and Marshall's clerks were busy helping their bosses formulate replies. One of Marshall's new clerks was Mark Tushnet, who would later become a leading constitutional scholar. He urged his justice to join in Blackmun's opinion but shared Marshall's concern that it allowed the state too much control in the first trimester. Marshall so informed Blackmun, who listened, and on December 11, circulated a memo agreeing to shift permissible state regulation back to the twenty-eighth week, when viability of the fetus could be ascertained. Viability was the old doctrine of quickening, and Blackmun must have encountered it repeatedly in his traverses through the medical literature of the past two hundred years. Still, "I do not wish to do so if it would alienate any Justice who has expressed to me, either by writing or orally, that he is in general agreement, on the merits, with the circulated [November 22] memorandum."

Tushnet prepared and Marshall emended a reply to the new memo: "I am inclined to agree that drawing the line at viability accommodates the interests at stake better than drawing it at the end of the first trimester." Many women simply did not know that they were pregnant until well into the first trimester, and limiting their abortion options to that time frame would have worked a hardship on them. A compromise would perhaps be to allow the state to begin regulating after the first trimester but not allow those regulations to dictate the mother's choice until after viability. Brennan's objections, though voiced equally gently, were more serious. If the state's historical interest had been the mother's health and welfare, then the state should not have the power to limit abortions until nearer the end of the pregnancy.

Burger now let his cat out of the bag. He agreed with the general direction of Blackmun's opinion but desired that it say something about the rights of husbands and parents of minors seeking abortions. These questions had not been discussed to any extent in conference, and Blackmun's memo thanking everyone for their help did not acknowledge Burger's specific concerns. Left out, Burger had to decide whether to sign on or join White's and Rehnquist's announced plans to dissent. On January 22, the Court announced the vote and released the opinion. Burger had joined the Blackmun opinion, then added a brief concurrence.

Blackmun intended to make an announcement before reading the opinion that the cases were "most sensitive, emotional and controversial" and that even after the decision came down, he expected, "the controversy will continue." He wished state legislatures in session to pay particular heed to the fact that the Court was not holding that the "Constitution compels abortion on demand" or that "a pregnant woman has an absolute right to an abortion." Unclear what purpose such an announcement would have (it was not part of the opinion, hence not law), Brennan convinced Blackmun not to make it, and the idea was dropped four days before the decision was promulgated in Court. Brennan no doubt saw what Blackmun had either concealed from himself or wished to conceal from a rapidly polarizing public opinion: *Roe* actually gave women the right and the power to obtain first-trimester abortions on demand, or request, or however their choice was phrased. On January 22, Blackmun did add a personal note to the announcement of the vote in Court, "of the deep and seemingly absolute convictions that the subject inspires."

Blackmun began his opinion for the Court with the stark reminder that Texas and Georgia had made abortion into crimes, although the two statutes had "a different cast," the latter reflecting "advancing medical knowledge, and . . . new thinking about an old issue." In the time between the passage of the former in 1857 and the adoption of the latter in 1968, changing legal and social ideas on population growth, pollution, poverty, and race had intervened. Social context mattered in law. The Court recognized the fundamentally differing views of the parties, and wished to avoid all imputation of emotion.

Part I of the opinion reported the Texas statute and part II the history of the three cases consolidated under *Roe*. Part III accepted jurisdiction, and part IV handled the justiciability, standing, and the Court's willingness to render a decision. The Court had no trouble with the use of pseudonyms or with the issue that *Roe* presented a genuine case or controversy. The Court did not require that Roe be pregnant for the entire period of the litigation or at its end, for pregnancy was a repeatable event. Thus she and the class she represented had standing. Hallford's case was dismissed and remanded to the state court. Blackmun did not buy the appellants' distinction between current and potential indictments (although striking down the statute would bar future indictments just as effectively as an injunction—a point he did not make). The Court's view of the Does' situation was simple: their fears were speculative, and their claim was dismissed (but again, if the Court struck down the statute, the real Marsha King would be able to get a legal abortion in Texas).

Parts V and VI presented a review of the history of abortion from a medical perspective—the fruits of Blackmun's research over the summer. The laws that made abortion a crime were "not of ancient or even common law origin." They came in the latter half of the nineteenth century. The Hippocratic oath did not deter the ancient Greek doctors who invented it from helping with abortions, for the Greeks did not regard the fetus as having life until separated from its mother. In the English common law, abortion attempted or completed before quickening was not an indictable offense. Even religious authorities assumed that the soul was implanted sometime between conception and birth. Prior to that, the fetus was a part of the woman's body. Abortion after quickening was a serious misdemeanor, but not a felony (a capital offense). Blackmun cited Blackstone as authority for the latter statement, ironic in light of Flowers's attempt to use Blackstone as authority for the personality of the unborn child. Blackmun cited Cyril Means's article as corroboration.

After 1803, abortion did become a serious crime, but in one form or another the quickening distinction lingered in the English law. Blackmun then cited *Rex v. Bourne* to show how broadly English courts were prepared to treat a doctor's assertion that the abortion was intended, in good faith, to preserve the health of the mother. In 1967, Parliament reformed English abortion law to permit abortion at any time that three doctors agreed it was necessary for the physical and mental health of the mother or any existing children of her family, or if the child was likely to be born with physical and mental deformities.

Blackmun believed that the American law paralleled the English law until the middle of the nineteenth century, in particular in preserving the quickening distinction. Over the course of the next hundred years, however, most states barred all abortions except to save the mother's life. History demonstrated that for the first half of our country's existence, "a woman enjoyed a substantially broader right to terminate a pregnancy than she does in most states today." What had happened? Blackmun concluded that the American Medical Association and leading doctors set out to suppress abortion, in 1871 issuing a blanket condemnation and asking states to make abortion a crime. Why? When these resolutions were passed, abortion was an extremely dangerous medical procedure. Anti-abortion statutes then had as their primary purpose protection of the mother's life.

But in 1972, abortion was much less dangerous than carrying a pregnancy to term. Thus, in 1970, the House of Delegates of the AMA changed its mind and decided that abortion should only be subject to the discretion of three licensed physicians. In 1972, the American Bar Association agreed: it left abortion before twenty weeks of pregnancy to the patient and her physician. Thereafter, the state might regulate abortion in the interest of the unborn child. Blackmun was uneasy resting the overturning of the Texas statute on vague penumbras of rights, the undefined content of the Ninth Amendment, and the intimate pleas of the women. But in the authority of the male medical and legal establishment he found comfort.

The remainder of the opinion surveyed the realm of privacy and private rights that the Court had enunciated in recent years, preferring to derive these from the Fourteenth Amendment rather than the Ninth Amendment (although Blackmun allowed that other justices might frame them differently). But privacy, however derived, did not grant the absolute right to abortion. States had a right that grew as the pregnancy continued, so that "at some point in time [in the pregnancy]" the state could assert a compelling interest in protecting the potential life of the fetus.

Neither Blackmun nor the majority of the Court for whom he wrote "was in a position to speculate" on the medical question of when life began, nor did the Court think that the states could turn religious or moral presumptions into medical facts, but it offered a formula to answer the legal question of when the state could restrict abortions. During the first trimester, the state was not to intrude into the doctor-patient relationship—the decision was "left to the medical judgment of the pregnant woman's attending physician." At some point during the next trimester, after "viability," the state might act in ways "reasonably related to maternal health" to restrict access to abortion or the conditions under which it was performed. In the final trimester, the state's interest in the potential life of the fetus could be "promoted" by partial bans on abortion, so long as these did not endanger the mother's health. The Texas and Georgia statutes failed to measure up to this standard, and so were void.

The trimester scheme had no basis in prior constitutional law. Years later, Weddington reported to the authors of this book that she was surprised by the formula. Critics of *Roe* pointed to the lack of precedent for the trimester apportioning of rights and interests as one of the weakest parts of the decision. But in seeking an injunction Weddington had inadvertently opened the door to Blackmun's novelty, for she had asked the Court to provide equitable relief for her clients, and equitable remedies need not have precedent in the language of the law or the prior rulings of courts. Such relief must only be narrowly tailored to do justice, and that is what Blackmun intended. A contemporary analogy lay close at hand: in the early 1970s, federal judges, frustrated by school boards' long delays in implementing *Brown*, were ordering the boards to bus minority children into all-white school districts. There was nothing in the *Brown* decision on busing. Nor did busing have a place in precedent on civil rights. The Judges relied on their powers to fashion appropriate equitable remedies to reach the solution fairest *to all parties*. That is the goal of equity, and that is what Blackmun thought he had done for appellants and appellee in *Roe*.

Blackmun had tailored his opinion to ensure that at least four other justices joined it. Then it would stand as the opinion of the Court and have full precedential weight. In fact, six other justices joined him, but three of them wrote concurring opinions to explain their own thinking. Chief Justice Burger's concurrence was barely longer than a page in print and agreed that the Texas and Georgia statutes violated the Fourteenth Amendment. Burger was also concerned that Texas admitted that its prosecutors looked the other way when abortions were performed on women who had been raped, leaving abortionists and women seeking abortions to the mercy of prosecutorial whim. Had he his way, he would have left in place some requirement that at least two doctors certify all abortions, but the majority had removed that barrier in the first trimester. What is more, he reassured White and Rehnquist, the Court's decision would not open the door to "abortion on demand" or corrupt the medical profession.

Douglas joined Blackmun but wrote a short concurrence of his own to lay the result squarely on the right of privacy that he had elucidated in *Griswold*. He even quoted at some length from his opinion in the latter case, then expanded upon the three liberties that he and Brennan had discussed in the spring: control over one's personality, the freedom of choice in the basic decisions of one's private life, including the right to be let alone (a phrase borrowed from Justice Brandeis in a 1920s wiretapping case), and the freedom from bodily restraint and compulsion. The last referred to the state effectually forcing a woman to remain pregnant. Such liberties might be curbed by a compelling state interest, but when the state took away a fundamental right, the scope of its intrusion must be "narrowly drawn." The Texas and Georgia statutes were not. They deprived women of their "preferred life style" and forced them to accept an "undesired future." These state's laws ignored the psychological debility that such coercion visited on women whose pregnancies were unwanted. They struck a balance between liberty and constraint "wholly in favor of the latter."

Justice Stewart entered a third concurrence. He was still troubled, as he had been in his *Griswold* dissent, with the recrudescence of substantive due process analysis. Then, he had resisted such an analysis. But now he conceded that it was proper. The meaning that the Court assigned to the word "liberty" in the Fourteenth Amendment had to change with the times. It had to be broader than the rights enumerated by name in the Bill of Rights. Justice Harlan was correct in his dissent in *Poe v. Ullman* that liberty must be a continuum, and the Court must see its future as well as its past. Freedom of choice was an idea whose time had come.

Justice White, as he had promised, dissented, Justice Rehnquist joining in the dissent. White was in the middle of a career that showed him a thoughtful realist, with no illusions about the Court's power to alter social mores or act as a super-legislature. But his dissent had an obdurate and bitter tone that surprised his friends and antagonized his opponents. Later he would say that he could find no basis in the Constitution for a right to abortion, and thus the decision of the Court was wholly "illegitimate."

White saw the crucial cases as those in which women simply wanted to end a pregnancy that did not endanger them. They might be motivated by shame, convenience, economics, or "dislike of children." The Court's majority had turned women's "whim or caprice" into a constitutional principle, although there was nothing in the Constitution's language to sustain that judgment. To convenience a mother, and for little more, the Court had "disentitled" the legislatures of all fifty states from weighing the "relative importance of the continued existence and development of the fetus on the one hand against a spectrum of possible impacts on the mother on the other hand." He would have the Court reverse both the Texas and the Georgia federal panels and leave the mothers to the judgments of the state legislatures. In other realms of law and on other cases in which he had dissented, White would often accept the majority opinion as the basis for later rulings. This is called the doctrine of *stare decisis* (Latin for "to stand by things decided"). White never recanted his dissent in *Roe* or accepted it as settled law.

Justice Rehnquist, the most junior of the justices, wrote the last opinion. It too was short, and like Stewart's and White's, powerfully phrased. Roe was not pregnant at the time of the decision, so the Court overreached itself in providing her with a relief she did not need and could not claim. There was no right of privacy involved, for the abortion was not a private act. If liberty was lost, it was lost through "due process of law." The state's regulation of abortion did not have to rest upon a compelling interest, only a rational one, and the states' statutes surely had a rational relationship to the goal of saving the unborn child.

———

But now it was done. The Court had pronounced on the right to an abortion. Justice Frankfurter was wont to warn his colleagues that the Court had only a certain amount of political capital that it might use to take controversial positions. Such capital had to be spent with great care. Doctrines like abstention based on mootness or lack of standing, deference to the Congress, deference to the states, and the refusal to hear "political questions" were all ways to avoid waste of that capital. As his views in *Poe* suggested, Frankfurter would undoubtedly have preferred to avoid deciding *Roe* on its merits.

Perhaps Frankfurter would have foreseen the storm coming, heard the winds of dissent in the state legislatures and Congress, and seen the pro-life marchers heading for the steps of the Supreme Court building. Perhaps he could have predicted that the case would return again and again, in other guises, to the High Court, for in over twenty abortion rights decisions between 1973 and 2000, the Court reviewed set after set of municipal, state, and federal regulations, and agonized over whether they required the Court to revisit the core holding of *Roe*. From his intimate experience with electoral and appointive politics from the Progressive Era of the 1910s through the New Deal right up to his own appointment to the Court in 1939, he surely might have guessed that politicians' and judges' positions on *Roe* would become a test of their acceptability to large segments of the voting population.

And all that would come to pass, from battles over the wording of abortion planks in national party platforms to elections for federal and state senators and representatives turning on that one issue, from radio and billboard campaigns showing fetuses after abortions to the murder of doctors who performed abortions. But for now, the limited, circumscribed, highly controverted right to an abortion was the law of the land.

CHAPTER 5

Roe Under Siege, 1973–1988

The Court's decision in *Roe* and *Doe* went beyond what the appellants expected. It swept away all but the basic medical regulations applicable to all surgeries and delighted the leaders of the women's movement. Coffee first heard the news driving to work in Dallas. Reporters' queries on Weddington's response to the decision were relayed to her by coworkers. The telegrams from the Supreme Court clerk arrived later in the day. Lucas's telegram missed him; he had moved with no forwarding address. NARAL leader Lawrence Lader called it "a thunderbolt." Pilpel was surprised as well. "It scaled the whole mountain," she later said to an interviewer. "We expected to get there, but not on the first trip." The *New York Times* editorialized that the decision was a vindication for the women's rights movement. In St. Louis, abortion rights activist Judy Widdicombe got over her delight quickly and set about recruiting doctors and nurses for a public abortion counseling facility.

Shortly after the decision was announced, African-American women's leaders also began deliberations on how best to utilize abortion benefits. The National Black Feminist Organization (NBFO), formed in New York during the fall of 1973, included in its board lawyers like Eleanor Holmes Norton, a founder of NOW, and Congresswoman Shirley Chisholm, an honorary chairwoman of NARAL. The NBFO strongly supported Dr. Kenneth Edelin, a black physician on trial for performing an illegal abortion, and some of the members trained to aid in abortion clinics. Byllye Avery, another original member of NBFO, not only helped refer women needing abortions to providers, but founded a clinic in Gainesville, Florida. She explained her motives simply: "[F]or poor women abortion is a matter of survival; if I have this one more child, it etches away my margin of survival."

But just as the darkest hour for abortion rights, in the 1920s, had in it the beginning of the revival of abortion reform agitation, so the liberal activists' celebrations of the Court's decision flew in the face of a growing storm of opposition to abortion rights. As Blackmun was writing his opinion, the November 1972 elections landed a series of blows on the abortion-rights advocates' shoulders. Referendums for repeal of state anti-abortion laws failed in Michigan and North Dakota by significant margins. Anti-abortion rights media in these states had found a most effective way to reach voters: radio spots featuring the "voices of the unborn" calling abortion murder. Weddington had won election to the Texas assembly from Austin, her fame and her political connections giving her a huge majority of the votes, but she saw little likelihood of overturning the state statute. Catholic magazines called for the excommunication of Justice Brennan, and Cardinal John Krol, president of the National Catholic Conference, warned that the Court was encouraging the "greatest slaughter of innocent life in the history of mankind." Her identity revealed, Norma McCorvey became the target of hate mail and threatening telephone calls. The tide of public opinion seemed to be turning against abortion rights.

One might have expected the liberal academic community to welcome *Roe,* but the sweep of Blackmun's opinion put off liberal jurisprudents like John Hart Ely. Ely, Chief Justice Warren's clerk when the Court heard *Poe v. Ullman,* worried that the Constitution did not provide for a right to privacy. His concern had not changed in the ensuing years, and he devoted an entire article in 1973 to lambasting *Roe.* He did not argue that the meaning of the Constitution was limited to its framers' ideas, but he insisted that in *Roe* the Court had gone too far. Better to leave abortion rights to the popularly elected branches. The article was vividly and forcefully written (so much so that ten years later Ely half apologized for his excessive ardor), but parts of its argument appealed to a wide array of liberal jurisprudents, including a number of liberal critics of *Roe* who worried that the Court was creating a new and formidable set of rights without express and substantive enabling language in the Constitution. As law professor Russell Coombs wrote to the authors of this book about his reaction at the time, "I always despised *Roe* for its violation of those Articles [III and V of the U.S. Constitution]" that limited the purview of the Court. He remains convinced that, even for those who favored the outcome, "the storm about *Roe* and later abortion cases has been fed in large part by the view of a great many people that the Supreme Court overstepped the bounds of its authority."

Ruth Bader Ginsburg, then a professor at Columbia University Law School and head of the ACLU women's rights project, was also convinced that the opinion was too sweeping, and thereby made all women's rights vulnerable. It short-circuited the growing legislative movement for repeal of the abortion laws. The country was not ready for the opinion; the legislative and political infrastructure was not in place. But if the Court was bent on finding grounds for a sweeping opinion, the Due Process Clause of the Fourteenth Amendment, with its attendant implication that the court was setting itself up as a super-legislature to revive "substantive due process," was not the place to look. The Texas law discriminated against women on the basis of their sex; better to knock it down for violating the Equal Protection Clause.

Lawyering for the ACLU, Ginsburg had successfully argued to the Court that sex-based distinctions like housing benefits for men in the armed services in excess of those given to women violated the Equal Protection Clause of the Constitution. In *Frontiero v. Richardson* (1973), the Court agreed, and four justices seemed willing to make sexual distinctions in the law a "suspect category." Other members of the Court were waiting for the ratification of the ERA to do that. Justice Rehnquist alone dissented. In other cases after 1973, federal courts and the Congress proved willing to measure sex discrimination in the law against an equal protection standard, but when cases involving discrimination on the basis of sex also involved pregnancy, for example when pregnant teachers were forced to take unpaid maternity leave, the Court found in their favor not on equal protection grounds, but on due process grounds.

Writing twelve years after the decision, from the vantage point of the D.C. Appeals Court bench, Ginsburg worried that because "doctrine in the two areas ... has evolved in discrete compartments," due process decisions like *Roe* had a devastating impact on "the woman who lacks resources to finance privately implementation of her personal choice to terminate her pregnancy." There were two reasons why this was so. The first was that such women were very often poor, young, and unmarried and belonged to an ethnic minority. They had less education, less travel experience, and less contact with lawyers and doctors. Indeed, they tended to see lawyers and doctors as agents for a hostile state, which denied to them the opportunities that *Roe* provided.

The second reason was that states continued to turn religious and moral precepts into anti-abortion law even after *Roe*. Reading the preambles to state laws, listening to the debates in the state legislatures, and following the media and street politics, one can see that anti–abortion rights advocates regarded pregnancy in one of two mutually exclusive and morally charged ways. A pregnancy within a marriage was good; a pregnancy outside of a marriage was bad. The unmarried woman who sought to terminate a pregnancy was a double sinner, first for the illicit sexual activity that led to the pregnancy, and second for the rejection of women's preordained role as mother. For pro-life partisans, legal limitations on the abortions sought by such women were morally discriminating rather than unjustly discriminatory acts.

The Court abetted these views, perhaps unwittingly, on technical grounds. For laypeople, the reasons courts give for their rulings may seem inordinately narrow. For lawyers, they are the soul of the law. The law reasons by analogy and classification, putting new cases in old boxes. If it did not, every case would be a case of "first instance" with nothing to guide the court, there would be little regularity or predictability to the outcome of court cases, and lawyers would have to confront a vast variety of outcomes from place to place and time to time. Lawyers and their clients would not know which decision to rely on. Precedent—the common-law rule that rulings of superior courts in prior cases are authority for present cases in lower courts—would not work.

The Due Process Clause of the Fourteenth Amendment was one of these boxes, and it was already overstuffed when the Court jammed *Roe* into it. But due process was negative in the way it delivered relief to the appellants—it stopped government from intruding into a fundamental liberty protected by the Constitution, but went no farther. It did not ensure that abortions would be available to those who sought them. For that matter, neither did the box labeled equal protection. It may have been a more appropriate category for cases that inherently entailed sex discrimination, but it still only barred government intrusion. For example, had *Roe* been decided, as Ginsburg preferred, on equal protection grounds, the states might still have claimed that *Roe* did not require them to fund abortions for the poor.

Sylvia Law, another feminist law professor, pushed the latter argument further. In a 1984 law review article that brought together the legal, social, historical, and cultural literature widely cited by other scholars, she argued that genuine equality could not come from "protection" of women (the old "weaker sex" argument) or from mere facial equality in law. The same "assumptions about biological difference and destiny [that had in the past] provided the prime justification for creating a separate, inferior status for women" would undo any gains under a regime of equality, for the old cultural norms were still in place. They told "every woman over thirty" that she should choose home, motherhood, and domesticity over all other life courses. A dry formal equality in law that did not take into account the realities of women's differences, in particular the special burdens they bore when they became pregnant, would be worse than useless. More than a decade after the submission of the New Women Lawyers' brief to the Court in *Roe,* Professor Law harkened back to its demand that women's autonomy as persons become the basis for women's rights in law. "The vision of equality advocated here [the vision absent from Blackmun's opinion in *Roe*] suggests that the appropriate function of the law is not to enforce a general vision of what men and women are really like, but rather to respect each person's authority to define herself or himself, free from sex-determined legal constraints."

More conservative jurisprudents like Brigham Young's Rex Lee and Harvard's Charles Fried had equally complex views on abortion rights. Lee, a Mormon, opposed *Roe* from its inception, but it was not the Church of Latter Day Saints' avowed opposition to abortion that motivated Lee to take his stand. Instead, he had a narrow view of the social role of courts. At the same time, when he was President Ronald Reagan's first solicitor general, he resisted asking the courts to overturn *Roe* outright. He thought it not the place of the solicitor general to lecture the Court on how to read the Constitution.

Fried, a law professor at Harvard Law School whose writings on private-law subjects like contracts showed both strong moralism and individualism, privately applauded *Roe*. Later, serving as solicitor general in President Ronald Reagan's administration, Fried did an about-face on abortion rights. In briefs he wrote for the government attacking the decision, he claimed that *Roe* had no textual basis in the Constitution and that the Court misused its authority to impose one set of social mores upon everyone. For a state legislature to do this might be deplorable, but it was a democratically elected body. For appointed federal court judges with life tenure to do it was a dangerous precedent. He had no trouble telling the Supreme Court that *Roe* was wrongly decided, because he viewed the solicitor general's job as advocacy of the president's position on the law.

Law Professor Mary Ann Glendon's opposition to *Roe* was of a subtler sort. In a comparison of American and European abortion regulations written in 1987, she concluded that *Roe* was so badly written and so sweeping that it had begun crumbling from within almost as soon as it was announced. For *Roe* had fostered a sense of embattlement on both sides in what Glendon read as its absolutist stance. Compromise rather than confrontation should have been the Court's goal.

The Religious Opposition Grows

Leading the opposition to *Roe* out of court and academia was the Roman Catholic hierarchy. In 1869 Pope Pius IX prohibited all abortions. The papacy renewed its opposition in a 1968 encyclical. From 1966 to 1973, the Family Life Bureau of the National Conference of Catholic Bishops (NCCB) kept watch on the reform efforts in states and helped prepare statements for Catholic clergy warning against the immorality of abortion. The hierarchy ordered that none of the more than six hundred Catholic hospitals in the country allow doctors, whether they wanted to or not, to perform abortions. As one director of the leading Catholic pro-life organization boasted, "The only reason we have a movement [against abortion] in this nation is because of the Catholic people and the Catholic Church."

In the late 1960s and early 1970s, the church hierarchy was effective in preventing reform in New Hampshire, Arizona, Minnesota, Michigan, and Pennsylvania, but sometimes its efforts misfired. In March 1970, the Hawaiian state legislature repealed all criminal sanctions against doctors who performed abortions. The Catholic Church had urged its parishioners, some 28 percent of the population, to oppose the law. The Knights of Columbus, Catholic Social Services, and diocesan organizations joined the lobbying effort. Bishop John Scanlon took a major role in the political process, sent his representatives to the assembly, and finally appeared himself. He failed. Catholic politicians like Governor John Burns, who refused to veto the bill, thought that abortion should be a matter of personal conscience and wanted a separation of church and state.

In 1973 the NCCB called for the formation of "grassroots pro-life organizations" and ordered the National Right to Life Committee to coordinate local and national protests against *Roe*. In the same year, Monsignor Robert Lynch organized a National Committee for a Human Life Amendment to be funded through a one-cent per Catholic assessment each year. Although the Roman Catholic laity was divided on the issue (Roman Catholic women constituted over 25 percent of those who sought abortions after *Roe*) and some Roman Catholic liberal spokesmen saw a danger in making the abortion issue the leading public question that the church addressed, Reverend Edward Bryce, the head of the Committee for Pro-Life Activities of the NCCB, told an interviewer in 1978 that the conference saw abortion as an issue that mobilized opinion within the church.

In Congress, eight days after *Roe* came down, Maryland representative Lawrence Hogan introduced a draft amendment to the Constitution to make the fetus a "person" under the Fourteenth Amendment. Fetal life and fetal legal rights were to begin with conception. New York's Senator James F. Buckley introduced a constitutional amendment to reverse *Roe* the next day. Roman Catholic cardinals appeared for the first time before congressional committees to argue for Buckley's right-to-life amendment to the Constitution. Within three years, more than fifty differently worded amendments to ban or cut back on abortion had reached the floor of Congress. Representatives of the Roman Catholic church kept watch over every bill introduced thereafter in Congress, objecting when the legislation seemed to further abortion rights or might have been interpreted by the courts to open the door wider to abortion. For example, in the case of the Civil Rights Restoration Act of 1988, intended to prevent discrimination against women in education, and the Religious Freedom Restoration Act of 1993, intended to protect the First Amendment rights of worshipers, the church insisted on the removal of language that might have abetted abortion services.

But even the Roman Catholic church would have allowed an exception to anti-abortion laws when the mother's life was at stake, something that the evangelical Christian Right political action committees eschewed. Leaders of the far right wing of the Christian Right would call such trimming compromises with the Devil. Among the leaders of the Christian Right, the decision in *Roe* was just as important and performed the same galvanizing psychological role as it did for the abortion rights forces. Because abortion law repeal embodied the autonomy and independence of the new woman, it had become the centerpiece of the women's rights movement. In the reverse mirror image, because abortion law repeal seemed to assault traditional values of family and religion, it politicized the religious right. For example, Jerry Falwell, an evangelical minister and, in 1979, the founder of the Moral Majority movement, recalled that *Roe* had awakened him from his slumbers. Not only did he preach against it, he realized that preaching would not be enough—the preachers would have to become politicians.

Roe had infuriated a lightly sleeping giant, and that giant rose up in wrath in the 1970s. The Christian evangelical movement—a loose coalition of southern and western preachers and their congregations numbering between 20 and 40 percent of Protestants who regularly attended church services—had not been particularly involved in politics before the 1960s, but the potential was there, for evangelical networks were national in scope. Evangelical preaching had been on the radio from the time of Aimee Semple McPherson in the 1920s and on television had followed the crusades of Billy Graham in the 1960s and 1970s. Religious programming such as Pat Robertson's *700 Club* and Falwell's *Old Time Gospel Hour* reached households all over the country. Christian publishing houses' mass marketing techniques could easily be turned to political uses.

In the early 1970s, Republican party managers on the New Right such as Phyllis Schlafly entered into an alliance with evangelical leaders. The differences between the two groups (the New Right had a far broader international agenda, was better educated, and had corporate backing) would ultimately strain the coalition, but New Right government priorities overlapped the moral concerns of the Christian Right, and a number of ministers such as Robertson assayed political careers for themselves or supported Republican leaders whose social and cultural values seemed to match the evangelical credo.

The Christian Right had a longstanding interest in the law when it touched the Bible. Evangelical groups were behind the banning of the teaching of evolution in school classrooms in Tennessee and other states during the 1920s, and had supported the introduction of creationist teachings in the 1960s. But evangelicals did not have a broadly based political agenda nor any desire to overturn existing institutions. Indeed, evangelicals felt strongly about a very narrow range of issues. These included opposition to gay and lesbian rights (or at least to laws forbidding discrimination against individuals based on their sexual orientation); support for prayer in the schools and the end of government regulation of evangelical private schools; the removal of offensive language and subjects from libraries, movies, and television; and the censorship of sexually explicit books and magazines. In a national poll conducted in 1981, significant numbers of Americans indicated their support for the Religious Right's position on school prayer and homosexuality. Behind these was a vision of conservative or traditional family values. For example, Robertson's television network was called "The Family Channel."

It was thus natural and perhaps inevitable that abortion rights—the issue that had galvanized the women's movement and became the center of their new legal paradigm—would also galvanize evangelical leaders. The "moral report card" issued by the movement's *Christian Voice* from 1980 rated congressmen on their views of abortion rights, among other issues of interest to evangelicals. Thus *Roe,* a legal decision meant to take abortion out of politics, had not only thrust abortion back into politics but made abortion into the central domestic political issue for the next quarter century. Many politicians found that their position on *Roe* became the single most important determinant in their political future.

The Abortion Political "Litmus Test"

It did not take *Roe* to make politicians' views on abortion crucial to their chances of election and reelection. Abortion was a litmus test for party membership and popular vote as early as the late 1960s, as the New York legislative debates had demonstrated. But *Roe* gave focus and urgency to the political efforts of both sides. In the states, grassroots organizations opposed to *Roe* tried to undermine it with a myriad of legislative regulations. Some 449 of these made it to the floor of statehouses within two years of *Roe*, and 58 became law. These included complicated licensing and inspection rules, requirements to report the numbers of abortions performed, bans on advertising, detailed informed-consent requirements for minors and married women, and denial of public funding. The purpose of these was to make abortion expensive, time-consuming, and difficult to obtain.

As Planned Parenthood reported in 1977, 80 percent of public hospitals and 70 percent of private hospitals refused to allow abortions on their premises. Because of the variety of the state rules, the crazy-quilt pattern of state law on abortions that preceded *Roe* continued after it, as on average over one-fourth of the women seeking abortions in the Dakotas, West Virginia, Wyoming, Arizona, Indiana, Iowa, Kentucky, Maryland, Mississippi, Missouri, New Mexico, and Oklahoma had to travel out of state to find facilities.

At first, rising grassroots opposition to abortion rights was well reported in the media but made little impact on federal policy. Federal spending for health care (Title X of the Family Planning Act of 1970) already excluded abortion counseling. President Gerald Ford urged the country to support an amendment to the Constitution allowing states to regulate abortion policy; but his wife, Betty, had publically announced her support for abortion rights, and his vice president, Nelson Rockefeller, had supported abortion rights when he was governor of New York. In April 1975, the U.S. Senate tabled a bill that would have ended all Medicaid funding for therapeutic abortions. In the fall of the year, the Senate also dropped all pending right-to-life amendments. Ford's reelection platform urged Americans to continue the dialogue on abortion and praised the sincere convictions of both sides.

But in 1976 the politics of abortion became enmeshed with the presidential election campaign. During the 1976 legislative session, Henry Hyde, a conservative Illinois Republican congressman, placed an amendment on the Department of Health, Education, and Welfare appropriations bill that would have banned all federal funding for abortions. From 1965, using Medicaid money, the federal government provided funds for states to spend on health care for their citizens. Beginning in 1970, these funds had underwritten the expenses of hundreds of birth control counseling and family planning centers. President Nixon had barred funding abortions unless they were a medical necessity. Hyde's bill would have closed that exception, in effect going even beyond Texas's old statute.

The Hyde amendment to the HEW appropriation passed the House without trouble, but the Senate version of the bill would have made exceptions for abortions to save the mother's life as well as in cases of rape and incest, resembling the pre-*Roe* reform abortion statutes. Hyde viewed the Senate version as a "sellout" and refused to compromise, but cooler heads prevailed, and the Senate version was adopted in the House and sent to President Ford. He vetoed it, but Congress overturned his veto.

The explosion of the abortion funding issue in the election campaign of 1976 dropped sparks into an already supercharged atmosphere. Ford's desire to continue the public dialogue may not have cost him votes, but it had unanticipated consequences. The Democratic nominee for the presidency, Jimmy Carter of Georgia, identified himself as a born-again Christian and announced during the Iowa presidential primary that he personally opposed abortion. His managers clashed with Democratic feminists at the national convention, and a fragile compromise not to seek the overturn of *Roe* pleased no one. Carter continued to make speeches calling abortion "wrong," but he did not make anti-abortion a central issue in his campaign. Nevertheless, he won with the support of southern evangelicals, whose views on abortion rights matched his.

In office, Carter selected Joseph Califano, a liberal Catholic, but an anti–abortion rights advocate, as his secretary of health, education, and welfare, the post responsible for funding and making policy in family planning. In response to the Hyde amendment and Supreme Court decisions upholding states' refusal to fund abortions, Carter and Califano agreed that the federal government should not try to support abortion the way it supported prenatal and birth care. Presidential advisor Midge Constanza and other women in the executive office were upset and held a meeting to urge Carter to change his position. Sarah Weddington, who was general counsel at the USDA and would later agree to serve as one of Carter's assistants, was there and recalled that he listened to every mention of abortion with a clenched jaw. Asked by the other women to try to change his mind, she identified herself as counsel for Roe before the High Court and explained why the women who needed abortion the most were also the women who could not pay for it. During the rest of his tenure in office and her service as an assistant, Carter and Weddington came to a working agreement: she would not badger him about funding and he would not make public statements against Roe. Again, it was a compromise that pleased neither side.

In the first year of Carter's administration, the Hyde amendment again won in the lower house, and again its sponsors wanted to ban abortion funding. They complained that allowing exceptions to protect the mother's health opened a loophole so wide that "you could get an abortion with an ingrown toenail." The Senate version would have allowed funding in cases of rape or incest. A long and bitter conference between the two houses led to adoption of the Senate bill, which Carter signed on December 9, 1977. The next year, the fight was on again, with the compromise measure of 1977 first winning by 181 to 167 in the lower house, and then being overturned by a 212 to 198 vote. The more liberal bill prevailed in the Senate, however, and in another bitter conference, the Senate draft was approved. In a variety of forms, the amendment passed every year during Carter's, Reagan's, and Bush's administrations, although Congress has refused to make the legislation permanent.

At the same time as Congress was cutting medicaid funding for all but a few abortions, it was overwhelmingly approving the Adolescent Health Services and Pregnancy Prevention and Care Act. Designed to prevent abortion among teenagers, the language of its supporters demonstrated that their objection to abortion funding was moralistic, not parsimonious. Teenage sexual activity out of wedlock was a sin, not a social problem, whether or not a pregnancy resulted.

The moralist legislative theme that the appropriate alternative to abortion was self-denial would result, in 1981, in the Adolescent Family Life Act. Openly called a law "to promote self discipline and chastity" by one of its drafters, Alabama Republican senator Jeremiah Denton, it allotted over thirty million dollars to private and public sex education groups. But they were forbidden to provide abortion counseling, even if adolescents or their parents requested it, and groups that had in the past promoted abortion were not to receive any funding under the new law. Nor were teachers engaged by the program to speak approvingly of abortion.

This kind of "gag rule" might seem to violate the First Amendment rights of counselors and teachers, but there was precedent for it. In the 1830s, the United States Congress was inundated with petitions from anti-slavery groups. The language of these petitions was highly inflammatory, and slave-holding congressmen were offended by it. Led by South Carolina senator John C. Calhoun and other southern legislators, Congress imposed a "gag rule" on its own members, forbidding them from reading the petitions aloud. The gag rule lasted for nearly a decade, added free speech issues to anti-slavery ones in the growing national crisis over the expansion of slavery, and earned southern leaders in Congress the nickname "the slaveocracy."

The Adolescent Family Life Act not only proscribed pro-abortion speech, it provided the counseling groups with literature that portrayed women as the mothers of the race, procreation as women's highest and sacred duty, and abortion as murder: "However confused the motives, abortion always takes an innocent, already existing life. Since human life is the highest form of life on earth, man's greatest responsibility lies in generating other human lives responsibly. However, once generated, even irresponsibly, the new life is as sacred as the lives of its generators." Under this theory, it was perfectly acceptable for the federal government through the Hyde amendment (and for any state that wished) to deny funding for abortion while sponsoring prenatal care and birth. The state had a right and a duty to prefer birth to abortion, *Roe* to the contrary notwithstanding.

Observing Ford's fate and Carter's problems with his own cabinet, a set of young, energetic, and able Republican party managers realized that the dwindling fortunes of the party after the Carter victory (only 20 percent of registered voters identified themselves as Republicans) could be resuscitated through use of the abortion issue. Richard Viguerie, Paul Weyrich, Howard Phillips, and Terry Dolan were all experienced campaign advisors. Phillips was a former official in the Nixon administration, Weyrich a founder of one of the first of the conservative think tanks, the Heritage Foundation, and Dolan an able fund raiser and innovator in negative campaigning. All but Phillips were Roman Catholics and believed that abortion was a moral wrong as well as a potential political windfall for the Republicans. Abortion rights, they realized, alienated otherwise liberal Catholic voters from liberal candidates and could bring numbers of evangelicals from the South and West into the Republican fold. The four convinced the national party to focus its energy on ousting congressmen and congresswomen who favored abortion rights. The blow fell on Republicans as well as Democrats who had supported *Roe*, such as liberal Republican senators Edward Brooke of Massachusetts, Clifford Case of New Jersey, and Charles Percy of Illinois. They lost their seats in 1978.

Abortion rights became a litmus test for candidates to the federal judiciary after 1980. President Ronald Reagan's justice department announced that it would be seeking to appoint anti–abortion rights judges to the lower federal bench. Over the course of his eight years in office, some three hundred of these appointments were made, and Reagan's legal advisors apparently kept their word. In addition, appointments to the Justice Department's own offices were measured against this yardstick. President George Bush chose two justices for the High Court; neither was expected to support *Roe*. Nor was it only anti–abortion rights forces that used the litmus test. President Bill Clinton's appointments to the Supreme Court were both pro-*Roe*, and he supported a Right to Choose act in Congress.

Abortion Returns to the Court

The U.S. Supreme Court does not have to hear cases on appeal from the lower courts, but in what amounted to its own version of the obsession the politicians and activists demonstrated over abortion, the

Court agreed to hear case after case that came its way on abortion after 1973. Opinions in these produced an almost impenetrable maze of doctrinal twists and turns, as abortion cases were reclassified as government spending cases, administrative law cases, free speech cases, and federalism cases.

Why did the Court entertain all these cases? There is no obvious answer. In certain kinds of litigation, notably voting rights cases of the early 1960s and after, the Court's decisions virtually invited disputants to continue to litigate because each redistricting plan raised new problems. In other kinds of cases, for example school desegregation, the Court left enforcement to lower courts using the injunctive power to compel school boards to comply, with the result that the High Court had to hear repeated challenges to lower courts' rulings. Abortion cases might have fallen into this category of recurring review because each new round of state regulations, responding to earlier Court decisions, raised sufficiently distinct issues to demand detailed resolution. Or it may be that members of the Court dissatisfied with the state of abortion law saw each new case as one more chance to revise *Roe*.

Another kind of explanation lies in the character of the counsel who directed challenges to state regulation. On the one hand, pro-life legal groups like Americans United for Life thought they could undermine *Roe* through a succession of increasingly restrictive state laws. From 1984 on, they pursued this strategy. On the other hand, pro-choice lawyers had a remarkable record of victories in the federal courts. Pro–abortion rights plaintiffs, often "repeat players" like the counsel for the ACLU and the PPFA, brought suits against every restrictive provision they could. The list of amici on the side of the abortion rights litigators, including elite legal, medical, and academic groups, attests to the intellectual pull of the pro-choice forces. Between 1977 and 1990, when pro-choice action groups were able to rally their forces, the district and circuit federal courts rendered pro-choice decisions. Finally, when the district and appellate courts enjoined states from enforcing their own regulations, the states had to appeal to the Supreme Court or concede the incapacity of their legislative process. No state will do the latter willingly.

The cases the Court took on fell into four categories: denial of funding, limitations on access to abortion services, restrictions on doctors' speech, and finally restraints on anti-abortion activity, including the speech of demonstrators. The first two of these dominated the 1970s and 1980s, the latter the 1990s. The state legislatures involved would obviously have preferred the Court to back away from or even reverse *Roe*, but at first the *Roe* majority seemed to be relatively firm, and all that anti-abortion state legislatures and later the Congress could do was to shift abortion counseling and procedures from public hospitals to private clinics.

The state of Missouri led the way. In the immediate aftermath of *Roe*, abortion rights advocates immediately announced plans for abortion counseling clinics and abortion services. In Missouri, where a suit in federal court against the state's abortion laws was slowly moving forward before *Roe*, Judy Widdicombe opened Reproductive Health Ser vices in downtown St. Louis. No longer would Missouri women seeking abortions have to travel to states like New York and California to gain medical help. She did not have to wait long for the first self-recruited doctor, Michael Freiman, to appear. He had, like so many other local interns and residents, seen more than enough botched abortions. He was joined by George Wulff, an obstetrics professor at Washington University Medical School. Individual gifts and some contributions from foundations and labor unions paid for the clinic.

But Widdicombe may have gone too far too fast, setting up a clinic in the shadow of St. Louis's massive Catholic Cathedral. By October, right-to-life protestors had made her office a target of their campaign, and the state passed legislation to limit what she and other reproductive services could do. In 1974, the state's house of representatives passed, by a 148 to 3 vote, a pro-life bill. The senate concurred, 27 to 5. Testimony before both houses featured spokesmen for the Catholic church and pro-life organizations. Only Widdicombe spoke for abortion rights. It was no contest.

In *Planned Parenthood of Missouri v. Danforth* (1976), Widdicombe's clinic brought a suit against the state of Missouri for imposing parental consent (for minors) and spousal consent (for married women) requirements on women seeking early-term abortions. The *Roe* majority (less Douglas, who had retired, and Burger, who now joined White and Rehnquist in dissent), struck down the state's spousal consent and parental consent requirements. Douglas's replacement, John Paul Stevens, sided with the majority. Stewart and Powell wrote separately to indicate they favored a parental consultation provision, and Stevens would have allowed the parental approval rule to stand—indications that the *Roe* ban on state regulation in the first trimester was already shaky.

Stevens was Chicago-born, -bred, and -educated, a former Supreme Court clerk and a moderate Republican. President Nixon had plucked Stevens from private practice and placed him on the Seventh Circuit bench, from which President Gerald Ford elevated him to the High Court in 1975. His opinions on both courts were frank, to the point, and self-confident. He fit into no block, made up his own mind, and, far more often than his political sponsors could have guessed, sided against government and with the poor, minorities, and aliens. His opinion in *Danforth* signaled his commitment to abortion as a right, but one that was subject to reasonable regulation. He did not regard such regulations as a covert way to deny women the power to choose an abortion, however.

If *Roe* seemed safe for the moment from direct assault, it was vulnerable to flank attack through denial of funding. The issue of funding had appeared in briefs and oral argument in both *Roe* and *Doe*. Appellants then had made the case that abortions would cost less than public support for unwanted children. But the Court in *Roe* did not require that states promote abortion by paying for it. Douglas and Marshall had been aware that denial of public funds would have a disparate impact on the poor similar to the problems they faced before legalization, when the rich could travel in search of a legal and safe abortion, but the poor had to stay home and have more children.

After *Roe,* states like Connecticut and Pennsylvania passed laws that required abortions take place only in fully equipped hospitals, which seemed on their face to protect the mothers' health but in fact were designed to reduce the number of abortions. For the same reason, the two states opted to deny the use of federal Medicaid funds for abortion at any stage of the pregnancy except when one or more doctors certified in writing that the abortion was necessary to save the life or health of the mother, when the fetus was likely to have crippling birth defects, or when the pregnancy was the result of rape or incest previously reported to the police. The same states used federal funds for prematernity and maternity care for the indigent, openly favoring continued pregnancy over abortion.

In *Maher v. Roe* (1977) in Connecticut, *Beal v. Doe* (1977) from Pennsylvania, and *Poelker v. Doe* (1977) involving a municipal regulation from St. Louis, Missouri, Powell, Stewart, and Burger from the *Roe* majority joined White, Stevens, and Rehnquist in upholding laws that restricted funding even in the first trimester. Powell wrote the decision in *Beal* and *Maher*. Both opinions claimed to leave the central holding in *Roe*—the right to choice—intact but concluded that a constitutionally protected right to seek an abortion was not the same as a constitutional mandate that abortion would be treated by municipalities and states in the same way they treated potential motherhood. Powell continued that the state laws did not create the poverty that may have made it impossible for some women to obtain abortions, nor was a government's preference for birth over abortion barred by *Roe*. Brennan, Blackmun, and Marshall dissented, seeing behind the face of the restrictive laws a blatant and cynical purpose to defeat *Roe* by making abortion difficult to obtain for many and impossible to obtain for some.

To understand the distinctions that the justices were making, one has to recall the formulas that the Court uses to assess constitutional challenges to state legislation. In *Roe,* the Texas statute made abortion a crime. It was unconstitutional on its face if women had a fundamental right to privacy and if the state's interest in fetal life was not compelling. So the Court found in *Roe*. But nowhere in the Constitution does one find the words "privacy" or "compelling." These are part of a judge-made, or "prudential," way of reading the Constitution. Judicially invented and imposed doctrines for interpreting the Constitution are allowed, indeed they are often necessary, because of the role that judges play in interpreting the meaning and application of legislation in our system and because of the relative terseness of the Constitution. Three of these judge-made rules applied in the funding cases. The first, as Stewart later wrote, was that when a suit could be decided by either constitutional or statutory means, the Court "ought not to pass on questions of constitutionality ... unless such adjudication is unavoidable." In other words, if a majority could uphold or knock down the statute without referring back to the Constitution, it would do so. In the funding cases, this led the Court to examine city and state abortion laws for their fit to the statutes authorizing federal Medicaid payments to the cities and states, including the Hyde Amendment as it applied to Medicaid funding for abortions, rather than to the Fourteenth Amendment.

The second prudential doctrine the Court deployed was the distinction between the levels of scrutiny that legislation must pass to be constitutional. In *Roe* the Court had deployed a two-pronged test. By 1977 there were three prongs. Under the old test, if the act did not burden a fundamental right or disfavor a "suspect class" such as race or religion, then all the act had to have to pass muster was a rational relation to a constitutionally permissible purpose. Again, "rationality" and "permissibility" were determined by the Court—the words did not appear in the Constitution. A middle range of scrutiny was introduced by the majority of the Court in *Craig v. Boren* (1976), a sex-discrimination case brought to lower the drinking age of men in Oklahoma from twenty-one to eighteen, the age at which women could drink. In this intermediate range, applicable to statutes that disfavored one sex over the other, the law "must serve important governmental objectives and must be substantially related to those objectives." Finally, if an act challenged in the federal courts singled out and disproportionately harmed a suspect class, the legislation must undergo an even higher level of scrutiny. The state must show that it has a compelling interest that the act is narrowly tailored to promote. Was denial of funding rationally related to the constitutionally permissible purpose of preferring fetal life to abortion? Was denial of funding a matter of sex discrimination, requiring the intermediate level of scrutiny? Was access to abortion a fundamental right, and were poor people who could not afford a private abortion a suspect class, invoking the highest level of scrutiny of laws denying funding?

The last prudential doctrine, implicit but not stated in the Constitution, was that the Court should defer to democratically elected bodies when an issue is one of policy or political choices. That was why Tolle had asked the federal panel in Texas to refrain from invalidating the state's law. The Constitution gives jurisdiction to the High Court, but does not deny jurisdiction—leaving it to the justices, in their wisdom and prudence, to regard such issues as the legislature's proper sphere. Lower federal courts had barred states and municipalities from denying public funding of abortion. The High Court's majority reversed these decisions, in effect recommending that pro–abortion rights forces seek their aims through the electoral rather than the litigation process.

Beal was the lead case. The federal district court had dismissed the plaintiffs' complaint against a Pennsylvania law barring funding for abortion except for medically documented cases that the pregnancy would damage the mother's health, would produce a deformed infant, or was the result of rape or incest. The state's requirement that the abortion take place in an accredited hospital also passed scrutiny. The district court struck down the state's requirement that two physicians in addition to the woman's own doctor sign the papers for all abortions, including those in the first trimester. The Court of Appeals for the Third Circuit found that the three-doctor requirement should not apply in either the first or the second trimester. Justice Powell, writing for Burger, Stewart, White, Rehnquist, and Stephens, reversed the lower courts in part and held that the entire state statute was within the guidelines of the federal funding program. It was not necessary to raise or answer constitutional issues, Powell decided.

The opinion turned instead on the provisions of the federal Medicaid laws. These required states to assist certain categories of "medically needy" persons, like the aged, blind, and disabled, but left to states the matters of how and how much to assist others. Pennsylvania had elected to use the funds to help those women who carried their pregnancies to term but not those who elected to abort their pregnancies. During oral argument, Norman Watkins, deputy attorney general of Pennsylvania, had told the Court that the state routinely allowed doctors great latitude in determining those conditions surrounding the pregnancy that might endanger the woman's health; that is to say, the law allowed funding for the class of abortions that would have fit the pre-*Roe* "therapeutic abortion." Thus the funding restrictions in the law still paid lip service to the expertise of the doctors and to the doctor-patient relationship.

Relying on the state's interpretation of its own laws, Powell concluded that the Equal Protection Clause of the Fourteenth Amendment did not prohibit the state from "the policy choice" of funding birth but not every abortion. States could not criminalize abortion across the board, but they did not have to encourage or underwrite it. Powell explicitly deferred such decisions to the states themselves: "through the normal processes of democracy." In the end, the message amounted to this: The governments involved could spend their money as they wished.

If plaintiffs wanted to win their suit against Pennsylvania under these constraints, they had to find a mandate for abortion funding in the federal Medicaid act that provided the funds for Pennsylvania. "But nothing in the [federal Medicaid] statute suggests that participating states are required to fund every medical procedure that falls within the delineated categories of medical care," Powell insisted. States need only have rational standards for including and excluding categories of medical assistance. It was reasonable, Powell continued, for the state to protect fetal life as much as it did, and to prefer live birth to abortion. That state interest was explicitly conceded in *Roe*. In fine, only a regulation that was "unduly burdensome" on the woman's right to elect an abortion would violate *Roe*. Powell opined that the three-doctor requirement might be unduly burdensome, and remanded the issue back to the lower court for a determination.

But what could have been more burdensome to the poor mother than denial of funding, Justice Brennan wondered in his dissent. "The Court's construction can only result as a practical matter in forcing penniless pregnant women to have children they would not have borne if the state had not weighted the scales against their choice to have abortions." Powell had read Brennan's dissent, in which Blackmun and Marshall joined, but Powell was not moved by the "vivid . . . anguish" of the dissent. The state did not cause the penury of the poor; it did not add any burden to their poverty that they had not voluntarily taken on themselves.

Marshall wrote a separate dissent, and its language was even more vivid than Brennan's. The majority was doing in *Beal* exactly what the Court in *Roe* said Texas could not do: imposing a moral viewpoint. He looked behind the facial neutrality of the state law to find that "the impact of the regulation here falls tragically upon those among us least able to help or defend themselves." The statistics did not lie, he claimed. The application of the law, if not its language, denied equal protection to poor minority women. To agree that the state had only to show the "rationality" of its law's provisions, was to apply the wrong test of constitutionality, for a woman's right to an abortion was fundamental, and the state's interest was not compelling. By the majority's sleight of hand "a fundamental right is no longer at stake and mere rationality become the appropriate model of analysis."

Blackmun wrote a third dissent to underline the last point in Marshall's: the Court "allows the states . . . to accomplish indirectly what the Court in *Roe* . . . said they could not do directly. The Court concedes the existence of a constitutional right but denies the realization and enjoyment of that right on the ground that existence and realization are separate and distinct." Blackmun was of course defending his opinion in *Roe,* but in a way it was his own fault, for he had already agreed, in *Roe,* that the Court should not order injunctive relief. How then could the Court require funding? The right and the remedy were already severed in *Roe.*

In *Beal* the issue was Pennsylvania's disbursement of federal funds. In *Maher,* the State of Connecticut refused to use its own funds on nontherapeutic abortions, including those in the first trimester. The federal district court had struck down portions of the law requiring certification of medical necessity, written application by pregnant women, and prior consent by the state's Department of Social Services. Powell and the majority reversed the lower court. "The Connecticut regulation places no obstacles—absolute or otherwise—in the pregnant woman's path to an abortion," for "it has imposed no restriction on access to abortions that was not already there." Consequently he could argue, "Our conclusion signals no retreat from *Roe* or the cases applying it. There is a basic difference between direct state interference with a protected activity and state encouragement of an alternative activity consonant with legislative policy."

Hidden behind the debate on abortion in the funding cases was an issue that had been part of the abortion law reform movement from its inception in the 1930s: the rich could afford to find and finance abortions; the poor could not. The poor would have their children and get poorer, or seek and sometimes die from illegal abortions or self-inflicted abortions. Powell confronted this perennial issue obliquely in *Maher:* The lower court had read the Constitution incorrectly—"this case involves no discrimination against a suspect class." The "indigent" did not belong in that "limited category." Had Powell agreed that the poor were a suspect class under the Constitution for the purposes of abortion funding, poor people could bring a shipload of cases arguing that all manner of state funding formulas favored the wealthy. But he drew back from the assertion that "financial need alone" created a "fundamental right" under the Fourteenth Amendment.

Brennan's dissent had accused the majority of "a distressing insensitivity to the plight of impoverished pregnant women." Although he was "not unsympathetic to the plight of an indigent woman who desires an abortion," Powell repeated that denial of funding did not constitute an "unduly burdensome" obstacle to the choice of an abortion, and ordering states to use their funds to pay for such procedures, just as ordering states to use discretionary federal funds to pay for nontherapeutic abortions, would open the door to court-imposed spending in a myriad of other areas. The Constitution did not allow courts to act in this fashion, Powell concluded.

Obscured but still visible in the controversy over public funding for abortion was a wider-ranging contemporary dispute over the role of government in social welfare matters. In the 1970s, legislative politics had shifted to the right, the beginning of a long-term change in the shape of public discourse over the role of the liberal state in everyday life. Abortion was not just women's cause, it also was a liberal cause. *Beal* and *Maher* arrived at the Court in a time when rural conservatives were joining with ethnic blue-collar workers to demand a return to family values and traditional ways. Even the labor unions, once bastions of liberal political activity, were shifting to the right. The rise of the Moral Majority, the creation of Virginia evangelical preacher Jerry Falwell, further shifted the dialogue over government policy in a conservative direction. The Moral Majority's testament of political faith would be Falwell's *Listen America!* (1980), an attack on liberal politics and "secular humanism," the ideology of liberal pluralism, in which abortion rights had found a place. In this atmosphere of reduced expectations and declining social commitments for government, funding for abortion and its obverse, refusal to fund abortions, fit perfectly.

Moralistic pronouncements accompanied all of the state and municipal limitations, but the Court had not allowed explicitly religious considerations to dictate the outcome of cases until it decided *Poelker*.

The two St. Louis municipal hospitals offered obstetrical services at little or no cost to indigent patients. The units were staffed by the medical students of nearby St. Louis University. The school was Jesuit-run, and its dean and trustees opposed abortion rights. In part at their request and in part because of his own strong opposition, Mayor John Poelker ordered the hospitals not to perform abortions unless the life of the mother was at stake. "It's a moral issue with me," he told reporters. The resulting ban allowed fewer exceptions than the Connecticut and Pennsylvania laws.

The Eighth Circuit Court of Appeals, sitting in the city, overturned the ban, but the same U.S. Supreme Court majority that had joined in *Beal* and *Maher* reversed the lower court and allowed the city to reimpose its ordinance. The majority likened the case to the other funding cases. Brennan, Blackmun, and Marshall again objected. The majority's opinion did not attempt to probe the motives of the mayor, the hospital administrators, or the doctors, the dissenters noted. But one can argue that the fact pattern itself in *Poelker* was so different from the state cases that the outcome of *Poelker* should not have been linked to the other two cases. Connecticut and Pennsylvania alleged sound medical practice as the basis for their regulations. St. Louis's decision was not a medical one but the embodiment of the will of a church, effectively establishing a city religion. The majority of the Court had rejected just such an argument when the state of Texas raised it in *Roe*, but here it was veiled behind the pleadings, and the Court's majority made no effort to raise the veil.

The stage was now set for the last of the funding cases to be decided, *McRae v. Harris* (1980). The suit began in New York as *McRae v. Califano* in 1977, when two women, unable to use New York Medicaid funds because the Hyde amendment barred the state from paying for all but life-saving abortions, sued the secretary of the Department of Health, Education, and Welfare. Over the course of the suit, the two plaintiffs were joined by women from a Methodist church women's group. Their intervention brought to the suit a First Amendment establishment claim that allowed plaintiffs to attack the religious motivations behind the funding ban directly. A district court judge stayed (halted) operation of the Hyde amendment. New York, whose attorney general had written an amicus brief in support of the plaintiffs, was happy with the temporary injunction, but the sponsors of the congressional action were not. The district court allowed Congressman Hyde and Senators James Buckley of New York and Jesse Helms of North Carolina to intervene as defendants, but after a lengthy trial, the court found the plaintiffs' claims persuasive and authorized payment for all abortions before twenty-four weeks (the period specified in the state law).

The solicitor general of the United States, Wade McCree, argued for the federal government, in support of the Hyde amendment, that the funding ban did not violate *Roe*. Rhonda Copelon argued for the original plaintiffs (here the appellees, since the federal government had brought the appeal). With her were Nancy Stearns, Sylvia Law, Ellen K. Sawyer, Janet Benshoof, Judith Levin, Harriet Pilpel, and Eve Paul. Justice Stewart, writing for Burger, Powell, Rehnquist, and White, found the issue settled by *Maher* and *Beal*. Teenage pregnant women were not a suspect class, even if they also were women of color. If states could constitutionally deny funding, so could the federal government. Medicaid was an "entitlement," not a right, and all governments had the authority to deny entitlements so long as denial did not violate a fundamental right. The right to have an abortion was not abridged by denying funding, for the government had not erected any obstacle that was not already there. The government did not create the indigency, therefore the Hyde amendment need only be a rational method to express a constitutionally permissible purpose. *Roe* itself had expressly stated that states had a legitimate interest in the protection of fetal life. All that the Hyde amendment did was to further this interest.

Was the majority right? Did the Court's holding in the earlier funding cases dictate the result in *Harris*? In the former cases the Court upheld the state's legislative preference to fund birth but not (nontherapeutic) abortions. In *Harris*, the Court denied the states that option, that is, it said that Congress could stop states like New York that wanted to use federal moneys to pay for abortions. Powell's reasoning in favor of allowing states to choose how to spend federal funds was based on a preference for democratic allocation of public finances; the state legislatures were free to spend or not spend because they were the democratically elected organs of the people's will. In *Harris*, the majority refused to defer to democratically elected legislatures. Whatever the validity of the Court's logic in upholding the Hyde amendment, that logic could not rest on the logic of *Beal* or *Maher*.

Stewart had merely asserted that the Court's rationale in the earlier funding cases disposed of the due process and equal protection arguments against the Hyde amendment, but the First Amendment complaint was a new one, and he devoted much of his time to deal with it. He conceded that "it is the appellees' view that the Hyde amendment violates the Establishment Clause [of the First Amendment, 'Congress shall make no law respecting the establishment of a religion'] because it incorporates into law the doctrines of the Roman Catholic Church concerning the sinfulness of abortion and the time at which life commences." Anyone reading the debates on the Hyde amendment in Congress would have found a religious purpose in the act, but the Court is not required to look at the intentions of the framers of an act to decide on its constitutionality. Indeed, one strong tradition of statutory interpretation having its roots in England argues that courts should never go behind the clear text of a statute to seek meaning in legislative debates. U.S. Supreme Court Justice Antonin Scalia has written that even when courts say that they are looking at legislative intent, they "do not really look for subjective [historical or contextual] legislative intent. [Judges] look for a sort of 'objectified intent,' that is, an intent that fits into the judge's own 'objectives and desires.'"

Stewart refused to consider the legislative intent behind the Hyde amendment. If an act had some secular purpose, the religious motives of its framers were irrelevant. The Hyde amendment had such a secular purpose—the protection of fetal life. Should one object that such a purpose was rooted not in secular values but in explicitly religious ideas, Stewart had a ready answer. *Roe* had found such a purpose legitimate, and that made the protection of fetal life a secular purpose. The logical sleight of hand, something like laundering mob money through a legitimate business, had the ironic outcome of making *Roe* into the justification for the Hyde amendment.

The appellees had also challenged the Hyde amendment under the Free Exercise Clause of the First Amendment ("Congress shall make no law . . . prohibiting the free exercise thereof"). But Stewart judged that the women who wanted the abortion did not do so for religious reasons, and the Methodist women did not want abortions. The Methodist church itself, which had joined the suit, had no standing, for it had no "personal stake" in the outcome. The church ladies could not represent poor women who wanted an abortion, and even if the latter represented a class for the purposes of the suit, such a class could not include the Methodist women. End result: the free exercise question they raised was not properly before the Court.

Brennan, Marshall, Blackmun, and Stevens dissented. Recognizing the technical facility of Stewart's dismissal of all claims, Brennan begged the Court to consider the "human terms" of the suit. It condemned women to remain pregnant. The opinion echoed the NOW amicus brief in support of *Roe:* in effect, the Hyde amendment forced reproductive servitude on poor women. Marshall again decried the road the Court was traveling—the poor must bear the onus of their own poverty, as though poverty itself was the original sin leading to all others. He wished the Court would at least employ the intermediate level of scrutiny introduced in *Craig v. Boren,* but even that was unavailing. Blackmun's dissent was only a paragraph long: the Court "condescended" to women in need in language that was indifferent to the reality of women's lives. Stevens, seeing where the Court was going, had now joined the dissenters. He too reviled "the Court's sterile equal protection analysis," in which the court had traveled so far from *Roe* that it could not recognize the fundamental right that *Roe* conferred on women.

In the midst of the hubbub over whether the right to an abortion imposed a financial obligation on the state, in the funding cases the Court had affirmed an unexplored implication of *Roe* and reversed a half-century-old precedent on what may be called the right to bear children. In *Buck v. Bell* (1927), the Court had allowed states to perform involuntary hysterectomies on women "imbeciles." In effect, the Court had decreed that there was no constitutional right to bear a child, at least no right that could stand against a state legislature's desire to practice eugenics. *Roe,* insofar as it confirmed the right of a pregnant woman to chose her reproductive future, conferred the right to have a child. In the funding cases, the Court not only confirmed that right, but treated it as an entitlement (inasmuch as the state committed itself to spend public funds to ensure a safe birth).

The Reagan Years, 1980–1988

Despite the dissenting justices' gloom over the funding cases, many other abortion controversy participants saw 1980 as "morning in America." Ronald Reagan, a former movie star and television pitchman who had become governor of California, sought election to the presidency in 1980, promising to bring back the nation's glory. Reagan's tenure as governor had been marked by his hostility to liberal causes and environmental protection, and a professed desire to take the government out of the everyday life of Californians. A superb public speaker when working from a prepared text, he persuaded many voters that his program was a much needed corrective to big government. Although it had achieved much in the realm of human rights at home and abroad, President Carter's administration had been fatally damaged by his failure to control inflation and his inability to rescue hostages from the American embassy in Teheran, Iran. With an election whose course seemed drawn along ideological lines, but whose outcome showed that most Americans preferred not to vote, Reagan won 51 percent of the popular vote and the electoral votes of every state but Minnesota, Georgia, West Virginia, Maryland, and Rhode Island.

The nomination and election of Ronald Reagan as Republican candidate for the presidency seemed to foretell the ultimate victory of the anti–abortion rights movement. Although Reagan had signed the California Abortion Reform Act in 1967, since that time he had become an outspoken foe of further reform. During the 1980 campaign, he sent a personal message to the National Right to Life Committee and courted ministers such as Falwell and Robertson, who had made anti-abortion a major issue. Not by accident, the platform on which he ran was the first in which the Republicans dropped their support for the ERA. Once elected, Reagan approved Utah senator Orrin Hatch's anti-abortion constitutional amendment in 1981 and North Carolina senator Jesse Helms's "right to life" legislation. When both of these initiatives died in Congress, the Reagan administration did not make anti-abortion its number-one priority, but Reagan's antipathy to the ERA helped doom it, and he appointed conservative women such as Elizabeth Dole and Jeanne Kirkpatrick to posts in his administration.

Another of these conservative appointments was Sandra Day O'Connor, an Arizona Court of Appeals (intermediate appellate) judge, to the Supreme Court. After receiving her law degree from Stanford University Law School in 1952 and marrying, she experienced the same difficulty finding a law firm job as did Sarah Weddington nearly twenty years later. Like Weddington, O'Connor served as a deputy county attorney and won election to the Arizona state senate. In government service, she became accustomed to narrow and specific holdings anchored by particular fact patterns. She was not well known for either her legal opinions or her ranking in judicial circles. She was, however, a highly skilled judicial craftsman and a regular Republican, and Reagan's talent spotters thought that her conservatism would make her a suitable if not an ideal woman for the High Court—fulfilling Reagan's promise to appoint a woman to its bench. On the Court, her willingness to allow certain kinds of state support of religious activities, her opposition to affirmative action programs, and her views on abortion seemed at first to repay Reagan's expectations.

The time seemed ripe for *Roe* to fall. Christian Right preachers denounced the supposed feminist agenda as a direct assault upon the New Testament tenets of women's subordination to men. Howard Phillips charged that feminists had invaded Washington, D.C., and wanted to make wives the equal of husbands. It was a staple of this literature that female-dominated households led to drug abuse and sexual license, and then abortion. Opponents of abortion rights sincerely hoped that, as Paul Weyrich wrote in 1980, feminists who wanted "the downgrading of the male or the father role in the family" would soon be on the run.

Anti–abortion rights leaders agreed that they must defeat the ERA to prevent all manner of calamities, including abortion on demand. When the deadline for ratification arrived in June 1982, with the amendment three states short of the needed thirty-eight, opponents celebrated with a party in Washington, D.C. Schlafly, Falwell, Senators Helms and Buckley, and forty-five others were given special awards for their efforts. All opposed abortion as well as the ERA. When the ERA was reintroduced in Congress during the 1983 session, it fell six votes short of the two-thirds it needed in the House of Representatives. The anti-abortion lobby was out in full force. The ERA, it told members of both houses, was nothing more than a front for abortion on demand.

The moralism of the forces opposing the ERA and abortion had a sharp edge. Schlafly wrote in her *Power of the Positive Woman* (1977) that there were two sides to every issue, and only two—the moral and the immoral; there was no middle ground. If one favored the ERA one favored all the parade of "horribles" that the ERA might bring—legal support for lesbianism, the end of all protective legislation for women, the derogation of men's roles, and, worst of all, abortion on demand. With charismatic leaders like Schlafly in the vanguard, it was no wonder that pro-life political action committees raised on average 60 percent more money than pro-choice groups from 1978 to 1988.

As important as it was in discrediting, or at least narrowing, the way people saw the ERA, the abortion issue was neither the core of the ERA nor the sole cause of its demise. One of the authors of this book, lobbying for ratification of the ERA in Georgia during the 1980 legislative session, does not recall that *Roe* was ever mentioned in the floor debate or the discussions with assemblymen in corridors. Still, the potent pro-life campaign against *Roe* hung over the heads of ERA supporters in the states. Some felt that they were in a race to gain ratification in states before pro–abortion rights litigators could file suits under state ERAs. If a few states like Connecticut found grounds in state ERAs to protect abortion rights, it was unlikely that the United States Supreme Court would use the proposed amendment to order abortion on demand. Some feminist supporters of the ERA hoped that its ratification would force the High Court to reverse its abortion funding decisions. If the ERA made sex a suspect category along with race and religion, analysis of the Hyde amendment would have to focus on whether states were impermissibly discriminating against women when they refused to fund an operation that applied only to women. Perhaps anti-abortion forces were right to agree with Rex Lee that "no one can say how the ERA will be interpreted."

In the meantime, emotions over the abortion issue had reached a fever pitch. Dr. Bernard Nathanson, a founder of NARAL who had since repudiated the pro-choice movement, released his *Silent Scream,* a videotaped ultrasound depiction of an actual abortion. When, at one point in the videotape, the fetus seemed to be opening its mouth, Nathanson, doubling as narrator, intoned "once again we see the child's mouth open in a silent scream." A supportive congressman introduced a description of the film into the *Congressional Record.* President Reagan urged every American to see it. Judy Widdicombe feared that it was the best piece of anti-abortion rights propaganda she had ever seen. NARAL countered with a portfolio of pictures of women who had died from unsafe abortions, but that was old stuff.

The ERA and the abortion controversy by the mid-1980s had cultivated among some men a virulent strain of anti-feminism that spilled over into a new type of anti-abortion organization. These were male-dominated street movements. They were confrontational and sometimes violent, capturing the anger and the frustration of men at the women's movement in general as well as at the immorality they saw in abortion. Typical of these feelings, John Willke, president of the National Right to Life Committee, wrote that abortion "removed the right of a husband to protect the life of the child he has fathered in his wife's womb." Willke's views echoed in suits fathers brought for fetal rights and state-imposed limitations on abortion practices.

Norma McCorvey, working at a birth control clinic in the late 1980s, recalled in her autobiography how she came face to face with anti-abortion rights masculinity. Inside the clinic, she recalled in 1994, "everyone is friendly." The gynecologist was a "kind and generous man." She believed that the clinic was a place where women could feel safe. Outside, the demonstrators were "mostly young, conservatively dressed men. "They carry pictures showing dead fetuses—photographs blown up hundreds of times—and placards saying that we dismember dead babies and store them in our freezer . . . shout and pray at the top of their lungs and try to scare our patients." One of the placards that McCorvey noticed said "future American soldiers killed here." It was a sentiment that nineteenth- and early-twentieth-century anti–birth control spokesmen would have found entirely appropriate.

For a handful of the demonstrators, the strident masculinity of the anti-abortion movement edged into violence. In 1982, the first bombing of an abortion clinic occurred. By 1984, the number had passed 25. By the end of the Reagan administration, 77 family planning and abortion clinics had been bombed, 117 were burned, 250 had received bomb threats, 231 were burglarized, and 224 were vandalized. The Reagan administration belatedly recognized that these were terrorist acts, but the FBI was still reluctant to devote much of its manpower to investigating the incidents. The government termed the bombings the work of individuals rather than groups, but no one could miss the warlike language of the new direct-action groups. As Willke told a convention in 1986, he would inflict "pain and fear" on the women who supported abortion rights.

The first bombings and burnings may have been the work of a few individuals, but an ideology that reached far beyond individual incidents united the new masculinity of the far right with the moral absolutism of the earlier anti-abortion movement in a way that transformed the confrontational rhetoric into action. Three men were responsible, and all saw anti-abortion as a means to express masculine goals. The first was a career officer's son and Naval Academy dropout, Michael Bray. The second was a former public relations man and Benedictine novice, Joseph Scheidler. The third was Randall Terry, a Pentecostal preacher and used-car salesman in upstate New York.

Bray found comfort in evangelical religion, but became impatient with passive resistance to what he saw as immorality. Men must act on their moral commitments, he decided. Such men, like puritan "saints" in the seventeenth century, knew that they were saved and that others were immovably wedded to sin. The anti–abortion rights movement was a field in which Bray could test his doctrines and himself, and he began to explore direct-action techniques to put abortion clinics out of business. By the mid-1980s, these methods grew more and more violent. By 1984, Bray was placing pipe bombs against clinic walls throughout the South. His tactics caused his religious mentors great anguish, and they disavowed his violence, but they could not deny that the language and the emotion of the anti–abortion rights movement could lead a committed protestor to such a course. He was convicted in May 1985, and spent nearly four years in prison.

Scheidler, a bear of a man, traveled from protest to protest throughout the 1980s. He was soon the anti-abortion leader most feared by pro-choice forces, and sometimes by pro-lifers as well. His Friends for Life group, a splinter organization in the pro-life movement, gained the reputation for outrageous tactics. At one demonstration he gleefully displayed fetuses stolen from a laboratory to make his point; at another he used a bullhorn to intimidate clinic patients. Conservative columnist Pat Buchanan called Friends for Life the "green berets" of the pro-life movement, aptly capturing the militaristic side of Scheidler's approach. Scheidler liked the nickname and included it in his literature.

In late 1983, he developed a manual of confrontational tactics and mailed instructions to anti-abortion groups on how to appear at every campaign stop that Democratic presidential candidate and abortion rights supporter Walter Mondale made in 1984. Scheidler's *Closed: Ninty-Nine Ways to Stop Abortion* explained how to jam the clinic's phone lines, block exits, and use pickets to intimidate women trying to enter clinics. The most controversial of the techniques, however, was the targeting of the doctors who worked in the clinics. Scheidler proposed using detectives to find out where the doctors lived and directly harassing them. But Scheidler shied away from personal participation in the confrontations. Gradually his mantle of leadership passed to Terry.

Terry and Scheidler had been allies in founding Operation Rescue, but Terry did share Scheidler's deep-seated fear of authority. Terry came from a family of strong-minded and liberated women, and although he would reject their ideals, he inherited their moral certitude. Among his aunts were the communications director of the Rochester, New York, chapter of Planned Parenthood and the leaders of the abortion reform movement in upstate New York. All had faced unwanted pregnancies when abortion was illegal. A youthful rebel himself, Terry wandered west in search of countercultural enlightenment and came home to find himself left out of the yuppie culture of his peers. He went to Bible school, married a bright young woman, had children, insisted that his wife stay home and care for them, and took the only jobs open to him—selling used cars and working at McDonald's.

The upstate region of New York has a long history of religious radicalism. In the nineteenth century it was the birthplace of the Church of Latter-day Saints and home to the Shakers and the Oneida Community, and in the early 1980s, Terry experienced his own conversion. With it came a vision of how to stop abortion, he recalled. By 1984 Terry was counseling pregnant women not to have abortions, and in his spare time, he joined in picketing of clinics. In 1986, he was arrested for locking himself inside one of the clinics in Buffalo, New York. In 1987, from these experiences and his own growing sense of what could be done with massive confrontation, he developed Operation Rescue, a program to shut down the clinics. It was ecumenical, bringing together Roman Catholic and evangelical groups. It was charismatic, Terry regarding his coworkers as brothers and sisters. It was cultish, for he had a charismatic attraction for his followers that went beyond their common goals. It was popular, involving at one time or another thousands of demonstrators. It also made him a media star.

He drew upon the tradition of massive resistance that the civil rights leaders of the 1950s and 1960s had introduced into American politics, featuring prayer meetings, vigils, and human chains to block streets. Terry promised his followers, "By doing massive rescues, we could create the tension needed to turn the tide. When government officials have to choose between jailing tens of thousands of good, decent citizens, or making child killing illegal again, they will choose the latter, partly because there are no jails big enough to hold us if we move together in large numbers."

But Terry's tactics fostered divisions within the anti–abortion rights movement. Terry's enthusiasm barely masked his intemperate and unsympathetic view of women. He was opposed to all forms of birth control, to premarital sex of any kind, and to all feminism. He denounced its program as the "destruction of the traditional family unit." Worse, he believed, feminism promoted lesbianism. Advocates of a gentler form of persuasion, such as Earl Paulk, an Atlanta pastor and long an opponent of legalized abortion, accused Terry of ignoring the anguish that pregnant women experienced when they sought abortions. Others rejected the breaking of laws. Southern Baptist spokesman Charles Stanley presciently worried, "Where does [the lawlessness] stop?" Other critics noticed that after the initial rush of enthusiasm, the number of pickets had declined to a hardy and hardened few, and they seemed to be growing angry at their lack of success.

Despite the massive press attention given Operation Rescue, public opinion polls showed little change in Americans' views of abortion. With some dips and bumps, from 1972 to 1988 a remarkably steady 38 to 39 percent of Americans believed that abortion should be legal under all circumstances, and only 3 to 9 percent opposed abortion in all circumstances. Over 75 percent of those polled thought that abortion ought to be available if a mother's health was in danger or if the fetus showed evidence of damage. More than half felt the abortion should be legal if the family could not support the child or the mother was unmarried.

At the same time, over three-fourths of Americans favored parental notification or consent requirements and the upgrading of clinic facilities. Not surprising in a country where regulation of medical procedures of all kinds had become the norm, Americans wanted legal but regulated abortion. Thus, Terry's exhortations to one side, Operation Rescue, even at its high tide in the late 1980s, when it nearly shut down clinics in New York City, Los Angeles, Atlanta, and elsewhere, did not have staying power.

Indictments of Terry and his followers for civil misconduct and fines for contempt of court for violating injunctions against sit-ins were accumulating. In court, Terry used every technique pioneered by anti–Vietnam War protestors to harass his prosecutors, but he could not win over every jury and was soon deeply in debt for his legal expenses. His slogan—that all abortion was murder—still resonated with many Americans, but the fear of prosecution had driven his most dedicated followers underground. Terry decided that, like Martin Luther King Jr., he would go to jail for his beliefs, but in a Georgia prison, he began to suffer a nervous breakdown. Rivalries within Operation Rescue exploded with Terry temporarily out of the picture, and when he returned, a rebellion among his former cohorts left the organization a shell of its former self. Meanwhile the number of arsons and bombings increased.

The Trimester Formula Fractures, 1983–1988

While the new masculinity of the anti-abortion protests led to increased violence in the streets, opponents of abortion in the states followed a quieter but equally effective strategy. They simply passed regulation after regulation to limit access to abortion. Some were similar to regulations that the High Court had already struck down. Others were even more restrictive than those voided by the Court. By 1983, ten years after *Roe* should have settled the issue, the Court had rendered opinions in fifteen major cases regarding abortion and remanded dozens more back to lower courts for further findings or decisions consonant with Court rulings.

The majority of the Court in the funding cases had explicitly announced that they thought the denial of support did not touch the essential constitutional holding in *Roe*. As Justice Powell, author of those opinions, wrote in 1983, "The doctrine of *stare decisis* [that the Court will adhere to prior decisions] . . . is a doctrine that demands respect in a society governed by the rule of law." Governments could spend their money as they wished, so long as the purposes of the expenditures were not constitutionally barred. They could use funds for birth and deny them for abortions. This was why Stewart and Powell, who had both signed on to Blackmun's opinion in *Roe,* were able to vote with the majority in the funding cases, and indeed why Burger, who joined them, assigned the opinions to them. But what if states and municipalities ignored the precise instructions of *Roe* and *Danforth* and passed regulations whose not so hidden purpose was to deny the right to an abortion?

Cases of this type were appearing all over the map, like weeds in an untended field. Often they took three to four years to come to the Court, after pro-choice litigators had won lower court injunctions against them. In 1983, three of these cases came to the Court together, from Akron, Ohio, Missouri, and Virginia. Virginia had punished a doctor for performing an abortion in an unlicensed facility late in the second trimester. The Court upheld the punishment. Missouri (whose legislators seemed indifferent to the Court's earlier rulings, even on cases that had originated in Missouri) had passed a law that required all second-trimester abortions be performed in a hospital—in effect denying patients the chance to use cheaper clinics. In *Planned Parenthood of Kansas City v. Ashcroft,* the Court struck the latter rule down but allowed the state to require pathology reports on the fetal tissue, to compel minors to get one parent's consent or, if the minor was already living away from home or had otherwise proved their independence from their families, consent of a juvenile court judge (called a judicial "by-pass"), and to insist that a second physician be present during the procedure to deal with the fetus if it was viable.

The Ohio litigation was particularly mischievous, for in 1978, the city council of Akron, Ohio, ignoring the clear signal of *Danforth,* passed a series of seventeen resolutions severely restricting abortion in the city's hospitals. The first of the resolutions claimed that all were necessary "for the protection of the life and health of the pregnant woman," then asserted "it is the finding of the Council that there is no point in time between the union of the sperm and egg . . . and the birth of the infant at which point we can say the unborn child is not a human life." The city council had declared that *Roe* did not apply in Akron.

The new regulations imposed on doctors in Akron an obligation to the viable unborn child: from the end of the first trimester (at about fourteen weeks) no abortion except in hospitals; no abortion without a twenty-four-hour waiting period; no abortion without seventy-two hours' notice to parents or guardians; no abortion without informed written consent, including that of one of the parents (or the order of a court). Even more burdensome: no abortion without the doctor reading to the pregnant woman (and her parents if she was a minor) a script that included all the agencies available to adopt children, all the dangers that might occur from an abortion (whether these were relevant to her medical situation or not), and all the techniques that might be required, including the most extreme, even if these were not likely to be used. No abortion unless the doctor arranged for the fetal remains to be disposed of "in a humane and sanitary manner." Although doctors had nothing to do with such disposals in other cases, the penalty for their failure to see to the "humane" disposal of the fetus was to be a criminal misdemeanor.

The federal district court barred Akron from enforcing the parental notice and consent provisions, the portions of the scripted statement on alternatives to abortion, and the requirement that doctors become undertakers. The Circuit Court of Appeals agreed. So did six of the Supreme Court's justices. Powell, writing for the majority, saw through these (admittedly translucent) subterfuges. They had the purpose of obstructing or dissuading the pregnant woman from exercising her right to chose to end her pregnancy in its early stages. Powell argued that the *Roe* trimester formula "continues to provide a reasonable legal framework for limiting a state's authority to regulate abortions." Written consent and informed consent were not bars to her right to choose; but innovations such as the script the city wrote for doctors to read "departed from accepted medical practice." The "litany" of horrors, unrelated to the patient's actual condition, could only have the purpose of deterring the patient from proceeding. The restriction of second-trimester abortions to hospitals brought additional expense and health risks, given that properly equipped abortion clinics were safe enough to supplant hospitals. In a brittle and pointed final note to the city, Powell told its council that they were "free, of course, to enact more carefully drawn regulations that further its legitimate interest in proper disposal of fetal remains."

During the oral argument, United States Solicitor General Rex Lee had sought and gained ten minutes to present the Reagan administration's support for the Akron restrictions. The Court almost automatically extends this courtesy to the United States when it wishes to go beyond an amicus brief and address the Court. In his presentation, Lee argued that the Court should abandon the trimester formula of *Roe,* in which the right to a first-trimester abortion was to be untrammeled, and adopt a test that Powell, writing in *Beal* and *Maher,* had incidentally introduced. Powell had suggested that denial of funding was not an undue burden on the right to choose to terminate a pregnancy. Lee elevated this into an "unduly burdensome" test for all limitations and regulations, perhaps hoping that Powell would join a Rehnquist, White, Burger, O'Connor majority to uphold the Akron regulations.

Blackmun was furious and asked Lee point-blank if the government wanted the Court to overrule *Roe.* Lee said no. Why not? Blackmun persisted, implying quite correctly that the "unduly burdensome" formula would totally upset his balancing act in *Roe.* If Lee's proposal won the approval of the High Court, states or municipalities might regulate first-trimester abortions out of reach—as Powell, unappreciative of Lee's choice of language, later wrote in his opinion. Added to Lee's personal reluctance to tell the Court how to regard its own precedents, Reagan's advisors knew that *Roe* itself, whatever effect it had on access to abortions, had gained a symbolic meaning. It had become the measure of women's reproductive independence, connected to birth control, equal rights, and the end of sex discrimination. Reagan had opposed the ERA, but he signed bills that guaranteed to widows the same insurance benefits that widowers would get, and put teeth in alimony and child support payment orders.

But Blackmun's rough treatment of Lee and the six-man majority striking the Akron regulations did not stop the newest justice, Sandra Day O'Connor, from speaking on the issue in a dissent, joined by White and Rehnquist. O'Connor's nomination to the Court in 1981 had been opposed by anti–abortion rights forces. They knew that she had voted to repeal Arizona's harsh anti-abortion laws in 1970, when she was in the state senate, and had supported a family planning measure that would have paid for certain "surgical services" for minors without parental consent. She explained at her confirmation hearings that the state laws were unduly severe and she did not think that the family planning bill included abortion. But she was a Goldwater Republican, did not believe in big government or in courts usurping the role of legislatures, and would have allowed the Akron regulations to stand.

Lee's formula appealed to O'Connor, and she made it her own. In her draft opinion, she castigated the trimester formula in *Roe* as "an unprincipled and completely unworkable method of accommodating the conflicting personal rights and compelling state interests that are involved in the abortion context." In her published opinion, she took out the "unprincipled." Otherwise, she made few concessions to the majority. Its medical facts were out of date—cases of infant survival at twenty-two weeks had been recorded since 1973. The state's compelling interest, conceded in *Roe,* was moving back in time, toward conception. It was foolish to insist that an arbitrary division of pregnancy into trimesters should govern a constitutional right— either the mother's or the fetus's—or that the latter's interest only began at some fixed point midway in the pregnancy. The only answer was to dump the trimester formula and replace it with Lee's "unduly burdensome" terminology. After all, no one argued that privacy, on which abortion rested, was an absolute right. Using the new standard, lower courts could engage in factual inquiries to determine if a regulation was "unduly burdensome." As far as Justice O'Connor and the other dissenters were concerned, nothing that Akron did was unduly burdensome.

Akron should have closed the issue, but anti–abortion rights forces wanted the Court to overturn *Roe.* Pennsylvania was not the only state to use subterfuge to undermine *Roe,* but the politics of abortion in it are instructive and in many ways typical. Pennsylvania's two great urban centers, Philadelphia and Pittsburgh, both heavily Roman Catholic, did not develop reform parties during the 1960s, nor did reformers gain control of the major party organizations in the state. In the absence of organized abortion rights groups working with such political blocs, the Pennsylvania Catholic Conference (PCC) had little trouble going on the offensive against abortion rights before *Roe* and keeping the offensive after the decision came down.

Efforts to pass reform legislation on abortion in Pennsylvania were easily defeated before 1973, and restrictive legislation was easily approved after 1973. The Abortion Control Act of 1974, for example, denied state funding for "unneeded and unnecessary" abortions (including those sought in the first trimester), and required spousal and parental consent. On its face, the bill violated *Roe,* but it passed with large majorities in both houses. Governor Milton Shapp, openly in favor of choice, vetoed the bill. After a vigorous campaign over the summer recess by the PCC, the legislature reconvened and overrode his veto. The federal district court struck down the funding and consent provisions but allowed the state to regulate abortions as it would any other potentially dangerous medical procedure.

In 1982, when the political and judicial climate had warmed to anti–abortion rights initiatives, Pennsylvania anti–abortion rights forces again struck at *Roe.* The PCC was no longer in charge, however. A broad-spectrum right-to-life movement had emerged, and its leaders created the Pennsylvania Pro Life Federation. They helped elect two governors, Richard Thornburgh and Robert Casey, the former a Republican and the latter a Democrat, who shared one important stance: they were opposed to abortion rights. Thornburgh would not accept the 1981 bill—it would have effectively banned abortion—but he did sign the 1982 Abortion Control Act, which reintroduced the 1974 provisions, in addition to some new ones aimed at forcing women seeking abortions to undergo tests on the viability of the fetus.

Thus the Supreme Court faced a reprise of the issues raised and decided once in *Akron* in *Thornburgh v. American College of Obstetricians and Gynecologists* (1986). Even the players were back again, but the majority was clearly tiring. Burger had again switched sides, now to join Rehnquist, White, and O'Connor. Blackmun wrote for the majority, Powell, Stevens, Marshall, and Brennan. It was the last time that the trimester formula would survive a court test, and Blackmun may have realized that fact. The district court issued a preliminary injunction against the new provisions, and the Third Circuit Court of Appeals had struck down portions of the 1982 law that resembled in many ways the Akron municipal ordinance, including the requirement that a physician (and only a physician) recite the dangers of all abortions, rather than tailor the information to the patient's condition, and tell the patient about alternatives to abortion (including state laws on men's responsibilities to care for children they have fathered out of wedlock). To Blackmun, this was a patent attempt "to wedge the commonwealth's message discouraging abortion into the privacy of the informed-consent dialogue between the woman and her physician."

The state had added to the list of physicians' duties the determination of the viability of the fetus and a report (which could be "copied" but was not a public record) of personal information on the patient. A second physician was to be present, not to protect the health of the mother, but to take control of the "child" (the language in the statute, which the Court quoted), and to make every effort to save it if possible, in effect turning the abortion into a birthing. Violation of this last requirement was a felony—turning back the clock to before *Roe*. No doctor was to choose a method of abortion that might prevent a live birth, though the statute provided that a doctor's oath that he acted in good faith to save the mother or that the fetus could not be saved was a defense to the charge. But what doctor would want to be placed in the precarious position of losing a license or having to defend against a felony charge?

Justice Stevens joined Blackmun and wrote a separate concurrence reminding the court of the basic constitutional rights at stake—the right to be left alone, the right of individual autonomy in matters of reproduction. Against Justice White's dissent in the present case, Stevens cited White's views in *Griswold*. White's fears here "reveals that his opinion may be influenced as much by his own value preferences" as by any matter of law. Instead, "the responsibility for nurturing the soul of the newly born, as well as the unborn, rest with individual parents, not with the State."

Burger dissented, but he had trouble combining his support for *Roe* and his support for state regulations. He did not see how the state's requirement that doctors disseminate information—just information— that women needed violated the privacy of the doctor-patient relationship, even when the doctor was not free to depart from a script written by anti-abortion lawmakers and lobbyists, or why the state's requirement that parents consent to a minor having an abortion violated *Roe*. He had raised the same point ten years before, when Blackmun drafted his opinion. After all, "parents, not judges or social workers, have the inherent right and responsibility to advise their children in matters of this sensitivity and consequence." Burger's simple faith in the unity and common purpose of families and the love and affection that parents and children had for one another's best interests recalled the idealized worldview of the 1950s.

White too dissented: ordinarily he respected *stare decisis,* but here he could not. *Roe,* "on reconsideration, [is] found to be mistaken." But he was not mistaken—he had never subscribed to *Roe.* There was no basis in the Constitution for a woman's right to an abortion at any stage of the pregnancy. No word or phrase contained that right. If a right were "deeply rooted" in the life of the nation, like the right of married people to decide when and if to have children, then such a right must exist in the Constitution (as he had agreed in *Griswold*), but abortion rights were not deeply rooted. That proved the majority was wrong to strike down Pennsylvania's perfectly reasonable regulations.

Justice O'Connor dissented: the majority had worked "a major distortion" in constitutional jurisprudence. It had allowed the abortion question to divide the Court so deeply that no compromise was possible. Again it was the technical apparatus of *Roe* that was the culprit, denying the state's attorneys the chance to present factual evidence in the district court that Pennsylvania's rules did not unduly burden women seeking abortions. The appeals court had erred in going to the merits (the constitutionality) of the state's regulations when it should only have ruled on the legality of the preliminary injunction the lower court had issued. The Supreme Court's rush to defend the trimester formula was an error as well. But such errors were inevitable when the Court clung to its unworkable abortion jurisprudence.

In her dissent in *Akron*, Justice O'Connor had opined that the same kind of medical advances in ensuring the safety of later-term abortions the majority sought to protect were also making possible the survival of infants only twenty-two to twenty-four weeks old when taken from the womb. The trimester scheme "was clearly on a collision course with itself." The answer, she proposed, was the "unduly burdensome" test, which she applied again in *Thornburgh*. Although O'Connor thought that she was saving *Roe* from itself, in fact she was dividing it into two cases.

The first was a decision that stated women had a qualified right to control their own bodies through, among other things, the choice of an abortion. Out of doors, supporters and critics of women's abortion rights focusing on this symbolic *Roe* could only assume that the Court was seesawing between *Roe* and its disavowal. That was not quite true. After fifteen years of siege, the symbolic *Roe* was bloodied but unbowed. Only Rehnquist and White on the Court avowed their intention to reverse it, and they had opposed it from the start. The long train of litigation, the many restrictions imposed on it in the states, and even the Hyde amendment could not sway the other justices to call for the end of the symbolic *Roe*.

The other, formal decision in *Roe* revolved about the precise trimester system that Blackmun had crafted, and despite his increasingly doleful warnings, the Court had steadily chipped away at the language of the formal *Roe*. Because he had conceded the legitimate state interest in fetal life, he could not stop the momentum of the Court from sliding toward O'Connor's quite different schema. The state regulations that left the symbolic *Roe* in place had eroded the Court's guarantee that government could not deny to women the fundamental right to terminate a pregnancy in its early stages. And if the formal *Roe* died from its many wounds, could the symbolic *Roe* survive?

By the end of Reagan's second administration, the fate of both *Roe*s lay in the hands of a very different Court from the one that had decided it in 1973. In 1986, Burger had stepped down, and Reagan wanted

Rehnquist as chief justice. In his fourteen years on the Court, Rehnquist, often dissenting alone, had established himself as the conservative voice on a wide range of topics. He was a legal positivist with a vengeance, believing that the law was what the government said it was. He invariably favored the government in free speech cases, voting against challenges to government action. He opposed claims of racial and sexual discrimination and supported the death penalty whenever it was under legal attack. He opposed the ban on school prayer and supported government aid to parochial schools. He protected property rights strongly against environmental and affirmative action challenges. He preferred to let states have their way when state and federal governments clashed and the states wanted to deny benefits conferred by the federal government. He used whatever instrumental tools he had at his disposal, including somewhat imaginative reconstructions of fact situations, earlier rulings of the Court, and his own dissents in previous cases to seek the result he desired.

After a raucous hearing process, in which Rehnquist's ethics as well as his ideology survived criticism from liberal Democrats in the Senate, he was confirmed as chief justice. His place as associate justice was taken by Antonin Scalia, whose view of the world, the courts, and the Constitution was if anything more ideologically driven than Rehnquist's. Scalia was brilliant, acerbic, and ironic—treating those who disagreed with him on the Court with barely concealed scorn. The son of an immigrant intellectual, his education abroad and at Harvard Law School had honed a mind that preferred clear rules and direct statements of his opinion. He had practiced with a firm in Cleveland, taught at three of the country's most prestigious law schools (Virginia, Chicago, and Georgetown) and served in the Nixon and Ford administrations. In 1982, he joined the D.C. Circuit Court as one of Reagan's promised phalanx of anti–abortion rights federal judges.

His opposition to *Roe* was relentless, but not out of keeping with his view that the Court should establish clear rules rather than balance interests or promulgate subtle tests and standards. The content of such absolute rules for him would be stridently conservative, protecting private property against government takings, for example, and denying that abortion had any constitutional protection. Only in freedom of speech cases did he favor claims of individuals against government regulation;

in abortion rights cases, he abandoned that pose. Scalia's very strengths—his ability to argue with force and write with clarity, his unwillingness to compromise, and his brusque manner—undercut his ability to make allies on the Court. Over time, he would alienate some of the justices whose opinions might have helped him overturn *Roe*.

The most obvious of these potential allies turned aside was the last of the Reagan appointees to the Court, Anthony Kennedy. Kennedy replaced Powell. After he failed to put D.C. Circuit Court Judge Robert Bork on the Court, in large measure because Bork's anti–abortion rights views were so well known, and Judge Douglas Ginsburg decided not to remain a candidate for the job, Reagan turned to Kennedy. Like O'Connor, Kennedy had graduated with honors from Stanford, and like Blackmun and Brennan, he had attended Harvard Law School. A native Californian, he practiced for a decade in his home town of Sacramento. In 1975, President Ford appointed Kennedy to the Ninth Circuit Court of Appeals. Although the circuit was the nation's most liberal and Kennedy often found himself dissenting, he was a respected jurist on the bench, and a number of his opinions were adopted by the High Court.

On the Supreme Court, he seemed to fit nicely into the emerging conservative majority. For example, like Scalia a devout Catholic, Kennedy found that display of a crèche (the nativity scene) in front of a public building did not violate the Establishment Clause, nor did a school district that used public funds to pay a sign language teacher at a Roman Catholic high school. But would he join Scalia and Rehnquist in overturning the formal *Roe*'s trimester test? Would he also vote to end the symbolic *Roe*?

CHAPTER 6

The Two *Roes*, 1989–1992

Another cycle: the "new woman" of the late 1980s and 1990s valued her feminism in a way that confounded the stereotypes of earlier generations. She embraced "Victoria's Secret" catalogues of elegant lingerie but complained about "glass ceilings" in business and the professions that kept the best women from rising to the top of their firms. For these women, the sometimes aggressive posturing of the women's movement of the 1960s and 1970s seemed antique and out-of-place.

In the meantime, a backlash against women who achieved success drew together men who resented women's advancement and women who rejected their new freedoms. Using the same organizing skills that the leaders of the women's movement had pioneered, Happiness of Motherhood Eternal (HOME), Females Opposed to Equality (FOE), and Women Who Want to be Women (WWWW) lobbied for their objectives in local and statewide elections. But even as the backlash grew, polls showed that fewer and fewer women identified homemaking and childrearing as the "best part of being a woman."

As full of irony and contradiction as the newest version of the new woman was, women's status in the workplace and the home was protected by laws that the movement had won. Despite the failure of the ERA, the movement's successes in court and legislature had so leveled the playing field that the movement itself could take a seat on the sidelines. Suits brought by feminist legal scholars and litigators had made sexual harassment into a justiciable cause of civil action in the federal courts, preventing employers and fellow workers from turning the work place into a hostile environment for the working woman. Businesses and educational institutions adopted sexual harassment codes that helped men and women report, mediate, and reduce harassment on the job. The movement identified the abused spouse as a victim in a crime that was as hidden as abortion once was, and made the battered wife a widely recognized figure in the law. Suits for equal pay for equal work and for pension, medical leave, and other long-neglected inequities in law gained women a measure of financial equality. Women also gained jobs through affirmative action programs when the employer had a long history of discriminating against women.

But in the flagship issue for the movement—abortion law reform— the backlash seemed on the verge of triumph. Justice Sandra Day O'Connor's dissents in *Akron* and *Thornburgh* had borrowed a phrase from Rex Lee's brief in *Akron,* in turn derived from Justice Lewis Powell's opinions in *Beal* and *Maher:* abortion regulations must not be unduly burdensome. Powell did not intend his phrasing to nullify *Roe.* Instead, he was engaged in the arcane art of connecting real world situations to the rarefied and general language of the Due Process Clause. Because the state had a legitimate interest in the health of the mother and the potential life of a fetus, it could regulate abortions. It could prefer birth to termination of pregnancy, but it could not impose insuperable obstacles in the path of a woman's choice.

But Powell could not dictate what others would do with his language—even when he sat on the Court—and the obverse of unduly burdensome was due burdens. The courts would have to decide what was, in the words of Justice Scalia, "due" or undue, assuming that they retained *Roe* at all. The door was open, should O'Connor find herself voting with the majority, to make undue burden, rather than Blackmun's trimester formula, the test of permissible state action. By allowing states and municipalities to deny funding and ordain extensive consent and notification procedures and one-day waiting periods for women seeking abortions before the end of the second trimester, the Court had left Blackmun's formula in tatters. O'Connor was only speaking plain facts when she said that *Roe* could survive only if the trimester scheme was dumped.

What would pro-choice advocates lose with the imposition of the new standard? Neither her nor Blackmun's test for the constitutionality of regulations rested on women's rights to control what happened to their bodies. The trimester scheme relied on the doctor-patient relationship and the expertise of doctors; the undue burden test was left to the Court to decide from above the fray, not women sitting in an abortion clinic waiting room. Thus the two prongs of the new paradigm of women in the law introduced in the 1960s—the paramountcy of choice and the legal empowerment of ordinary women's voices—had already receded from the Court's deliberations.

The real danger to women's rights promoters in the shift of the Court's reasoning was that, framed in the language of undue burden, choice was no longer a "fundamental right" of privacy as enunciated in *Griswold* and extended in *Roe*. The trimester formula protected choice in the first weeks, but Chief Justice Rehnquist had long found no evidence of a fundamental right to an abortion anywhere in the Constitution, and now the Supreme Court was his Court. What was more, his allies in what Court observers called the "move to the right" were a majority on the bench. It should have been easy to return control of abortion to the state legislatures and Congress and take it off the table in the justices' conference room.

Roe owed its survival in part to the doctrine of *stare decisis,* but Justices White and Scalia agreed that the Court had decided *Roe* wrongly. White had great respect for the idea of precedent, but a case wrongly decided initially should not owe its continuing influence to the fact that the Court had decided it incorrectly. Scalia, by contrast, had no commitment to *stare decisis* and said so pointedly. But if *Roe* went down, its constitutional underpinnings could be exposed to attack. The fundamental right of privacy that *Roe* extended to abortion might also be rolled back, endangering *Griswold*. This was not acceptable to Justice Kennedy. In his statement to the Senate Judiciary Committee during hearings on his appointment, he made clear that "the concept of liberty in the Due Process Clause is quite expansive, quite sufficient, to protect the values of privacy that Americans legitimately think are part of their constitutional heritage." He even referred approvingly to the "substantive component" of the Fourteenth Amendment.

When Kennedy offered his support to *Griswold*, he based his views in part on the idea that Americans had come to see privacy as a fundamental right. He thus hinted that there might be another kind of precedential value that a signal case like *Griswold* and *Roe* possessed, a social *stare decisis,* on which Americans relied. Contraception was part of the social landscape, affecting the everyday sexual decisions of millions of women.

Were abortion rights part of this landscape as well? Counselor Frank Susman told the Court in 1989, "[T]he fact is that abortion, through its nationwide legalization sixteen years ago, has become so assimilated into the fabric of society as to become 'deeply rooted.'" He had the facts at hand: since 1973, twenty million women had "exercised this right." One-third of all pregnancies in America ended in abortions, and abortion was the most common elective surgery in the country. Women had come of age and "literally lived their entire childbearing years with the option of safe, legal abortion in the event of an unwanted pregnancy." The regulations of states and municipalities had a chilling effect on doctors and a deterrent effect on women (as the rules were intended to have), but women traveled across state lines and with the aid of abortion counselors and clinics found a way to terminate their pregnancies. Yet was this the same line of argument, based on long-established and legally sanctioned social usages, that had been used by southern defenders of segregation when they objected to *Brown v. Board of Education*? So Justice Scalia warned on more than one occasion.

As Justice Blackmun related to an audience at the University of Arkansas in September 1988, he "could count the votes," and he feared that *Roe* was doomed. Lower federal courts in Massachusetts, Kentucky, Colorado, and Missouri had protected *Roe* by knocking down overly restrictive state regulations, but other federal courts, in Louisiana, Illinois, and New York, had upheld variations of these same regulations. The diversity in the states' rules, the disparities in the courts' reading of the states' rules, and the inability (or unwillingness) of state and federal courts to apply Supreme Court holdings bewildered both supporters and opponents of abortion rights. Both sides were yearning for a knockout blow in the Congress or the courts, but privately funded abortion clinics had outflanked the Hyde amendment, and the High Court, thus far, had forbidden states to legislate abortion out of existence.

Webster v. Reproductive Health Services (1989)

In 1986, Missouri enacted the third generation of its anti-abortion laws. The new statute included twenty provisions, seven of which, based upon right-to-life lobbyists' models that had been adopted in the city of Akron and struck down by the Court in 1983 in *Planned Parenthood v. Ashcroft*, were openly designed to discourage abortion. There was a preamble to the act, labeled a "finding" by the legislature, that the "life of each human being begins at conception" and "unborn children have protectable interests in life, health, and well-being." In itself, this was unobjectionable, but applied to abortions, it had unpredictable consequences. Was it meant as a mere expression of pro-life sentiment? The state would later argue that the preamble did not violate *Roe*, for "these findings . . . do not serve as any substantive right. They impose no substantive responsibility." If so, then what purpose did they serve? They were clearly admonitory and hortatory—expressing a sense of shared moral repugnance to expansive abortion rights—reminiscent of the first state laws on abortion.

Was that expression a religious one—and if so, did it violate the First and Fourteenth Amendments? Did it also fly in the face of *Roe's* admonition to Texas not to put a religious concept of "life" into a secular law? But did it not also have a secular purpose (one to which *Roe* had assented) of recounting the state's legitimate interest in the life of the fetus that would make the preamble, under the *Harris* doctrine, constitutionally permissible?

The next provision of the Missouri Law required that all abortions after the sixteenth week be performed in hospitals. This created a problem for both doctors and their patients, given a third provision that no public hospital or public hospital worker was to take part in an abortion nor were public hospitals to expend funds on abortions. The former had already been struck down in *Ashcroft*. State legislatures are subject to the rulings of the Supreme Court, and the Missouri legislature knew about the latter case for three years before it passed its revised abortion law. It was a certainty that the federal district court would strike down the sixteen-week/hospital section of the law.

Why then did the state include the sixteenth-week requirements? After the Supreme Court decisions in the school desegregation cases barring state-ordered separation of students by race, southern state legislatures stonewalled the High Court. This flagrant defiance of the law of the land was part of a strategy of "massive resistance" that included the open use of violence to discourage young black boys and girls and their parents from crossing over "the color line." Was Missouri engaging in a legislative "massive resistance" against *Roe*?

Missouri's provisions against public funding of abortions had been approved by the Supreme Court in *Beal* and its companion cases, but the ban on anyone using the public facilities for abortions was new. It meant that public hospitals and doctors on public pay could not aid in abortions, even when the patient could pay for them. In effect, it left private clinics as the only second-trimester abortion providers. In his testimony before the Court, the attorney general of Missouri, William Webster, would argue that the ten private abortion clinics in his state would take up the slack and were already doing a land-office business.

The next set of provisions applied to all abortion clinics as well as public facilities—a series of rules forbidding doctors from advising anyone to have an abortion or telling them that an abortion was available or that one might be advisable, even if the pregnancy was in trouble. This was part of the legislatively scripted "informed consent" that the doctor was required to read to the patient and the patient sign, although again such scripts had been rejected by the Court in *Akron* and *Thornburgh*.

A final provision required doctors to ascertain, through a series of tests, whether a fetus was viable. This was unobjectionable, but the means were not. The High Court had already ruled that the state could not dictate which tests were to be used to determine fetal age, but Missouri required its physicians to determine lung size, and the only sure test for lung size, amniocentesis, was both expensive and dangerous to the mother and the fetus. In effect, the state was telling doctors that it was more important to the state to determine the viability of the fetus than to ensure the health of the woman patient, or rather, that the potentially viable fetus was the doctor's primary patient until proven otherwise.

Plaintiffs challenging the act were three doctors and two nurses who worked in a public facility (the Truman Memorial Hospital) and two clinic providers of abortions. None of these individuals or institutions had yet felt the weight of the act. They sought declaratory and injunctive relief to prevent the act from going into effect, for once *Roe* was in place, pro-choice forces could file proactively. The Court in *Roe* refused the injunction appellants sought because Dr. Hallford was already under indictment, and federal courts hesitated to intrude into ongoing state criminal proceedings. But in cases like *Webster,* the penalties for violating the state law were not criminal fines or imprisonment, and no indictments had been issued.

After a hearing, the federal district court issued a temporary injunction barring enforcement of seven provisions of the act. The purpose of the injunction was to prevent irreparable harm to the plaintiffs and their patients during the rest of the litigation. The district court had reasoned that because the state's new rules might have prevented women from gaining abortions to which they were constitutionally entitled, such an injunction was warranted. The district court then held a trial. It found that the seven provisions were unconstitutional on their face. That meant that under no construction—no interpretation by the state of its own act—could the provisions be constitutional. The lower court also refused to sever the unconstitutional portions of a provision from the language nearby—that is, if a provision was in any way unconstitutional, the entire provision failed. The Eighth Circuit Court of Appeals affirmed the district court's ruling and made the injunction permanent. The state appealed the lower courts' findings on the preamble, the twentieth-week testing, and use of public personnel, but did not contest the loss of the scripted informed consent or the ban on the use of hospitals after the sixteenth week of pregnancy.

The case should have been easy—either the provisions would be reinstated (a reversal of the lower courts) or were gone (affirming the lower courts)—but for one part of the state's brief. Webster argued that the state's provisions did not unduly burden the rights of women under *Roe,* but if the High Court found that the state's provisions conflicted with *Roe* as a matter of law, then the Court should reverse *Roe.* The state was asking the Court to allow the state's rules under *Roe* or to throw out *Roe.*

Missouri's tactic raised the stakes of winning and losing for everyone except the state. For anti–abortion rights forces outside of Missouri, the end of *Roe* would mean a victory without a venture; every state in which anti–abortion rights coalitions controlled the legislature would immediately begin restricting if not banning abortion. For pro-choice forces, the stakes were even higher. A loss would mean a protracted battle in every state legislature to protect rights that had been assured by *Roe*. The justices too saw that a direct challenge to *Roe* was a challenge to the Court to find a consensus or fragment into sharp-edged pieces, for debate within the Court over abortion was jagged and harsh.

Only the state stood neither to gain nor to lose by forcing the Court to review *Roe*. In other words, it was unnecessary for the Court to go back to *Roe* in order to settle the issues that *Webster* raised. If the majority of the Court was willing to reverse *Roe*, the same majority surely would have been willing to allow Missouri its limitations on abortion. If a majority agreed to save *Roe*, they still might have ruled for the state. Missouri neither lost nor gained by asking the Court to revisit *Roe*— unless of course the brief, like the newly imposed regulations themselves, had the core purpose of overturning *Roe*. Then, and only then, the attorney general's proposal to revisit *Roe* would not have been a superfluous gesture or a gratuitous aside, but a major purpose of the appeal.

Both sides recognized the importance of the case. Operation Rescue staged demonstrations in the District of Columbia, and the National Right to Life Committee joined in the publicity campaign. In January 1989, 65,000 pro-life marchers filled the streets of the District. Three months later, NOW and NARAL staged their own march, attracting half a million pro-choice supporters to the Capitol steps and the Mall. Seventy-eight amici submitted briefs, twenty more than any previous case. One of the briefs in favor of upholding the circuit court rested heavily on the work of historian James Mohr, and it had gained support from 286 other historians. The majority of the amici, however, called for reversal of the lower courts' decisions, and public support for the right to an abortion had slipped from over 70 percent to 60 percent (though the same polls showed that only 9 percent of the respondents thought that abortion should always be illegal.)

Attorney General Webster appeared in person to argue Missouri's case. Webster's oral presentation on the morning of April 26, 1989, began in a polished and assured tone. He ably connected the ban on public health officials aiding abortions with the ban on public funding already approved by the High Court. The state was not obligated to become an advocate for abortion, and that applied to all state-funded employees, whether they be doctors or not. By recasting doctors as public employees, Webster countered the doctor-patient privilege argument of the pro-choice advocates that went back to *Roe*.

To Justice Stevens's query about penalties in the statute for violating the aiding or performing provisions, Webster said there was no criminal sanction against doctors who violated the law. The penalty was denial of funding. Pressed by Stevens (because the language of the statute seemed to make the doctor's misconduct a misdemeanor), Webster conceded that "arguably" it was a misdemeanor, but he hastened to add, "We wouldn't view that violation as a misdemeanor." Surely the lawmakers would have, however—a point that Stevens, like a bulldog with a bone, would not surrender: "[S]o it would be a misdemeanor?" Justice Kennedy did not like Webster's waffling, and jumped in. "[T]he statute says it shall be unlawful." Justice Scalia, seeking to repair the growing damage of Webster's ragged explanation of punishment, offered a helpful hint on the question of penalties: "It might also be that the official who expends the funds, knowing they are going to be used in violation of the statute, is liable for the funds." Webster welcomed the friendly suggestion: "[T]hat certainly would be one of the appropriate remedies."

Webster defended the preamble by admitting that it was an "abstract, philosophical statement that . . . doesn't affect anyone." None of the justices—not even the supportive Scalia—touched that one. Webster continued that legislatures prefaced all sorts of bills with preambles "in the non-abortion area," whatever that might be. But the lack of response from the bench meant that Webster had probably won his way on this point, and it was a critical blow to the pro-choice faction.

He had harder work justifying the tests for age, weight, and lung capacity. Even Scalia pressed him on whether that information—required when the fetus was twenty weeks old—was of any use, since the tests at that age were generally inconclusive and one of them, amniocentesis, posed risks to the pregnant woman. Webster replied that doctors were not to depart from the professional standards of care in deciding if the tests were required as well as in their performance of the tests. He conceded that, at twenty weeks, amniocentesis would "show nothing," and thus would not be required. Stevens was first off the mark: "You are saying that the doctor, if he thinks it unnecessary, doesn't have to perform the lung test?" Webster seemed to agree. Stevens persisted: what if the doctor determined, after the first test (an ultrasound test to determine approximate age of the fetus) that the other two tests were unnecessary? Could he skip them? Webster reversed himself: the statute required "findings" by the doctor, and findings included lung capacity. Did that mean amniocentesis, Stevens demanded. No, Webster flipped back. But did the statute still require a finding on lung capacity? Well yes, Webster flopped again: even if the doctor found that the fetus was not viable, he had to go forward with all three tests, "if the first two tests don't indicate viability, they would need to" perform the third. In effect, the doctor could stop testing if he or she found the fetus viable but had to persevere with all three tests to prove the fetus had not quickened. And if the doctor thought it unnecessary to perform the third test? Stevens still wanted to know. Webster changed his line for the last time: "I don't believe the statute requires the physician to perform any tests that are unnecessary." Stevens could not have been satisfied, for there was no way to know from Webster's confused presentation what the statute required.

Webster was followed by Fried, the departing solicitor general. He no longer held a position in the government but appeared by special permission since he had prepared the government's brief supporting Missouri. Where Webster had tiptoed, Fried stomped: he asked the Court to overturn *Roe*. He did not want the Court to roll back all the privacy rights—he did not challenge *Griswold*—but rather "to pull this one thread." Kennedy wanted to know why privacy should be upheld, for surely *Griswold* had no more justification in the exact language of the Constitution than did *Roe*. Fried had an answer, and it was a powerful one: because *Griswold* rested on "a whole fabric [the textile metaphor again, but here mixed] of concrete matters." It was not an abstraction like "the right to control one's body." Why control of one's body was an abstraction seemed to puzzle Kennedy. He asked again, was not *Griswold* about the fundamental right to choose whether or not to procreate? No, retorted Fried, *Griswold* was about the intimacy of marriage.

No one at the time cited *Baird v. Eisenstadt*, in which the Court extended the right to practice contraception to unmarried people (which would have undercut Fried's argument), but Justice O'Connor asked, "[D]o you say there is no fundamental right to decide whether to have a child or not? . . . [D]o you deny the Constitution protects that right?" Fried shot back, "I would hesitate to formulate the right in such abstract terms," just as the Court had hesitated to do so in *Griswold*.

O'Connor tried a hypothetical on Fried. Hypotheticals are contrary-to-fact suppositions commonly used in law school teaching to force students to think about the consequences and limitations of their comments. For O'Connor to try out a hypothetical on Fried (on leave from his duties as a professor of law at Harvard Law School) was something of a turnabout. She began, if there was no fundamental right to decide whether to procreate, could a state, in the future, order people not to have children? (China, for example, long had enforced a one-child policy on families.) Could the state in furtherance of the legitimate goal of limiting population require abortions? What would stop the state? Fried opined that the Due Process Clause of the Fourteenth Amendment would serve. O'Connor then continued, and would the Due Process Clause apply because women had a liberty interest to their own bodies? And wasn't this the same reasoning that *Roe* used to protect abortion? With the trap sprung on Fried, he could only repeat, "Now if the Court does not in this case in its prudence decide to reconsider *Roe,* I would ask at least that it say nothing here that would further entrench this decision."

Frank Susman next rose for the plaintiff appellees. The tall, thin, former army drill sergeant was carrying on a family tradition in representing local clients. His acquaintance with abortion rights cases went back to 1971, when he and cocounsel Charlotte Thayer represented Samuel Rodgers, an African-American obstetrician and medical school professor, along with nine other clients seeking a declaratory judgment against Missouri's highly restrictive abortion law. Before a Missouri circuit court judge, Susman and Thayer won their case: the Missouri law was deemed unconstitutionally vague. The state had no compelling interests to protect, none that warranted denying pregnant women and doctors their constitutional rights. He had argued *Ashcroft* before the U.S. Supreme Court and won, argued *Poelker* and lost. Now he represented St. Louis's oldest abortion clinic, Reproductive Health Services, in its battle against Missouri's latest round of restrictions on abortion. Judy Widdicombe had tired of the abortion wars, but Susman convinced her that this fight had to be won. As was true in the prior cases, he had carried the day in the lower courts—but knew that the composition of the Supreme Court made victory this time more difficult.

He began with an ad lib reposte to Fried's metaphorical "single thread." Susman's experience was that when he pulled a thread the whole sleeve unraveled. That is what would happen to privacy rights if *Roe* were reversed. But Justice Scalia wanted to know how Susman could find no distinction between *Griswold* and *Roe,* and Susman offered that many of the most common methods of contraception, including intrauterine devices and birth control pills, were actually abortifacients and were labeled as such by the Food and Drug Administration. Science had obliterated the "bright line" distinction between contraception and abortion. Constitutional scholars hanker after bright line distinctions, and Justice Scalia was particularly fond of them. There was no doubt that Susman intended his comments to strike at Scalia's own jurisprudence. This was a dangerous tactic with such an able adversary, however, and Scalia would return to the fray with a vengeance in a few moments.

In the meantime, Justice Kennedy wanted to know how far Susman's analogy between contraception and abortion would stretch. Did the state have a right to forbid abortions (except to save the life of the mother) when the pregnancy was eight months along? Susman replied that the health of the mother was always paramount. But if the health of the mother was not in jeopardy? Then yes, *Roe* granted states that right. Wasn't that a bright line, Kennedy persisted. Susman surrendered: it was, but it was just the line drawn at quickening in the nineteenth-century statutes, and not the same as the state's preamble, which placed the beginning of fetal life at conception.

O'Connor joined in the colloquy. Some observers of the Court have argued that the visibly renewed commitment of the women's movement to *Roe* as *Webster* neared its day in court put pressure on Justice O'Connor. In cases involving discrimination on the basis of sex, she had already shown more liberal leanings than in other matters. She was, in addition, well aware that she was the only woman on the Court. Perhaps more important, she wanted to find a way to accommodate the increasingly strident differences of opinion on abortion. Her formative experiences and great success as a state legislator had taught her how important consensus was for the functioning of any institution.

She sought a middle position in the battle over *Webster* when she asked Susman if there was a difference between quickening and viability. Not much, he thought, for one cannot pinpoint viability with much more precision than a woman could feel the independent motion of the fetus. But the question gave Susman the chance to fall back on the authority of the American College of Obstetricians and Gynecologists, which had for nearly twenty years written amicus briefs in support of doctors performing abortions. What was more, Susman could turn to the historians' brief Sylvia Law and Clyde Spillenger submitted based on Mohr's 1979 book on the history of abortion in America. Mohr sought to prove that the first anti-abortion laws were not intended to protect fetal life, but the health of mothers. In these laws, all of the states accepted the fact that fetal life began after quickening.

The chief justice doubted that abortion could claim the same historical privileges—"deeply rooted traditions"—as the doctor-patient relationship and the marital relationship. Wasn't abortion a crime in the nineteenth century? Susman did not have the time (his thirty minutes was nearly up) nor did the Court have the inclination to listen to a nuanced scholarly argument. He could only ask the Court to go back and examine the reasons for the first statutes. Rehnquist brushed past that homework assignment to aver that if the state intervened, there could not be a "deeply rooted tradition of freedom." Susman had a reply ready, but it too, given the shortness of time available, sounded almost like a hypothetical. Was there not a deeply rooted tradition of free labor in the first half of the nineteenth century at the same time as the slave states vigorously policed the "peculiar institution" with laws? Was there not state legislation reinforcing Jim Crow (segregation) even after *Brown v. Board of Education?*

Justice Scalia returned to the oral argument here to remind Susman that pro-life amici had written their own historical briefs contradicting Mohr's views. Susman conceded that "there are briefs on both sides" and tried to rebuild his case by suggesting that the historians who signed Mohr's brief were more reputable than those in the pro-life briefs, in the same way that the American College of Obstetricians and Gynecologists' opinion deserved more weight than pro-life amici like the Wyoming Nurses for Life.

But if history was no guide, what was? Where did one get fundamental rights? Scalia supposed that one could find them in the text of the Constitution, but nothing in the text told men of good will when life began. Susman agreed, "I think that is the basic question." Both sides could agree on the "physiological facts": when brain waves could be detected; when heartbeats were loud enough to be heard. "But when you come to try to place emotional labels on what you call that collection of physiological facts," Susman worried, "that is where people part company. . . . It is a question verifiable only by reliance upon faith." Scalia was listening: "I agree with you entirely, but what conclusion does that lead you to?" Did it lead to a fundamental right to destroy "this thing," the fetus? "People have to make up their minds the best they can."

Susman replied simply, "When you have an issue that is so divisive and so emotional and so personal, and so intimate, it must be left as a fundamental right to the individual to make that choice." Speaking now not as a skilled advocate for one side but as a longtime observer of the abortion rights wars, Susman continued, "The very debate that went on outside this morning, outside this building, and has gone on in various towns and communities across our nation is the same debate that every woman who becomes pregnant and doesn't wish to be pregnant has with herself."

There are moments when counsel and justices seem to put aside the game of question and answer and grope toward some deeper understanding of the human condition. No one listening to the exchange between Scalia and Susman could have missed where they stood, but for a few minutes two very bright lawyers who were tired of going through case after case explained themselves to one another. It was a rare moment in part because both men dropped what Judge John T. Noonan has called the "masks of the law" and spoke in plain language. But the moment passed, and the oral argument ended.

Chief Justice Rehnquist had waited seventeen years for this case, since he had dissented in *Roe*. For seventeen years he had endured in silence the obloquy of liberal jurisprudents who swirled over his opinions like hawks seeking prey. For many of those years, he had dissented alone, or joined Justice White. More recently, he had secured a majority to limit *Roe* or to question its trimester formula. But never, not until *Webster,* had a state attorney general and a former U.S. solicitor general stood before the bench and asked that *Roe* be overturned.

At the conference on April 28, he spoke first and announced that he "disagreed with *Roe.*" Also, the lower courts' rulings on *Webster* should be reversed. White agreed, but O'Connor was hesitant. She would stand by her earlier views. *Roe* should not be overturned. Scalia joined Rehnquist and White. Kennedy thought that the Missouri rules passed muster, but he had qualms about saying more, for *Roe* was a long-settled precedent, and he believed in *stare decisis.* Stevens seemed to waver— perhaps Missouri had not gone too far. Only Blackmun, Brennan, and Marshall would have upheld the lower courts' injunctions.

But Rehnquist, for all his geniality in chambers and easygoing ways, was not the court politician that his old adversary, Brennan, was. He happily assigned himself the opinion but could only muster White and Kennedy to uphold all of the provisions that the state wanted to retain. Worse, he could not get a majority to topple *Roe.* Only Scalia was willing to join White and the chief in that position. In response to Rehnquist's first draft, Stevens was upset. He sent a memo charging Rehnquist with trying to gut *Roe* by leaving out any mention of women's fundamental right to an abortion. In the end, Stevens would vote to allow the ban on public funding, but affirm the circuit court on the rest of its holding.

Rehnquist had a five-justice majority to retain the preamble to the Missouri law, but he conceded, as had the state in oral argument, that the preamble had no operative weight. Likewise, he had a majority of the Court for the ban on use of public facilities, which extended slightly what the Court had already conceded in *Beal* and *Maher,* and for the three tests for viability. But he could not get O'Connor and Scalia to agree with his reasoning. He offered that the requirement of testing did not force doctors to impose tests they thought were unnecessary, a view that endorsed the very last of Webster's pronouncements on the issue and satisfied O'Connor only.

Near the end of his opinion, in the middle of his discussion of the three tests doctors were to perform, Rehnquist added dictum that the "rigid" trimester formula of *Roe* made it impossible for the Court to escape endless and fruitless discussion of concepts that had no basis in the Constitution. Nor did he see why, in spite of *Roe,* the state's interest in fetal life should not commence with conception. But he did not carry the logic of the dictum to its natural end. Instead of writing that the Court must overrule *Roe,* he backpedaled: the "facts of the present case, however, differ from those at issue in *Roe.* Then the state had made all abortions a crime. Here the state had merely regulated abortion." He and his fellow justices "would narrow and limit *Roe,*" but not overturn it.

O'Connor's refusal to join any opinion overturning *Roe* had reduced Rehnquist's core following from five to four members of the Court. Her concurring opinion agreed that the tests were permissible, but she did not read them to narrow *Roe* at all. The lower courts had misunderstood the language of the statute: the tests only made sense if the doctor thought they would be necessary. There was no compulsion involved; a doctor could skip one or more of the tests if he did not need them. And if done properly, they did not impose an undue burden on a woman's choice. The preamble would have no effect on women's rights. The rest of Rehnquist's opinion, she believed, derived from a long chain of earlier Court rulings. She approvingly noted his reference to her "undue burden" test and reiterated that it did not conflict with *Roe.*

Scalia was furious, not so much at O'Connor's defection from the majority as at what he perceived to be the illogic of her reasoning. Like a law professor correcting a sub-par student performance, he aimed his entire opinion at her. He agreed with Stevens's memo and Blackmun's draft dissent that the effect of the chief justice's opinion was to disembowel *Roe,* but Scalia wanted that evisceration performed with a broadsword rather than a scalpel. He rejected the "judicial statesmanship" of the chief justice, for it "needlessly prolonged" the Court's entrapment in a field "where it has little proper business." The abortion question was to Scalia a political one, not a legal one, and best left to the legislatures. This posture would allow Missouri to pass any law on abortion, including a permanent and total ban. O'Connor's praise of judicial restraint (whether her own or Rehnquist's) in refusing to overrule *Roe* "cannot be taken seriously." He then cited a series of O'Connor opinions overruling earlier Court holdings.

As painful as it might have been for the remaining justices to write another dissent, in one way each was easier than its predecessors, for all the justices had to do was quote their own earlier words. But by now, their misgivings and admonitions had a repetitive dullness, and their prose was brittle and worn. Even their capacity for indignation seemed muted. They had all but conceded that *Roe* was dead, one way or another. It might yet be overturned by the Court, a new majority admitting the error of the Court in 1973. If that were to occur, *Roe* would join a handful of cases in a gallery of infamy. These included *Dred Scott v. Sanford* (1857), holding that neither congressional laws nor the courts of the free states could emancipate a slave once he had returned to a slave state, and no African American could ever be a citizen; *Plessy v. Ferguson* (1896), holding that so long as states provided "separate but equal" public facilities for African Americans, states might segregate such facilities; and *Korematsu v. United States* (1944), holding that a federal plan to sweep up the Japanese and intern them in concentration camps was a lawful wartime measure. Or the Court might simply limit the reach of *Roe* to its own fact pattern: striking down only those state laws that viewed all abortions as a crime, save those to save the mother's life.

The writings of justices live beyond their tenure on the Court, because in a system of common-law precedent the words in a High Court opinion are the singing reason of the law, detached from the time and place and the person who wrote them. They can be summoned up and used decades later in cases entirely different from those the words decided. Yet as the abortion cases had proved, the words of the justices were very much a part of their time and place—and the justices' politics. The language of the *Roe* majority, each year more dimly echoed in the pleas of the dissenters in *Maher, Harris,* and now *Webster,* seemed destined to die with their authors' departure from the bench. Blackmun, Brennan, and Marshall, all in their eighties, remained, but as Brennan quipped, the three of them were just "old men."

Understandably, then, Blackmun's dissent had a vexatious, quarrelsome tone, conveying his sense that the foremost achievement of his career on the bench would soon be trashed. "Never in my memory has a plurality announced a judgment of this Court that so foments disregard for the law and for our standing decisions." The plurality had acted in a deceptive fashion, denying to reveal its obvious purpose. But Blackmun was not above some politicking of his own. He and O'Connor had talked, and he made a concession to her when he wrote that "the viability testing provision imposes a burden on second-trimester abortions" that was unacceptable. Only a "wooden reading" (a comeback to Rehnquist's characterization of the trimester formula as "rigid") of *Roe* would fail to see how the trimester formula relates to the Missouri rules. And if *Roe* had to bow because the Constitution did not mention abortion or privacy, then most of the Court's jurisprudence would have to be discarded, for little of it appeared in the language of the Constitution. When he continued that the plurality virtually "was inviting" state legislatures to pass more and more restrictive laws, Blackmun knew that certain of these were already on their way to the High Court, and any one of them might lead to the death of *Roe*.

From *Webster* to *Planned Parenthood of Eastern Pennsylvania v. Casey* (1992)

Nineteen hundred and ninety marked the beginning of the high tide of anti-abortion in the High Court. In the next two years, President Bush, an avowed opponent of *Roe,* would name two new justices to replace Brennan and Marshall, both *Roe* supporters. In 1971, during his tenure as a congressman from Texas, Bush had introduced the bill that made contraception legal in Washington, D.C., and he then spoke in favor of women's right to an abortion. But in his 1988 campaign run against Democratic Massachusetts governor Michael Dukakis, Bush changed his views. Dukakis's support for *Roe* was strong, and Massachusetts, despite the unswerving opposition of the Roman Catholic church, had passed legislation guaranteeing access to abortion clinics. In the 1980s the Massachusetts Supreme Judicial Court had ruled that the state's constitution provided ample room to accommodate abortion—indeed, a more expansive abortion right than women had under *Roe*. Bush's advisors sensed that Dukakis might be vulnerable on this issue and that Bush could gain support from Christian Right leaders like Falwell if Bush changed his views and announced his opposition to abortion. He did, and he won. As president, Bush pushed for denial of funding for abortions and stronger notice and consent provisions.

Three days after Justice Brennan announced his retirement from the Court, in July 1990, Bush named his replacement: former New Hampshire Supreme Court Justice David Souter. Surprised, Marshall asked who Souter was—he had never heard the name. In fact, Souter had just been appointed to the First Circuit Court of Appeals sitting in Boston when he was summoned to D.C. to meet with Bush.

Souter was reared in a Boston suburb but spent his teenage years in the New Hampshire town of Weare. Just as O'Connor grew up on a prosperous ranch in Arizona, and imbibed there many of her notions of individualism, Souter loved the lifestyle of small-town New England. Everyone knew everyone's business, but no one intruded in it. As photojournalist David Plowden wrote in *Small Town America* about his own home in Putney, Vermont: "In small towns, every person had a place, no matter how insignificant. People knew each other by their first names, not by their telephone numbers or fax numbers. They knew where each other lived, and who their fathers and mothers were." Souter was a scholastic star in high school, at Harvard College, and at Harvard Law School, a voracious reader of history and law before he became a lawyer, and a meticulous legal craftsman on the bench. His long and loyal friendship with New Hampshire Attorney General, later Republican Senator, Warren Rudman led Bush's chief advisor John Sununu, a former Republican governor of New Hampshire, to urge Bush to name Souter to the High Court.

Souter later revealed that when asked about abortion by the president's representatives, he replied that he had nothing to say about issues on which he might have to rule, and if they persisted in wanting an answer, they could count him out of the running. All during his interview with the president's aides and with Bush himself, the subject never came up. Bush later remarked, "You might just think that the whole nomination had something to do with abortion . . . it's something much broader than that. I have too much respect for the Supreme Court for that."

But five minutes into his Senate confirmation hearing, Souter faced the abortion question. Senator Joseph Biden of Delaware wanted to know where Souter stood. For the rest of his testimony he repeatedly told the Senate Judiciary Committee what he had told the president. He would wait for the cases to come and then make up his mind on the merits. But he believed that the Fourteenth Amendment "does recognize and protect an unenumerated [that is, unstated] right of privacy." He would not, thus, touch *Griswold* and did not subscribe to the notion that the Bill of Rights and the Fourteenth Amendment must be read literally. Faye Wattleton, president of the PPFA, was not re-assured by Souter's "days of evasive answers and filibusters," but anti–abortion rights leaders were also unsure of Souter's stance: "You bring guys like this on the Court," one reportedly said, "and they have a tendency to pull a Harry Blackmun on you."

Souter voted with the chief justice, Scalia, White, and Kennedy in the first abortion case the Court heard after Souter's elevation to the bench. In 1970, the federal government had established a program for family planning under Title X of the Public Health Services Act. It was intended as an alternative to abortion counseling, and one of its provisions required that no funds could go to abortion clinics. In 1988, the last year of Reagan's administration, personnel, including doctors, at clinics receiving federal money were told that they were not to mention abortion. If asked about it by a client, the health care or so-cial work professional had to say that the clinic did not consider abor-tion an "appropriate method" of birth control.

Doctor Irving Rust, a New York City practitioner and a recipient of Title X funds, sued Secretary of Health and Human Services Louis Sullivan, alleging that the regulations the secretary promulgated under authority of the act violated the terms of the act itself as well as Dr. Rust's and his patients' free speech and due process rights under the Constitution. The suit was a class action. The question before the courts was twofold: did the secretary exceed his discretion under the act, and did he violate the rights of the Title X funding recipients?

The Second Circuit Court of Appeals, sitting in New York City, upheld the restrictions on abortion speech (called a "gag rule" by their opponents) after the First and Third Circuit Courts of Appeals had struck down the same regulations for violating the constitutional rights of the doctors and their patients. When the case came to the High Court, the Commonwealth of Massachusetts filed as a friend of the court in support of the plaintiff, as did fifty-five other organizations, including a number of women's groups concerned about the restriction of free speech and the baneful effects of the regulations on the doctor-patient relationship. Professor Lawrence Tribe of Harvard Law School argued for Rust, joined by Janet Benshoof and Kathryn Kolbert, among others.

Solicitor General Kenneth Starr, who some years later would earn far more fame as a special counsel in a series of matters involving President Bill Clinton, argued for the federal government, supported by amici from a variety of religious faiths, including the Catholics United for Life, the National Organization of Episcopalians for Life, Presbyterians Pro-Life, and Southern Baptists for Life. The amici, like the counsel of record, talked past one another, the pro-choice briefs stressing the dangers of government-imposed censorship of free speech, the pro-life briefs countering that abortion speech was dangerous speech, for it counseled death. The former saw *Roe* protecting fundamental rights for women, including women's health; the latter opposed *Roe* because it violated the fundamental rights of the unborn.

Rehnquist wrote for the majority, including Souter, White, Kennedy, and Scalia. The act itself was ambiguous on the question of abortion counseling. In light of the ambiguity, the Court had to defer to the interpretation of the statute given it by the federal agency (Health and Human Services) charged with administering the act. The majority found that the secretary's interpretation was in line with the general purposes of the act and did not violate the free speech rights of the doctors but simply required that referral to abortion services be made outside of the confines of the Title X–funded clinic. The doctor-patient relationship might be protected by the First Amendment, but the Court did not have to consider that question because the regulations on doctor's speech did not violate the First Amendment. Nor was the patient's right to an abortion constrained, for she could always go to a family planning center that was not underwritten by federal funds—the same option she would have if Title X did not fund any clinics.

Souter and Kennedy had joined the chief's opinion, but O'Connor dissented. In a single-page opinion she stated that the secretary had wrongly interpreted his duties under the statute. He had no business telling doctors they could not advise women who needed an abortion that they ought to have one. It was unnecessary to go to the larger political issue (for of course the secretary only did what the president told him to do) or to the constitutionality of the delegation of authority that Congress gave to the executive branch under the statute.

O'Connor also joined the first part of the Blackmun and Marshall dissent. They insisted that the government could not attach an unconstitutional requirement to a funding bill and then say, in effect, if you don't want to give up your constitutional rights, don't apply for the funding. They cited *Akron* and *Thornburgh*, both of which denied governments the right to dictate to doctors what they should say to patients. The two justices continued, with Stevens now signing on, that the government was using funding as a way to promote one viewpoint on abortion. With heavy-handed irony, they quoted Rehnquist and Scalia dissents that had called free speech a fundamental right. What was more, the dissenters continued, the gag rule prevented women from getting an answer to their questions about abortion, even when these questions touched matters of immediate and permanent medical concerns. Women relying on doctors in these clinics would be placed in peril if the doctors could not warn them that their medical condition might require an abortion. Women misled in this fashion were not in the same position they would have been in if Title X clinics never existed.

This last question greatly influenced Stevens's own dissent, for he believed that the denial of complete and timely counseling by doctors violated the preamble of the 1970 federal law: to "promote public health and welfare." The woman who had high blood pressure or other serious medical conditions that continued pregnancy would aggravate could not be told so by the doctor she saw at the Title X family planning clinic. She walked away with false information, the silence conveying the impression that she was safe in continuing the pregnancy.

A month after *Rust* was announced, President Bush introduced to the press corps his next appointment to the Court. Marshall's dissent in *Rust* was his last official judicial act. Although O'Connor's defection in *Rust* suggested she was no longer a sure member of the anti-*Roe* majority, Souter's apparent support for Rehnquist's position and Bush's chance to appoint an anti–abortion rights replacement for Marshall should have written the last chapter of the *Roe* story.

On July 1, 1991, Bush named Clarence Thomas to replace Marshall. Thomas, like Marshall an African American, was born in Georgia and knew firsthand the sting of racism, but there the comparison to Marshall ended. Unlike Marshall's parents, Thomas's separated when he was a child, and he was raised by a disciplinarian grandfather and sent to an all-black Catholic elementary school and then an all-white parochial boarding school. For a time, at Holy Cross College, Thomas was a active antiracist dissident, but during his days at Yale Law School, he moved from strongly liberal to strongly conservative positions. His association with conservative Missouri attorney general Thomas C. Danforth after graduation influenced Thomas's nascent judicial philosophy as well. He was not against civil rights and affirmative action per se, but would use the strong arm of government only when an individual could prove that he or she had actually suffered discrimination. Thomas refused to regard groups, whether races, sexes, or other categories, as the proper recipients of relief. In addition, his strong attachment to Roman Catholicism, with its ideals of natural rights and the sanctity of all life from the moment of conception, reinforced his views on abortion.

When Danforth went on to the U.S. Senate, he helped Thomas find a post in the Reagan administration. There Thomas espoused the "get the government off the backs of the people" approach of his mentors. Indeed, as chief of the Equal Employment Opportunities office, Thomas had avoided litigating women's claims unless the complainant could show intentional harm. Appointed to the D.C. Court of Appeals, he confirmed his record in opposition to racial categorization, whether "benign" like affirmative action, or malign.

The abortion issue was the sticking point when he came before the Senate for confirmation of his nomination to the Court. He had left a "paper trail," a series of talks, articles, and published comments on the matter, all opposed to *Roe*. In one of these, he had reasoned that the Declaration of Independence, with its ringing trinity of life, liberty, and the pursuit of happiness, dictated a pro-life stance. In the hearings, he deliberately softened those views, recalling that he had thought little about *Roe* in the years since it came down, hard for some of the senators to believe given his writings on the subject, its importance in a number of his law school classes, his ties to Missouri (recall that

Danforth—in which Thomas's mentor was a named appellant—was the leading abortion case of 1976 and was again good law in 1991), and the general importance of the case in the early 1990s. The District of Columbia where he sat had many abortion clinics, and episodes of violent confrontation between demonstrators and police at these were featured in the local newspapers.

His opponents in the Senate would not allow him to evade the issue. Seventy-one times during his five days of confirmation hearings, he had to answer questions on abortion. When one senator expressed his incredulity that Thomas had no opinion on abortion to share with the committee, Thomas simply stared ahead and said nothing more. Sarah Weddington, testifying before the committee during the Thomas confirmation hearings, was so frustrated by his tactics that she held up a poster of Thomas pregnant. (She later remarked that she had heard that he had a sense of humor, and hoped that he would not be offended).

For his refusal to explain his earlier remarks on *Roe,* intimations that he was not intellectually prepared for the High Court, and accusations of sexual harassment from a former employee at the EEOC, his confirmation nearly failed, passing only fifty-two to forty-eight. He had won, however, and as he told another Bush appointee later, that was all that mattered. Marshall was quietly appalled that his seat would go to Thomas, and publically offered Thomas advice on how to decide racial discrimination cases, advice to which Thomas refused to reply. His vote should have been sufficient to topple *Roe* and send abortion back to the state legislatures, where it had been before the Supreme Court heard the Texas appeal. The case in which to do it was rapidly approaching the High Court.

When news of the voiding of its 1982 anti-abortion statute reached the Pennsylvania state legislature, its majority reacted by passing another restrictive act. The governor, a pro-life Democrat named Robert Casey, foresaw another round of court battles ending in the overturn of the bill and vetoed it, but he helped draft its successor, which passed in 1988. The newest act included provisions that the Supreme Court had nullified in earlier cases, including a twenty-four-hour waiting period and a scripted informed consent in which the doctor was to review all the alternatives to abortion for his patient and remind her that the state could gain child support from the father. The statute also provided for notification of parents (with a judicial bypass), the patient's written statement that she had notified or tried to notify her spouse, and the compiling of information on patients that could, under certain circumstance, become public.

The statute was challenged by three abortion providers and counselors, including Planned Parenthood of Eastern Pennsylvania and a doctor who filled a class action suit on behalf of all doctors who performed abortions in the state. *Planned Parenthood v. Casey* arrived at the Supreme Court in 1992, and given the makeup of the High Court, seemed to be the case that Rehnquist and White, joined now by Scalia, Kennedy, Souter, and Thomas (if not O'Connor) needed to reverse *Roe*.

Oral argument followed the familiar pattern. Kathryn Kolbert argued for the appellants (this time the circuit court, relying on *Webster*, had upheld the state regulations) that the effect of the new law was to force women to remain pregnant. Their "fundamental" right to choose was so vitiated by the regulations on them and on their doctors that it had, in all important respects, vanished. To allow Pennsylvania to go ahead was tantamount to overturning *Roe*. It was a bold strategy, especially in the face of a Court that in *Webster* had verged on doing just what Kolbert feared, but it forced the justices to decide if the symbolic *Roe*, the *Roe* that had come to mean so much to so many women, could be discarded.

Kolbert continued in a solemn, searing tone: the lower court had dumped *Akron* and *Thornburgh* (in which regulations like those before the Court in *Casey* were voided) and had abandoned the strict scrutiny test, which fundamental rights supposedly imposed upon state legislation. The lower court ignored the doctrine of *stare decisis*. "Never before has this Court bestowed and taken back a fundamental right that has been part of the settled rights and expectations of literally millions of Americans for nearly two decades." *Roe* was progress toward a new vision of women's rights. Would the Court now "regress"? The powerful linearity of her argument—an upward curve of "the autonomy of individuals to make life choices"—linked *Roe* to the civil rights and civil liberty cases of the 1960s and 1970s.

Attorney General Ernie Preate of Pennylvania followed. Kolbert had spoken for seven uninterrupted minutes before O'Connor asked the first question. Preate was almost immediately stopped by Blackmun.

Had Preate read *Roe*? Did he think it provided for abortion "on demand"? Preate replied that Pennsylvania did not believe that its law violated *Roe*. He simply wished the Court to replace the trimester formula with the undue burden standard. He suggested in passing that if the provisions proved to impose insuperable obstacles, petitioners could come back into court and make that argument. Justice O'Connor was not sure that the spousal notice provision did not impose such a burden and wanted to know what state interest it protected. The child's, Preate returned. Why was it then limited to husbands and not all fathers? Why not all men with whom the mother had sexual intercourse? Preate had brushed off the danger that battered wives might face from the regulation, a point raised in the amicus briefs against the law, but O'Connor was not persuaded. The other justices homed in on this question, concerned about how a state would determine what did and what did not constitute an undue burden. Scalia joined in the contest for the opposite reason—to show how indeterminate, hence unworkable, the undue burden test was.

Solicitor General Kenneth Starr had returned to represent the president's support for the Pennsylvania regulations. He worried that after twenty years of *Roe* the Court still did not have a governing standard for reviewing abortion cases and hoped that the plurality opinion in *Webster* would become that standard. In light of *Roe*'s holding that the state was not to impose a definition of life, Stevens wanted to know if Starr had a position on whether a fetus was a person under the Fourteenth Amendment. He hedged, but Stevens and then O'Connor pressed. The Court had said that the fetus was not a person; did Starr mean to change that statement? Starr hedged some more, "I think *Roe* goes this far ... that there is a legitimate interest of the state in the potential life *in utero* throughout pregnancy." Then, did the government believe that the interest of the state was "compelling" throughout the pregnancy? Yes, Starr answered. Stevens then sprung the trap: what was the constitutional text that supported this interest? If the argument for the fundamental right to an abortion failed for lack of explicit language in the Constitution, did not the argument for state interest in the potential life of the fetus fail for the same reason? Justice White stepped in to take Starr's argument in the opposite direction—why let *Roe* stand at all if the state had an interest in the life of the fetus from its inception? If the state's interest was rational, would not a total prohibition on abortion follow?

By this time, oral argument in the abortion rights cases was no longer a chance for justices to learn about the issues, engage counsel in debate, test one another by firing salvos over the heads of counsel, or even hone arguments that would later appear in their opinions. Intellectual exhaustion had set in. It was almost as though the precise nature of the regulations no longer mattered, as if argument about them was shadowboxing in the foregone conclusion that a majority would overrule *Roe*. In the conference after the case was argued, Kennedy and Souter seemed ready to join Rehnquist, White, Thomas, and Scalia to uphold the regulations and strike down *Roe*. But something happened, not so much in the law (which was already so overlaid with interpretations and precedents as to be almost immobile) as in the chemistry of the Court itself a sense among some of the justices that the symbolic *Roe* must be saved even if Blackmun's trimester formula was no longer meaningful.

O'Connor held out on the issue of the spousal notification, an issue that made sense in light of the growing concern with battered spouse syndrome. She had always accepted the symbolic importance of *Roe* to women. In a 1990 Minnesota case, she had almost joined the Blackmun-Marshall-Brennan-Stevens opinion striking down a rule that both parents of a minor had to be notified. In the end, she accepted the state's provision of a judicial bypass for the dual notification, showing her independence from both sides in the increasingly hostile atmosphere that abortion cases generated. But that case proved her more and more willing to stake out her own turf, a stand firmly grounded in specific fact situations and likely factual outcomes.

Without revealing their mutual effort to anyone else on the Court, Justices Kennedy, O'Connor, and Souter began to meet and soon determined to write a "joint opinion" upholding both *Roe* and the Pennsylvania statute. They hoped, perhaps, to take the case out of the political arena—a forlorn hope, but one worthy of exploration. When he learned of their plan, and the fact that *Roe* would not fall, Justice Scalia compared their naïveté to the Taney Court majority's in its 1857 decision in *Dred Scott v. Sanford*. Taney, too, hoped that a sweeping opinion in favor of the slaveholder's rights to his property would end the slavery controversy that was dividing the nation. Scalia's unflattering comparison found its way into his dissenting opinion. But when the three justices read their joint opinion to the assemblage in the Supreme Court building, even veteran "Court watchers" were deeply moved. They knew that they were seeing something rarely seen before—three appointees expected to join in the demise of *Roe* had jointly authored an opinion that reaffirmed the symbolic value of *Roe* and the right to choose.

The opinion of the Court, that is, the opinion that had a majority, split into two parts. Both parts were written jointly by Kennedy, Souter, and O'Connor (its sections in that order). The first part upheld *Roe* and was joined by Stevens and Blackmun. Although it was carefully crafted and at times eloquent in its exposition of legal ideas, it was also frankly presentist, recognizing the immense political pressure under which the Court operated and the need for *stare decisis* in the light of that pressure. The second part of the Kennedy-Souter-O'Connor opinion, adhered to by Rehnquist, Thomas, Scalia, and White, upheld all of the disputed Pennsylvania provisions save the spousal notification, claiming that they did not violate an "undue burden" test. Thus the whole of the joint opinion fully satisfied only the three authors.

Blackmun wrote an opinion concurring in part and dissenting in part. He knew it was his swan song, and it was a deeply moving elegy for the *Roe* he had written and at the same time a song of praise for the "courage" of the three authors. Rehnquist similarly concurred in part and dissented in part, calling the joint opinion little more than a movieset facade behind which *Roe* had vanished.

The most chilling dissenting opinion was Scalia's. In a way it was also the most brilliant, finding all the flaws in the joint opinion and exposing them mercilessly. But that very brutality of prose cost the opinion its power to compel adherence. It had no humanity, though it may have been superb law—or rather, it revealed that what remained of *Roe* now rested more on compassion than on constitutional reasoning. And that may have been, in the end, why *Roe* survived, even as a shell of its former self, in a Court whose majority was far to the political right of the Court that wrote *Roe*.

Kennedy opened the joint opinion with a recital of the history of the case with words that surprised everyone in the courtroom, delighting some, and infuriating others. "A jurisprudence of doubt" pervaded the Court's rulings on abortion. In six cases over the past decade the federal government had asked the Court to void the liberty interest of women enunciated in *Roe*. Both sides in the oral argument had intimated that the provisions could be upheld only if *Roe* were overruled. The opinion that the chief justice had written (assuming when he wrote it that it was to be the opinion of the Court) took the same pose. State regulations of abortion had only to be rational to pass muster. But the authors of the joint opinion (joined here by Stevens and Blackmun) differed: "[T]he essential holding of *Roe v. Wade* should be retained and once again reaffirmed."

Kennedy read that holding to have three equally important parts. The first was the right to abort a fetus in the first trimester "without undue interference from the state." This formulation led naturally to the next principle, that the state had an interest in the potential life of the fetus from conception, and so undid Blackmun's formula completely, only holding the state to a rational standard of regulation. It could not prohibit an abortion, but it could heavily regulate the conditions for abortions. The third principle was that after "fetal viability," the state could "restrict abortions," subject only to exceptions for the mother's life or health.

In his dissent from this part of the joint opinion, Rehnquist asserted that "the joint opinion, following its newly-minted version of *stare decisis*, retains the outer shell of *Roe v. Wade* but beats a wholesale retreat from the substance of that case." Did the substitution of the *Webster* test for the *Roe* formula amount to the demise of *Roe*, and should the joint opinion's authors have admitted openly what they had done by stealth? The chief justice had either missed what the joint authors were trying to do or dismissed what motivated them.

As Kennedy continued, the Fourteenth Amendment not only protected those liberties that existed in legal discourse in 1868, when the amendment was ratified, but the liberties that women and men had come to associate with modern life. For example, privacy in marriage, mentioned nowhere in the Constitution, was one of those evolving concepts, which the Court had only discovered in 1965.

Kennedy called the Court's ongoing elaboration of these liberties "reasoned judgment," but for the past twenty years Rehnquist had known and loathed it under another name: the "living Constitution." Justice Brennan had adopted that term to connote a Constitution that grew and took on new meanings without changing its size or adding new words. Under a living Constitution, wherein due process was not frozen in time, the liberty interests of women could expand to encompass reproductive autonomy. Kennedy followed with a paean to motherhood that concluded differently from those found in the public discourse a hundred years before. Instead of asserting that the state knew what was best for women, or that men knew what was moral for women, he wrote: "Her suffering [in pregnancy] is too intimate and personal for the State to insist . . . upon its own vision of the woman's role, however dominant that vision has been in the course of our history and our culture. The destiny of the woman must be shaped to a large extent on her own conception of her spiritual imperatives and her place in society." In this sense, the abortion decision was only one step removed from the contraception decision on a continuum of choices.

Souter's portion on *stare decisis* followed. Its tone was less elevated and more straightforward than Kennedy's, as one might expect in a discourse on such a dry subject, but thoroughgoing meticulousness was already Souter's hallmark. When confronted with a call to overturn well-settled precedent, the Court must engage in "a series of prudential and pragmatic considerations." In particular, had related principles of law so changed or the world so altered that the old rule no longer had "significant application or justification"? He read *Roe* to limit state power rather than to establish a fundamental right, which, again as the chief justice later noted, was an odd reading of *Roe* at best and perhaps also disingenuous. But Souter knew that his take on the case differed from that of *Roe's* author, and like Kennedy he reached outside the confines of the law books for his authority. "The inquiry into reliance counts the cost of a rule's repudiation as it would fall on those who have relied reasonably on the rule's continued application." An unwanted or forcible pregnancy was not like a contract dispute. "The ability of women to participate equally in the economic and social life of the Nation has been facilitated by their ability to control their reproductive lives." Insofar as the "Constitution serves human values," to undo *Roe* would be to betray the hopes and plans of millions.

This ulterior motivation revealed, Souter returned to the law books to find that *Roe* was still good law, fitting well other cases in which the Court protected "personal autonomy and bodily integrity." Even if the state had gained some ground in its power to regulate abortion practice, a shift in "time limits," the essential liberty of women to terminate a pregnancy was not jeopardized by the string of decisions following *Roe*. There was no need to overrule *Roe*. The Court had, of course, overturned some notorious holdings—for example *Plessy* was effectually repudiated by *Brown v. Board of Education*. But comparing *Roe* to *Plessy* made no sense, for *Plessy* was wrong when it was decided. What was more, the legitimacy of the Court itself would suffer if it abandoned *Roe*, for it would seem that the clamor of one side in a partisan duel, rather than principle, had swayed the Court. The greater the political tumult, the more wary the Court should be of overturning precedent.

Justice O'Connor concluded the joint opinion with the reasons why the provisions of the Pennsylvania law (less the spousal notification requirement) passed muster under the undue burden test. Indeed, although her portion was the longest, it was the easiest to explain, for she had merely to recite, like a mantra, that "a finding of undue burden is a shorthand for the conclusion that a state regulation has the purpose or effect of placing a substantial burden in the path of a woman seeking an abortion of a non-viable fetus." In the rest of her portion she merely "refined" the analysis of the circuit court whose opinion she and the other joint authors, now joined by Rehnquist, Thomas, Scalia, and White, affirmed. The majority opinions in *Akron* and *Thornburgh* vanished as if they had never existed.

O'Connor paused the litany of affirmation of the circuit court to go back to the testimony of expert witnesses at the district court trial that women forced to consult their husbands before an abortion might have much to fear from such notification. The statute exempted women who feared bodily injury from husbands, but it did not bar husbands from using the information against a wife in a child custody battle, nor from publicizing the woman's choice, nor from inflicting bodily harm on children or relatives of the woman, nor from using control over family finances to punish her for her decision. The American Medical Association worried about these possibilities, and so did O'Connor. The spousal notification provision was an undue burden, and it must give way.

O'Connor seemed particularly aware of matters of fact in her portion of the joint opinion. Some scholars suggest that the joint opinion reflected O'Connor's general approach to law and lawmaking on the Court as well as her particular view of *Roe*. Clearly the joint opinion expressed her strong commitment to the importance of the integrity of the Court as well as her belief that ordinary people must be able to rely on the Court when settled interests like privacy were at stake. Her cautious, fact-based jurisprudence, with its aversion to stark, bright line rules (the very opposite of Scalia's jurisprudence), runs through all parts of the joint opinion. Moreover, she had become Brennan's successor as the coalition-builder on the Court, the role that Scalia might have attained but eschewed.

Not only did she recognize the pressure that both sides were putting on the Court (after all she too had to pass through the throngs of demonstrators), but she no doubt knew that the politics of abortion had reached a boiling point in Arizona. There pro-life forces had written a referendum (Proposition 110) barring all but a handful of abortions to save the life of the mother and in cases of rape. Her old mentor, former senator Barry Goldwater, opposed the referendum, saying that "I'm a great believer in a woman's choice," a switch from his advocacy of a right-to-life amendment when he was a senator. The League of Women Voters announced its opposition as well. Six months after the joint opinion closed the *Casey* litigation, the referendum had its own day in court, at the November 1992 polling booths. The result was a stunning defeat for the proposition in every category of the state's voting population except born-again Protestants, including the 22 percent of the state's population that was Catholic.

Blackmun joined in the first two parts of the joint opinion saving the symbolic *Roe* but dissented on some of the Pennsylvania provisions. Poignantly, in view of his age and the few years left to him on the Court, he warned that "all that remained [after *Webster*] between the promise of *Roe* and the darkness of the plurality [decision in *Webster*] was a single flickering flame. . . . But now, when many expected the darkness to fall, the flame has grown bright." If only one vote still saved any of *Roe,* in *Casey* the joint authors had committed an act "of personal courage and constitutional principle" in saving the essence of *Roe*. Blackmun may have engaged in wishful thinking in writing that the joint opinion "require[d] that a state's abortion decisions be subjected to the strictest judicial scrutiny," for the joint opinion had discarded that high level of review. Indeed, Blackmun could not cite anything in the joint opinion in support of his claim; he had to fall back on *Griswold* and *Roe*. He ended his dissent with the plain fact that he could not stay on the Court forever. Just one vote switch, and both *Roes* would be gone.

Blackmun had castigated Rehnquist's views as a "stunted conception of individual liberty." Blackmun's harsh judgment on Rehnquist had some truth—the chief did tend to defer to government—but his frustration at what he saw as the evasive tactics of the authors of the joint opinion stood on firm ground. It seemed to him that they had assayed an "unjustified constitutional compromise," leaving the Court open to another twenty years of minute examination of state regulations. Comparing what they had said about the Pennsylvania rules to *Roe* showed that they had jettisoned the "fundamental" character of the abortion right. The "undue burden" test appeared nowhere in *Roe* and was fabricated of "whole cloth." They had mischaracterized *stare decisis* and left *Roe* like a "storefront on a western movie set." Like *Plessy*, *Roe* had run its course and should be discarded.

Scalia's dissent, joined by Thomas, White, and Rehnquist, graded the joint opinion a C, in law schools a devastating assessment. To a point-by-point refutation of the joint opinion, Scalia added some substantive judgments of his own, responding to Blackmun's sweeping valedictory. Like Kennedy, Souter, and O'Connor, Scalia took notice of the five hundred thousand women marching on the Capitol in support of abortion rights, but he read that march differently from the authors of the joint opinion. Before *Roe*, he believed, "national politics were not plagued by abortion protests, national abortion lobbying, or abortion marches on Congress." There was disagreement, but "that disagreement was being worked out at the state level." Before *Roe*, he thought, political compromise was possible. All this changed with *Roe*'s "mandate for abortion on demand." Roe "fanned into life an issue that has inflamed our national politics in general, and has obscured with its smoke the selection of justices to this Court in particular, ever since." *Roe* was an excuse for and an example of the rise to the "Imperial Judi-

ciary . . . this Nietzschian vision of us unelected, life-tenured judges"
running ahead of the democratic process and mystically divining what
is good for all the people. Worst of all, *Roe* had created a new class of
consumers for the immorality of abortion. Scalia's history lesson was
flawed, but his passion was genuine.

———

Overcoming all challenges, *Roe* had survived. In *Webster* and *Casey*,
however, the operational core of the decision had changed. As a symbol, *Roe* remained bright, but it had become clear that state regulations
almost invariably passed muster. Only states such as Louisiana, Utah,
and Wyoming, determined to flout federal law by banning all abortions, faced reversal in the courts. What was left, then—the shouting
in the streets, the intransigence of the two sides? Was access to a safe
and inexpensive abortion still there?

    Casey's joint opinion, grounded in what Justices Scalia and Blackmun
agreed was the most fragile and jimcrack of compromises, could not
protect *Roe* against the very political forces that the authors of the joint
opinion sought to keep at bay. Were President Bush reelected, the
imminent retirement of Justices Blackmun and White would bring
another shift of personnel on the Court, and might doom even the
symbolic *Roe*. Politics, not law, held abortion rights in its grasp.

Epilogue: *Roe* in the Clinton Years,
1993–2000

Casey was announced on June 29, 1992, before proponents of Arizona Proposition 110 lost their bid to ban all abortions and before the election of a liberal Democratic president who favored *Roe*. If it is true that the judges read the election returns, it is also true that they can forecast the impact of those elections. Both Blackmun and Scalia could appreciate how much the election of Bill Clinton would affect abortion rights. Only a few weeks after he had taken his oath of office, he lifted the gag rule on Title X fund recipients, influenced Congress in 1993 to alter the language of the Hyde amendment to include funding for "wrongful pregnancies" resulting from rape and incest, and allowed abortions on American military bases.

With the election of a pro-choice president in 1992, the battle over the survival of *Roe* cooled. President Clinton's two appointments to the Court were both supporters of the symbolism of the decision, as well as the right of women to terminate their pregnancies at an early stage. The first, named on June 13, 1993, was Ruth Bader Ginsburg. At the top of her class at Cornell, and then at Columbia Law School, like O'Connor she found no openings in major East Coast firms for a woman. As she later recalled, "I had three strikes against me. I was Jewish, I was a woman, and I was a mother." She nevertheless found a career in law teaching. While on the faculty at Columbia Law School, she became the head litigator in sex discrimination cases for the ACLU. In the 1970s, she won six women's rights cases before the High Court, using the remarkable tactic of arguing that the laws involved deprived men of equal rights. Criticized by both radical feminists and conservatives for her view that men and women should be treated strictly equally, she replied that her victories in court had helped to end the confinement of women to a separate, inferior sphere of life. But as a judge on the D.C. Circuit Court of Appeals, to which President Carter appointed her, she showed great caution on the role that courts could play in social reform.

She was not a great fan of the logic of the Court in *Roe,* and at the time of her confirmation was certain that the abortion issue would fade from public view as pills like RU 486 (the so-called morning-after pill) came on the market and reduced the number of unwanted pregnancies. When asked about *Roe* at her confirmation hearings, she reasserted what she had written years before: the Constitution must protect a woman's right to choose to terminate a pregnancy. She was confirmed ninety-six to three, the only vocal opposition coming from pro-life groups. As Phyllis Schlafly told a law school conference at Stanford University almost a year after the nomination was announced, "Ruth Bader Ginsburg's elevation to the U.S. Supreme Court represents the affirmation of the radical feminist agenda for which she had been the most articulate advocate for more than twenty years," a somewhat exaggerated depiction of Ginsburg's feminism.

In July 1994, President Clinton's second nominee to the High Court, First Circuit Court of Appeals Chief Judge Stephen G. Breyer, also sailed through the confirmation process. Breyer, a former Harvard Law School professor and something of a conservative economic theorist, came from and married into wealth. A few witnesses, notably the consumer activist Ralph Nader, accused Breyer of favoring wealthy corporations over small businesses and individuals, but many conservatives were content that Breyer seemed to lack any ideological predilections. As Texas Republican senator Phil Gramm said in an interview during the hearings, "The chances of [a liberal Democratic president] nominating anyone more conservative than Judge Breyer... were almost zero." Although his hearings did not focus on abortion (he simply remarked that *Roe* was settled law), and he was confirmed by a vote of eighty-seven to nine on July 29, 1994, all of his opponents were outspoken pro-life politicians. Paige Comstock Cunningham, president of Americans United for Life, thought that Breyer must have "passed President Clinton's abortion litmus test." Plainly, for its partisans, the abortion issue was not about to fade.

If the symbolic *Roe* now seemed relatively secure in the courts, the prospects for women seeking abortions and doctors willing to provide them were less certain. The results of the Scheidler and Terry program to harass abortion doctors had become all too evident by 1993. Although Scheidler did not advocate violence and Terry renounced physical attacks on doctors, those who followed the Operation Rescue example did not always content themselves with telephone calls and placards. On March 10, 1993, Dr. David Gunn, already the target of death threats, was murdered during a Pensacola, Florida, anti-abortion rally. Michael F. Griffin shot Dr. Gunn in the back three times. Operation Rescue had printed Gunn's photograph, home number, and address on a "wanted poster" the year before. On August 19, 1993, Dr. George Tiller was shot in both arms by Rachelle Shannon, a protestor at a Wichita, Kansas, anti-abortion rally. She had been sending letters of support to the jailed Griffin and hailed the murderer of Dr. Gunn as a "hero of our time." The next day, Dr. George Patterson, owner of four southeastern abortion clinics, was bushwhacked. His killer has never been caught. On July 29, 1994, former evangelical minister Paul Hill, director of the anti-abortion group Defensive Action, murdered Dr. John Britton and his elderly escort, James H. Barrett, outside a Pensacola clinic. A woman who was also chaperoning the doctor was badly wounded. Hill had chosen a twelve-gauge shotgun as his weapon and fired it at point-blank range. Convinced that the "infants" he was saving from the abortionist justified the murder of the doctor and his escorts, Hill was unrepentant at his trial and sentencing.

Pro-choice groups did not idly watch the escalating violence at the clinics. In 1989, NOW filed suit in federal court against Operation Rescue, arguing that the picketing, shouting, harassment, and threats continued a conspiracy in violation of the clinic personnel's and the patients' civil rights. The law under which NOW sought relief was the so-called Ku Klux Klan Act passed by Congress in 1871 to make Klan violence against freedmen and women into a federal offense. The lower federal courts accepted the analogy between the women seeking abortions and the freedmen seeking to exercise their newfound rights as citizens. The Supreme Court in *Bray v. Alexandria Health Clinic* (1993), Justice Scalia writing for himself, Chief Justice Rehnquist, and Justices Thomas, Kennedy, and White, found that the women did not fit the category that Congress intended to protect with the act, and abortion was not a protected right under it. Justices Souter (in part), and Blackmun, Stevens, and O'Connor dissented.

At the same time, NOW assayed the use of the federal RICO (racketeer-influenced and corrupt organization) Act, likening the methods and aims of anti-abortion groups to those of gangs. Again the key was the racketeering nature (defined in the law as "any act or threat involving murder, kidnaping, gambling, arson, robbery, bribery, extortion") of the demonstrators' conduct. They had threatened murder and arson, and some among them had carried out the threats. When petitioners could prove that anti-abortion groups had destroyed clinic property, as in one Pennsylvania case, lower federal courts accepted the analogy, deciding that a criminal conspiracy indictable under RICO did not have to have an economic purpose. In *NOW v. Joseph Scheidler* (1994) the High Court unanimously refused to rule out RICO prosecutions of anti–abortion rights groups.

Pro-choice litigators also used state courts to gain injunctions against anti–abortion rights protestors. In Florida, where the protests were vehement and violent, a state court imposed and the state's highest court upheld an order barring protestors from coming within thirty-six feet of the clinic's entrances or within three hundred feet of individuals entering and leaving, unless the latter indicated their willingness to talk with the protestors. The demonstrators filed suit with the federal courts, alleging that the ban was a violation of their free speech rights. In *Madsen v. Women's Health Center* (1994), the Supreme Court (with Rehnquist writing for himself and Justices Blackmun, O'Connor, Souter, and Ginsburg, as well as Stevens in part), found that the ban was an acceptable restraint of the demonstrators' speech so long as the ban burdened speech no more than was necessary to serve a "significant government interest." The three-hundred-foot distance between demonstrators and persons using the clinic was not required, nor was a buffer zone between demonstrators and nonaccess areas.

Scalia, Thomas, and Kennedy dissented, arguing that the demonstrators were not engaging in criminal activity and were unlawfully deprived of their free speech rights under the First Amendment. In *Schenck v. Pro-Choice Network* (1997), the Court, voting eight to one, invalidated a New York court's "floating buffer zone" of fifteen feet between persons seeking to enter or leave a clinic and all demonstrators. That imposition burdened speech too much. But a fifteen-foot fixed space around entrances was acceptable.

In January 2000, a federal judge in Washington, D.C., had to order demonstrators to stand twenty feet away from the entrances to District abortion clinics. Earlier Supreme Court rulings on how far anti–abortion rights picketers must stay from clinic doors did not deter the protestors. Colorado's statute, requiring only eight feet of separation, came before the High Court in January 2000 *(Hill v. Colorado)*, on an appeal from the Colorado Supreme Court's decision upholding the law. Eighteen states with similar laws joined Colorado as amici, as did the College of Obstetricians and Gynecologists, seeking to protect doctors' offices in abortion clinics. On the other side were arrayed abortion rights opponents, animal rights activists (who use similar tactics of confrontation), and the AFL-CIO, seeking to protect the tactics of labor picketers.

The Court, in a six to three opinion, upheld the statute on June 28, 2000. During oral argument, and in his dissent, Justice Scalia asked why a statute could single out anti-abortion protestors for restrictions that did not apply to other individuals exercising their right to free speech. When the decision was announced, he read his impassioned dissent in Court. Justices Thomas and Kennedy joined him in dissent, Kennedy reading another dissenting opinion aloud. At the oral argument, Justices Breyer and O'Connor had doubted that eight feet of separation prevented free speech, when angry voices carried much farther. Justice Stevens wrote the majority opinion, joined by the chief justice and Justices Souter and O'Connor as well as Breyer and Ginsburg. Observers thought that the passions the case evoked were a proxy for another decision on abortion rights announced the same day, on partial-birth abortion.

The pro-choice forces had their victories in Congress. In 1993, influenced by the violence at the clinics and the uncertainty of the KKK Act and RICO analogies that the pro-choice movement relied on to curb the violence, Congress moved to protect lawful providers of abortions with the Freedom of Access to Clinic Entrances Act. FACE provided that "whoever by force or threat of force or by physical obstruction, intentionally injures, intimidates, or interferes with or attempts to injure, intimidate or interfere with any person . . . [to hinder that person or class of persons] from obtaining or providing reproductive health services shall be subject to criminal penalties and civil remedies." The latter included injunctive relief and monetary damages. Clinton signed the bill into law in 1994, saying that "this bill is designed to eliminate violence and coercion. It is not a strike against the First Amendment.... We simply cannot, we must not continue to allow the attacks, the incidents of arson, the campaigns of intimidation upon law-abiding citizens that has given rise to this law."

Pro-life groups immediately challenged the law's constitutionality as well as its application to their activities. In a series of cases, notably *Terry v. Reno* and *American Life League v. Reno,* federal courts held that the statute did not violate the First Amendment, and in *U.S. v. Dinwiddie* the courts held that the statute did not exceed Congress's authority under the Commerce Clause of the Constitution. As of 1999, in fifteen out of seventeen criminal prosecutions the Department of Justice had brought under the law, defendants were convicted. In fourteen out of seventeen cases seeking civil damages, courts found defendants liable. The U.S. Supreme Court has declined to review these cases. The law has not stopped the violence, however, and may have even intensified it by driving some pro-life extremists underground.

The battle over abortion rights in Congress shifted once again when pro-life Republicans won a majority of the House of Representatives in 1994. In 1995, the lower house voted to reverse the 1993 extension of funding to rape and incest victims, but the Senate refused to concur. The House tried again in 1996, and again the Senate blocked the re-turn to the more restrictive funding formula. Thereafter, the pro-life representatives shifted to legislation that would prevent all federally funded health care professionals from providing information about or referrals to abortion clinics. The anti–abortion rights leaders also drafted a "Child Custody Protection Act" that would make it a fed-eral crime for any person other than a parent to knowingly transport a minor across state lines for the purpose of obtaining an abortion, if the minor had not complied with the state of origin's laws regarding parental notification and consent.

In response, from 1996 to 1999, Clinton supported a "Family Plan-ning and Choice Protection Act" that would have increased funding for family planning clinics under Title X, permanently removed the gag rule on counseling contraceptive and abortion services when ap-propriate, required health insurance plans to cover contraception, and protected women's access to abortion clinics. The act would also have repealed funding limitations on abortions for women in prisons, the military, and various indigent medical care programs, in effect reversing the Hyde amendment. Although the act had substantial support in Congress, it did not pass during his eight years in office.

By 2000, the law regarding abortion had grown even more bewildering than it was before *Roe*. Following a 1975 act of Congress allowing individuals or institutions receiving federal funds to refrain from participating in abortions without facing loss of federal funds (so-called conscience clauses), forty-six states passed laws exempting such men and women from performing abortions. Men and women had merely to claim a religious or moral objection to the procedure. Some states have extended this to pharmacists who do not want to fill prescriptions for medications that might be used as abortifacients.

In the matter of parental notification or consent for minors to have abortions, only Utah and Idaho, whose legislatures are strongly influenced by the Mormon Church, which is opposed to all abortions, and Texas require and enforce consent rules. Among the states with the highest rates of minors seeking abortions, New Jersey (where 58 percent of teenage pregnancies end in abortion), New York (56 percent), Massachusetts (53 percent), Connecticut (50 percent), and Rhode Island (43 percent), there are no notification or consent rules. Nor does one find them in New Hampshire, Vermont, Florida, Oklahoma, Oregon, or Washington State. Eight states have adopted consent rules that federal courts approved. Twenty-five states have notification and consent regulations for minors, but these can be bypassed if the minor can convince a judge that she is mature enough to understand what she is doing and that notification of her parents would not be in her best interest. Reports from these states indicate that bypasses are not easy to obtain, nor have judges been consistent in issuing them. In short, the crazy-quilt pattern of the laws—a diversity that resembles the diversity of state law during the "reform" period of the late 1960s—seems to invite minors to cross state lines in search of a more favorable climate for an abortion.

Finally, pro-life lawmakers in Congress attempted to deny federal funding to any doctor using the dilate and extraction (D and X) method of abortion (called by abortion opponents a "partial-birth" abortion because the last portion of the procedure takes place in the birth canal rather than the uterus). Pro-life advocates likened the extraction to an "infanticide." Pro-choice advocates replied that the procedure is used only in early pregnancy, and has nothing to do with birth, for the fetus is not viable at that stage. President Clinton vetoed the congressional partial-birth abortion bills.

Nevertheless, thirty states passed bans on D and X operations. Federal courts struck down most of the laws. After Congress enlarged the exceptions to the ban on funding abortions to include wrongful pregnancies, more than one-third of the states refused to comply. Federal courts issued orders in twelve of these cases, but as of the beginning of 2000 three states, Alabama, Mississippi, and South Dakota, still refused to fund abortions in cases of rape and incest, despite federal court orders to do so.

The first of the so-called partial-birth abortion statutes, from Nebraska, finally reached the Court in the spring of 2000. Nebraska's law was so vaguely worded and involved such severe criminal penalties that it resembled the Texas law voided in *Roe*. In defense of his state's statute, Nebraska attorney general Donald Stenberg offered that the statute did not deny a woman the right to choose an abortion, but merely informed doctors that they may not use this particular method to accomplish that goal. Still, when an assembly member had offered an amendment to make the law more precise, the motion was defeated. Plainly the majority wanted an end to abortion, not merely to D and X surgeries.

Doctors like Leroy Carhart, who brought the suit against the Nebraska law, along with other doctors, replied that the D and X method is the safest for women and that the fetuses are not viable in any case so early in the pregnancy. Thus the Nebraska law not only was too vague for doctors to interpret, it violated their rights and women's rights under any interpretation of *Roe*. The district court and the Eighth Circuit Court of Appeals struck down the law on the grounds of its vagueness—the language might be applied to any abortion procedure. Nebraska appealed to the Supreme Court, and on April 25, 2000, the Court heard oral argument.

The questions of the justices raised the old issues and revealed how they would vote when the time came. Why was the state's act not a permissible way to protect fetal life, Justice Scalia wanted to know, as he recounted the horrific details of the procedure. Did it not pull off arms and legs and crush the skull by sucking out the infant's brain? Was there no way that it could be interpreted to fit under *Casey*? (Carhart's attorneys had brought a facial challenge—they had to show that no construction of the law would be permissible.) Justice Ginsburg approached from a different direction. Why bar the D and X when the state allowed doctors to use equally draconian procedures to do the same thing when the fetus was inside the uterus? Did not the act ignore the High Court's earlier instructions to states to let doctors do their jobs according to their best professional judgment, Justice Ginsburg inquired. Justices Souter and Stevens reminded Stenberg that Nebraska had a statute on the books barring late-term abortions; what did this law add to that? Justice O'Connor worried that the law was so vague it might bar the older dilation and evacuation, or D and E, procedure, effectively denying women any surgical aid. Attorney General Stenberg persisted that the state legislature, not the courts, best determined abortion restrictions.

The decision came down on June 28, 2000. In a five to four opinion written for the majority by Justice Breyer, the Court overturned the Nebraska statute. Breyer agreed with the lower court that the statute was impermissibly vague, but went on to argue that no matter how it was rewritten, it would have imposed an undue burden on a woman seeking a safe abortion. The law had no regard for the "health of the mother," which the D and X procedure, when medically indicated, was designed to protect. Breyer argued that the majority view was merely an application of the Court's opinion in *Casey*, but he had added a measure of deference to the discretion of doctors absent from *Casey*. By denying that Nebraska could revise its partial-birth abortion ban, Breyer no doubt hoped to avoid Nebraska doing what Pennsylvania did after *Thornburgh*—merely tightening the language of the law, and perhaps adding a few new provisions, to see how far they would get in the courts.

Justice Kennedy joined Justices Rehnquist, Scalia, and Thomas in dissent, arguing that the majority had misinterpreted *Casey* by unnecessarily diminishing the interest of the state in the life of the fetus. Justice Scalia's dissent was a scathing attack on the jurisprudence of the majority view but did not cover any new ground. Justice Thomas, writing in dissent, once again rejected the core opinion in *Roe:* "Although a state may permit abortion, nothing in the Constitution dictates that a state must do so." But Thomas's unwillingness to accept as precedent all the cases between *Roe* and *Carhart*, including *Webster* and *Casey*, and his explicit attack on Justice O'Connor for "twist[ing]" the meaning of those precedents, was not the harshest of the dissenting opinions. Justice Scalia's dissent was an even more scathing attack on the jurisprudence of the majority view. In the orgy of bad feeling (all the justices but Souter wrote opinions), Justice Breyer's calm tone was all but lost.

The Court had become as polarized and as intransigent as the demonstrators in the streets. The revived intransigence of the justices left *Roe* again at risk. As Roger K. Evans of the Planned Parenthood Federal of America wrote for the *National Law Journal* on July 10, 2000, "within the Nebraska decision are the seeds of a substantial shift in the terrain of the abortion right in the future." But Evans was wrong: insofar as women availed themselves of that right, the slide began not with *Stenberg v. Carhart* but with *Webster* and *Casey*. According to the Congressional Information Service, in the three years before *Webster* was decided, for every 1,000 live births, there were a little over 400 abortions. After *Webster*, that number began a slow but steady decline, to 350 abortions for every 1,000 live births. At the same time, the Gallup polls showed the steady erosion of popular support for abortion rights. Perhaps the declining abortion figures reflected the success of the much publicized campaign against sexual activity and the increased access to contraceptive devices in high school, but studies of individual regions, particularly those in the states with newly imposed and especially severe restrictions on abortion, suggest an alternative cause of the decline. Data from rural counties in Pennsylvania assembled for the years 1975 to 1994, and presented in 1997, showed a dramatic drop in the number of hospital-performed abortions. Mary Beliveau, director of the Pennsylvania Pro-Life Federation, opined that the cause of the decline was the educational impact of the rules upheld in *Casey*. Karin Mariner, an abortion rights advocate based in Philadelphia, disagreed. Questionnaires filled out by the hospitals in the region indicated that they were using the new rules to dissuade pregnant women from gaining abortions.

Indeed, the words "undue burden" had themselves taken on a double meaning. In the courts, the doctrine subtly but surely shifted the initial burden of proof onto the shoulders of those challenging state regulation of abortions. Under *Roe* as first propounded, the right to choose an abortion in the first trimester was fundamental and compromised only by the state's interest in the health of the pregnant woman. The state assumed the task of establishing that the interest any of its other regulations protected was compelling enough to outweigh a fundamental right. Under the undue burden test of *Webster, Casey,* and their progeny, by contrast, the choice of the abortion was no longer a fundamental right, and the plaintiff/abortion provider bore the initial burden of convincing a court that any particular regulation was unduly burdensome.

The second undue burden was felt by every abortion provider. Although the choice of an abortion remained legal and private donations kept the doors of abortion clinics open, doctors, nurses, counselors, and employees at the clinics faced the prospect of verbal abuse, physical assault, and worse every day. Federal and state authorities searched for James Charles Kopp in connection with the sniper murder of abortionist Dr. Barnett Slepian. Kopp was a deeply religious man in his early forties who traveled from city to city with anti-abortion demonstrators. His own descent into personal disappointment and violence seemed to parallel that of some of the anti–abortion rights movements, torn from their nonviolent moorings by the belligerence of a few of their members. With the threat of criminal prosecution under federal and state laws hanging over them, the most violent of these "rescuers," the "Army of God," continued the bombing and arson of the 1980s, and worse. In 1994, 1995, and again in 1997, doctors were ambushed in their homes by a sniper. He stalked them and patiently waited for his shot. In 1998 the sniper killed Slepian. Kopp is in custody, but the sniper has become a symbol to some of the righteousness of violence and to others of the dangers of fanaticism.

The violence has its impact on the doctors who work in the clinics. Their number thinned sharply during the early 1990s as the cohort of men and women who had known the horrors of illegal abortions during the pre-*Roe* era retired from practice and few young doctors volunteered to replace the retirees. Abortion skills were left out of the great majority of obstetrical teaching programs, so much so that the Accreditation Council of Graduate Medical Education, along with the American College of Obstetrics and Gynecology, had to rewrite the training rules for medical schools. Even so, the new rules allowed Catholic schools and hospitals, as well as individual teachers, to opt out of the new accreditation standards if abortion offended their morals. Pro-life members of Congress then called for legislation that would bar the professional organizations from requiring the teaching of abortion in medical schools. The American Medical Association, which had approved *Roe* but favored state regulation of the procedure, jumped into the fray to protect the autonomy of medical schools and professional self-accreditation.

But the Food and Drug Administration may have had the last word: on September 28, 2000, it approved, with little fanfare and few restrictions, RU 486, the postcoital birth control device that Justice Ginsburg had prophesied, seven years before, would make *Roe* obsolete and most surgical abortions unnecessary. As FDA Commissioner Jane Henney remarked, "For those who choose to have an early termination of their pregnancy, this is a reasonable alternative." The pills would be distributed through doctors, and the treatment would require at least two visits. The pills were effective only within forty-nine days of the patient's last menstrual cycle, and in 5 to 8 percent of the cases, surgery might still be required to fully expel the fetus or to stop excess bleeding. Yet even these administrative regulations, so long in coming, faced political tests, for as Judie Brown, of the American Life League, an anti–abortion rights action group, warned: "We will not tolerate the FDA's decision to approve the destructions of innocent human persons through chemical abortion." Henney and Brown both knew that appointments to the FDA were the prerogative of the president and the Senate, an election was coming, and all FDA regulations could be revisited.

A bitter and tumultuous presidential election in 2000 brought all of these issues into stark relief, but not to resolution. Though the issue was understated by one of the candidates and dodged by the other, voters knew where both candidates stood on the abortion rights issue. On Election Day, voters' stance on the abortion rights issue turned out to be one of the strongest determinants of how they cast their ballots. The size of the turnout and the closeness of the result implied that the debate over abortion rights would continue to roil American politics, and events in the first days of President George W. Bush's administration have shown that the abortion rights debate will grow even hotter in the days to come.

Conclusion: The Never-Ending Story

In 2001, the wheel turns again: Bill Clinton out, George W. Bush in; the reimposition of gag rules and funding restrictions on reproductive counseling centers abroad that facilitate abortions; pro-life organizations celebrating; NOW warning about the anti–abortion rights posture of the new administration. John Ashcroft, who as state legislator, attorney general, governor, and senator from Missouri opposed all abortion except to save the mother's life, is confirmed as U.S. attorney general. He promises to uphold the law as it stands when it is "settled," but does not indicate whether he regards *Roe* as falling in this category. His supporters hope that he will promote the interests of the unborn. Norma McCorvey, who in the early 1990s proudly revealed her service in an abortion clinic, now runs the Roe No More Ministry in Dallas, a referral service for speakers against the decision.

The battle over *Roe* goes on and on: new regulations, new challenges, new cases, old protests, old alignments, old arguments, because neither side—and there are only two sides, no middle—can find a way to compromise or quit. Why is there no closure? Perhaps history can explain. The purpose of the Landmark Law Cases and American Society series is to use cases to open a window into life and ideas in our past. What does *Roe* tell us about that past?

We have argued that Justice Blackmun's opinion in *Roe* was meant to do justice to all parties—an equitable solution to a complex conflict. The recognition of a fundamental right of reproductive choice did not preclude the state's interest in unborn life. But that interest arose after viability. Blackmun had reached deep into the history of the abortion question, to the old doctrine of quickening, hoping that it still provided a scale in which to balance the competing claims. He did not incorporate the new paradigm of women' s voice in the law, instead restating the older, paternalistic, medically driven argument that doctors should be free of state interference in taking care of their pregnant patients. But again, he left open the door that the state could regard the fetus as a legal person at some time in its gestation.

The trimester scheme that embodied that balance of women's fundamental right and states' arising interest survived state challenges through the 1970s and 1980s, but the Court did not deem federal and state limitations on access to public funding and hospital care for abortion an "undue burden" on the right to choose to terminate a pregnancy in its earliest stages. By the end of the 1980s, state requirements of parental notice and the evaluation of fetuses for viability also passed the test of constitutionality. Federal rules barring the discussion of abortion in federally funded facilities similarly gained judicial approval. The Court shifted to the undue burden standard, rather than the trimester formula, to weigh state and federal regulations. *Roe* survived as a concept; the majority of the Court insisted that its core had become an essential part of American constitutional jurisprudence. But its core was gutted. Or was it?

Was this majority right? Or was the dissent—that *Roe* invented rights that the Constitution never mentioned, and gave to courts the power that democratic legislatures were supposed to exercise—better law and wiser policy? Americans have looked to the Court itself for an answer, but *Roe* and its progeny are written in a language that ordinary Americans cannot easily understand. The majority and the minority of the Court certainly had a good deal to say, then and afterward, but their words were part of a specialized, arcane vocabulary that had its own rules of grammar and usage. They intoned the words of appellate law courts, not the words of ordinary people. On occasion, one or another of the justices (usually Brennan or Marshall) made a plea for the Court to hear the voices and see the plight of ordinary people, but that plea was itself part of a complex and highly technical argument. How could it be otherwise? The justices are all skilled lawyers whose job it is to transform the experience of ordinary life into the rarefied language of the law. The court battle over the rights of women to choose abortions and the rights of government to protect fetal life will always be fought in the oxygen-poor altitude of lofty constitutional concepts like due process and equal protection.

What is more, the choice of one of these constitutional categories often concealed others equally applicable. For example, to treat abortion as a privacy right under the Due Process Clause might deny that abortion rights restrictions were a form of sex discrimination (Ruth Bader Ginsburg's argument). But when the Court shifts to viewing abortion questions as matters of sex discrimination it may well lump together all women instead of looking at the different needs and capacities of rich women and poor women. In other words, emphasis on gender tends to obscure crucial differences in class-based attitudes toward abortion and doctors.

In the same fashion, just looking at the socioeconomic status of women (for example in the funding cases) may blur vital distinctions among women from different ethnic heritages and ancestries. The white upper-class woman may regard her doctor in a different way than does the working-class woman of color—with the result that the doctor's reading of an informed consent message may have a completely different impact on the two women's choice of an abortion. Seen in this light, the categorical thinking of the Court so badly mangles the complex multiplicity of real-life factors in abortion decisions that its holdings on abortion from *Roe* to *Casey* increase rather than allay confusion.

Or it may be that the opinions lack the grit of everyday life because men and women simply do not hear the harmonics of one another's voices when it comes to abortion. In 1968, writing under the pen name Jeffrey Hudson, the novelist Michael Crichton published an abortion murder mystery titled *A Case of Need*. At the end, Crichton, a trained physician, stepped back and listed six reasons for reforming the (then) criminal law of abortion and six reasons to leave the law as it was. Only one of the first six touched women's right to choose or raised questions of reproductive autonomy from a woman's point of view. The last of the twelve, based on controversial evidence about DNA development, summed them all: forming a "commentary on modern man that he must justify his morality on the basis of the molecular mechanisms at work within a single cell of his body." Modern man's body—not a woman's body, and not what happened in her body, but what happened in the body of the fetus—mattered. Crichton was not unsympathetic to the plight of women who wanted or needed abortions, he just did not see it from their point of view or at least adopt their perspective to describe their plight.

Compare his supposedly neutral, objective, dry assessment with another doctor's, an abortionist and general practitioner named Elizabeth Karlin. In the face of escalating violence, she continued to go to her clinic, interview and counsel women, and help, when they were ready, with their abortions. She recalled, "It is very important to me to know that I am not alone doing abortions. . . . Patients stop for a hug on the way home. Women stop me in the supermarket and, with tears in their eyes, thank me for what I do . . . and I know, even being hated, that I'm in good company."

To enlarge on Karlin's point: Adrienne Rich, the poet, writes that "some ideas are not really new but keep having to be affirmed from the ground up. Over and over. One of these is the apparently simple idea that women are as intrinsically human as men, that . . . experience shapes us, randomness shapes us, the stars and the weather, our own accommodations and rebellions, above all, the social order around us." The central fact of that order was the exploitation of women's bodies, as laborers, as "wombs" for a man's children. So Rich can propose, "Procreative choice is for women an equivalent of the demand for the legally limited working day" for men, a statement that is as unlikely to appear in an opinion of the High Court as a volume of her poetry would be in the middle of the United States Code Annotated. It may be that gendered voice matters in court as well: counsel on the briefs of the state and the federal government in favor of curtailment of *Roe* were almost invariably entirely male. Counsel arguing against restriction of the abortion right invariably included men and women, with the latter often addressing the Supreme Court in oral argument.

Crichton assumed that a male doctor was a neutral scientific observer and an aid to the pregnant woman patient, but recent studies of doctors' views of female patients in difficult pregnancies show what Rich intuited: that male doctors are not neutral, and they view their female patients with less than objectivity. A 1987 survey of the heads of programs in fetal medicine revealed that nearly half thought that mothers who wished to carry their labor through without surgical intervention, against the doctor's advice, should be "detained in hospitals or other facilities so that compliance could be ensured." Slightly over one-fourth of these doctors wanted state surveillance of women in the third trimester who stay outside of the hospital system. Keeping women in "other facilities" against their will is a form of "preventive detention" that even the most conservative of state legislatures have not considered.

Another study of male doctors' attitudes toward women patients that brings into question the assumption of their neutrality and objectivity found that doctors regarded poor women and women of color as more likely to be "difficult patients," and such patients were more likely to receive substandard medical care. Some of this can be explained by poverty itself (having a private doctor ensured better care than relying upon the staff of a public hospital), but the responses of the doctors demonstrated that they had opinions closely reacting to their patients' ethnic and economic status, even when the source of payment for the care was not an issue.

Thus *Roe* does not speak to us in either plain or neutral language. We speak to it. We fit it into a historical context. That understood, we need to reframe and enlarge the question, "What does *Roe* tell us?" to make it more supple and realistic. One way to do this is to pose three historical questions. The first is, what made *Roe* and abortion so important in the early 1970s? The second is, why was the debate so bitter and the two sides so intractable? The third is, what do the politics and law of *Roe* reveal about fundamental American values?

Abortion was not a central issue in American politics and abortion cases were not so important in nineteenth- and early-twentieth-century American history because women had little say in lawmaking. The dominant legal paradigm viewed women as inferiors, whose primary function in society was mothering. Women were the virtuous bearers and nurturers of the next generation. The right to abortion challenged those values, but without a say in the law women could not overcome laws passed against abortion.

Over the course of the twentieth century, however, the role and influence of women in society changed. Women entered the professions, amassed wealth, gained the vote, and won government office. At first, despite these gains, the paradigm of women's place in the law remained unchanged. Thus, women had to bring leading male doctors and lawyers into the reproductive rights movement and persuade them that the laws against contraception and abortion were unfair, thereby convincing men to take the lead in "reforming" abortion laws. In the reform movement that men led, abortion was an important but not a defining issue of law. Men aided the women in the fight for control of their own bodies, but it was a battle on the periphery of the law.

It was only when the women's movement of the 1960s emerged and began to formulate a new conception of women's place in the law that abortion became a major national issue. For women reformers saw that the key to legal equality was choice, and the crucial test of choice for women was access to abortion. As the women's movement made abortion rights politically visible, abortion rights advocates added a second strand to the argument for women's rights generally. Abortion rights promoters brought to the courtroom a new, direct, everyday voice. They wove the records of this voice into the dry, technical, formal presentations of law. Abortion rights, absorbing both the ideal of choice and autonomy and the plain style of speaking, became the centerpiece of a new paradigm of women's place in the law. When abortion rights were challenged, narrowed, and endangered, advocates saw an assault not only on a newly won legal right but on the entire system of emancipated feminist thought that right symbolized.

The storm that formed during and after *Roe* was so bitter because both sides saw abortion not as a simple, limited legal issue, but as one that represented two opposing moral worlds. As Justice Breyer wrote in his opinion on partial-birth abortion, pro-life and pro–abortion rights seemed "virtually irreconcilable points of view." We are an intensely moralistic nation. We frame our foreign affairs and our wars, our politics and our economics, in terms of moral precepts. For pro–abortion rights forces, choice was a moral principle that went far beyond abortion rights; for anti–abortion rights groups, fetal life was a moral principle that reached out to the sacred memory of traditional families and motherhood.

Both sides rooted their arguments in older American values. Both sides believed fervently in their cause because they saw themselves as moral preceptors. Their language and their tactics grew more strident because they were radicalized by their participation in the abortion rights wars. Abortion rights rhetoric served as a political litmus test, and entire political campaigns turned on abortion planks.

In the face of the political storm, it was inevitable that the High Court become politicized. Appointment to the federal bench was more and more based on the nominees' views of *Roe*, and debates over *Roe* bent the entire shape of the judiciary in a way similar to abortion rights' impact on local and national elections. The justices of the Supreme Court began to use stronger and stronger language in their opinions, accusing one another of improper purposes and unsound readings of statutes and the Constitution. The polarization of the legal debate and the legal community could hardly be laid to the door of the majority in *Roe*, particularly Justice Blackmun, who tailored his opinion to win the support of all of his colleagues and who wanted *Roe* to take abortion out of politics. But when politics becomes the handmaiden of morality, no branch of government will be safe from political partisanship.

In the courtroom and the convention hall, *Roe* demonstrated that the wall of separation between church and state is translucent if not invisible. This theme too is deeply embedded in our history. Although some religious groups, such as the National Conference of Christians and Jews, supported *Roe*, the opposition to *Roe* was profoundly religious, expressed in religious terms and led by clergymen or those trained for the ministry. In its ability to bring together evangelical and liturgical leaders, pro-life indeed came as close to an ecumenical movement as American history has seen.

Roe also proved that movements for liberal reform and equality in American history, such as the women's movement, are matched against an equally powerful cultural and social conservatism. Had the opposition to *Roe* been all male, one might have ascribed it to the struggle for political and economic power between the sexes. Had it been a quarrel among women, we might attribute it to a deep divide in women's views of their place. In fact, men and women on either side saw abortion as part of a larger scheme, in which change or resistance to change was crucial. Legal issues often become the foci of such free-floating cultural schisms; the creation-evolution controversy is another of them.

Third, the battle over *Roe* proved how powerful the media is and how easily, in some cases, it can manipulate or manufacture opinion.

This may seem a cynical judgment on the close tie between democracy and demagoguery, but from the first efforts of the doctors in the 1840s and 1850s to criminalize abortion, through the eugenics movement of the 1920s, to the demonization of abortion providers in the 1990s, the role of mass communication and the unstable emotional currents it unleashes are integral to the abortion rights story.

Finally, *Roe* proved that the course of the law is not linear, making itself pure over time, but loops back and twists and turns. As near as *Roe* has come to extinction, it has survived not because its technical formulas were impervious to criticism. They were not, and no longer suffice. *Roe* still stands because it symbolized an idea whose time had come—the idea that women's bodies belong to women, not men, not doctors, not pressure groups, not Congress, not lobbyists, and certainly not judges and justices in court. In this sense, the symbolic sense, the persistence of *Roe* proves that the arcane tracings of legal language survive only when they conform to larger social and cultural realities.

1803	English Omnibus Crime Act (Lord Ellenborough's Act) makes abortion criminal at any stage of the pregnancy.
1821	First American state legislation on abortion, designed to protect mothers.
1857	Texas legislature makes abortion or attempted abortion on "woman with child" a felony; state courts later interpret this as applying to any stage of the pregnancy.
1873	So-called Comstock laws (anti-obscenity) in Congress make importation of contraceptive devices, advertisement of contraceptive services, and use of the mails to send contraceptive devices a federal offense. State Comstock laws follow. These not repealed until mid–twentieth century.
1876	Georgia state legislature makes abortion or attempted abortion a felony.
1916	Margaret Sanger opens first birth control clinic in New York City.
1921–1923	Sanger founds the American Birth Control League and tours world supporting birth control.
1936	In *U.S. v. One Package,* Judge Augustus Hand voids a portion of the federal Comstock laws.
1937	American Medical Association comes out in favor of birth control.
1942	American Birth Control League becomes Planned Parenthood Federation of America (PPFA), with affiliates all over the country.
1950–1970	Abortion law "reform" movement launched to increase the number of "therapeutic exceptions" to include mother's mental and physical health. Conferences in 1952 and 1955 by doctors and Planned Parenthood discuss abortion options.
1960	American Medical Association reports that abortion ban is unenforceable.

1962   American Law Institute approves Model Penal Code with therapeutic abortion provisions. Sherri Finkbein case (thalidomide pregnancy).

1963   Publication of Betty Friedan's best-selling feminist book, *The Feminine Mystique.*

1965   Rubella epidemic increases demands for therapeutic abortions; Planned Parenthood League of Connecticut and PPFA win suit against Connecticut's anti-contraception laws in *Griswold v. Connecticut.* In 7 to 2 decision on the Court, Justice William O. Douglas finds a fundamental right to privacy in the Due Process Clause of the Fourteenth Amendment and the Ninth Amendment's promise of unenumerated rights.

1966   Founding of National Organization of Women (NOW).

1967   Colorado, North Carolina, and California enact Model Penal Code type reformed abortion laws.

1969   Founding of National Abortion Rights Action League (NARAL). New York City "speak out" on abortion. *Belous* in California and *Vuitch* case in Washington, D.C., expand definition of therapeutic exception to abortion laws.

1970   Linda Coffee and Sarah Weddington file *Roe v. Wade;* federal court rules against Texas abortion law. Margie Pitts Hames files *Doe v. Bolton* in Georgia and wins in lower federal court. Both cases appealed to U.S. Supreme Court. Federal "Title X" funds for family planning exclude payments for abortions.

1971   Supreme Court hears first round of oral argument in *Roe* and *Doe,* which have been consolidated. Dr. Jane Hodgson convicted for performing in-hospital abortion (the only such conviction in modern period).

1972   Justices Lewis Powell and William Rehnquist added to Supreme Court. Second round of oral arguments in *Roe* and *Doe. Baird v. Eisenstadt* extends privacy right to unmarried couples.

1973   High Court decision in *Roe* announced, with opinion by Justice Harry Blackmun, that the right to abortion can be found in the Due Process Clause, that the state has an interest in life of fetus from after first trimester, but that state regulations must pass "strict scrutiny" standard. Justices Byron White and William Rehnquist dissent. Founding of American Right to Life Committee.

1976 *Planned Parenthood v. Danforth,* first of state regulation cases, arrives at Supreme Court; Court allows written informed consent requirements. Hyde amendment introduced in Congress to deny federal funds to abortions, passed over President Gerald Ford's veto. Jimmy Carter wins presidential race running as pro-life candidate. Justice John Paul Stevens joins the Court and will almost invariably support *Roe* thereafter.

1977 Hyde amendment again passed in Congress and signed into law by President Carter. In so-called funding cases of *Beal v. Doe, Maher v. Roe,* and *Poelker v. Doe,* High Court upholds state and municipal decisions to deny public funding of abortions, with Justice Powell joining the majority of Chief Justice Warren Burger and Justices Rehnquist, White, and Potter Stewart.

1980 Supreme Court upholds federal ban on abortion funding through Hyde amendment in *Harris v. McRae.* Republicans add right-to-life plank to their platform, and Republican candidate Ronald Reagan wins presidency calling for constitutional amendment to ban abortion.

1981 Justice Sandra Day O'Connor joins the Court. Her vote will be the swing vote in abortion rights cases to come.

1982 First abortion clinic bombing.

1983 Court holds that city and state regulations in *City of Akron v. Akron Center for Reproductive Health* and *Ashcroft v. Planned Parenthood* are violations of standard in *Roe;* O'Connor joins the dissent, arguing that the proper standard for review should be "undue burden" rather than the *Roe* trimester schema.

1986 In a 5 to 4 decision *(Thornburgh v. American College of Obstetricians and Gynecologists),* the last to uphold the trimester formula in *Roe,* the Court strikes down a series of Pennsylvania abortion regulations. Chief Justice Burger retires and is replaced by Rehnquist. Antonin Scalia is added to the Court, and will become *Roe's* most articulate and persistent critic.

1987 Randall Terry leads first "rescue." Operation Rescue formally founded the next year.

1988 Anthony Kennedy is added to the Court. Rules for federal Title X family planning clinics amended to bar any employee from discussing abortion.

1989	In *Webster v. Reproductive Services* a majority of the Court upholds Missouri restrictions on abortions; the majority opinion drops the "fundamental right" language of *Roe* and requires instead that state regulations be rational; Justices Rehnquist, Kennedy, and White seem ready to jettison *Roe,* but O'Connor refuses to follow that course.
1991	Justice David Souter added to Court. Court finds that instructions limiting speech in family planning clinics receiving federal funds under Title X *(Rust v. Sullivan)* are constitutional; O'Connor joins the dissenters.
1992	Justice Clarence Thomas added to Court and votes with majority in upholding stringent Pennsylvania rules on abortion in *Casey v. Planned Parenthood.* Attempt by Justices Rehnquist, White, Scalia, and Thomas to reverse *Roe* fails when Kennedy, O'Connor, and Souter author a joint opinion upholding the principle of *Roe,* which Justices Stevens and Blackmun join. William Jefferson Clinton wins presidency, vowing a pro-choice program.
1993	Clinton lifts gag rule in Title X clinics. In *Bray v. Alexandria Women's Health Clinic,* Court holds that NOW cannot use the Ku Klux Klan Act of 1871 to seek damages against pro-life demonstrators. Justice Ruth Bader Ginsburg added to the Court. Congress allows federal funding for abortion cases where rape and incest have been reported. Violence against abortion clinics and doctors escalates, as Dr. David Gunn, abortion clinic practitioner, is murdered.
1994	Congress passes Freedom of Access to Clinic Entrances Act (FACE). Justice Stephen G. Breyer appointed to Court. Court in *Madsen v. Women's Health Center* finds that buffer zone around abortion clinic entrances is not violation of free speech rights of protestors. In *NOW v. Scheidler,* Court agrees that federal anti-racketeering laws (RICO) can be used against anti-abortion conspiracies. Paul Hill murders Dr. John Britton and his volunteer escort, James Barrett.
1995–1999	House of Representatives attempts to narrow federal funding for abortions to save life of mother only. Supreme Court refuses to hear challenges to prosecution of anti-abortion protestors under FACE. Pro-life majority in Congress passes

"partial-birth abortion" (dilate and extraction procedure) ban, which President Clinton twice vetoes. States pass anti–partial-birth abortion acts, which lower federal courts strike down as "unduly burdensome." Fourth doctor and two clinic receptionists killed by pro-life assassins.

2000   In *Stenberg v. Carhart,* Supreme Court voids Nebraska's partial-birth abortion ban in bitterly divided vote.

2001   Newly elected President George W. Bush reinstates rules against funding of overseas family planning clinics that discuss abortion options. Attorney General John Ashcroft promises Congress he will enforce all laws, including the legality of abortion, although he is in favor of a return to the pre-*Roe* abortion regime.

BIBLIOGRAPHICAL ESSAY

Note from the Series Editors: The following bibliographical essay contains the major primary and secondary sources the author consulted for this volume. We have asked all authors in the series to omit formal citations in order to make our volumes more readable, inexpensive, and appealing for students and general readers. In adopting this format, Landmark Law Cases and American Society follows the precedent of a number of highly regarded and widely consulted series.

Our purpose in this short bibliographical essay is twofold. We want to credit the authors whose work we have found most useful in guiding our thinking, and we want to point students to sources they will find most accessible and easy to understand. For this reason, the essay is highly selective.

The district court cases we discuss can be found in the West Law Reporter called the Federal Supplement (abbreviated F. Supp). For example, *Roe v. Wade* is 314 F. Supp 1217 (1970), which, translated, means that the court's opinion starts on page 1217 of volume 314 of the reporter. *Doe v. Bolton,* the companion case from Georgia, is 319 F. Supp 1048 (1970). The first opinion was handed down on June 17, the latter on July 31, but five volumes of federal district court cases separate them in the reporter—evidence of the immense business of the federal trial courts. In addition, we counted over two dozen Supreme Court cases on abortion after *Roe.*

The three United States Supreme Court cases that are the centerpiece of this book, *Roe v. Wade* 410 U.S. 113 (1973), *Webster v. Reproductive Health Services* 487 U.S. 490 (1989), and *Planned Parenthood of Southeastern Pennsylvania v. Casey* 505 U.S. 833 (1992), tell so many stories it is hard to know how to disentangle them and present them in a coherent manner. The cases invariably began with a district court decision, and the latter cases were also heard by a circuit court of appeals (the United States has eleven of these regional intermediate appellate courts). When parties appealed to the U.S. Supreme Court, they first filed a jurisdictional statement laying out the history of the case in the courts and explaining why the High Court should take jurisdiction over the case. When the High Court noted probable jurisdiction, the parties filed full briefs arguing the constitutional and statutory points of law. In addition, so-called friends of the court (amicus curiae) were also allowed to file briefs supporting one side or the other. On numerous occasions, the United States government was one of the amici. All the briefs of the parties, including a selection from the friends of the court, verbatim transcripts of the oral arguments of counsel for the parties before the High Court, and the opinions of the Supreme Court justices in these cases appear in volumes of *Landmark Briefs and Arguments of the Supreme Court of the United States: Constitutional Law,* ed. Philip B. Kurland and Gerhard Casper. In addition, an audiotape of selections of the oral arguments in *Roe, Webster, Casey,* and other abortion-related cases appears as a supplement to Stephanie Guitton and Peter Irons's collection, *May It Please the Court* (1993). The cassettes, available from the New Press, are narrated by Irons, Sylvia Law, Eleanor Holmes Norton, and Nadine Stroesser.

There are too many accounts, firsthand and scholarly, of *Roe* and its progeny to list here. Many are excellent. The ones we have relied on include David Garrow, *Liberty and Sexuality: The Right to Privacy and the Making of* Roe v. Wade (1994), a voluminously detailed account of the story from its origins in the Connecticut Planned Parenthood League's war on the anti–birth control statutes of the state through the arguments in *Casey.* The extensive bibliography of the book alone is worth the price.

Cynthia Gorney's *Articles of Faith: A Frontline History of the Abortion Wars* (1998) follows an even more personal approach than Garrow, and her anecdotes and insight make the story truly come alive, particularly in Missouri, the focal point of her inquiry and the source of many of the cases on abortion. One of these, in 1970, might well have been the pivotal case had it not been for *Roe.* Bob Woodward and Scott Armstrong, *The Brethren: Inside the Supreme Court* (1979) includes a gossipy account of the case based largely on interviews with the justices' clerks. The lead counsel in *Roe,* Sarah Weddington, tells her own story in *A Question of Choice* (1992). Norma McCorvey revealed personal details in McCorvey and Andy Meisler, *I Am Roe: My Life,* Roe v. Wade, *and Freedom of Choice* (1994). A highly readable journalistic essay on *Roe* and its immediate effects is Marian Faux, Roe v. Wade: *The Untold Story*

of the Landmark Supreme Court Decision That Made Abortion Legal (1988).
On the *Webster* and *Casey* cases in the Rehnquist Court, one may see
David G. Savage, *Turning Right: The Making of the Rehnquist Supreme Court*
(1992); James F. Simon, *The Center Holds: The Power Struggle Within the
Rehnquist Court* (1995); and Tinsley E. Yarbrough, *The Rehnquist Court
and the Constitution* (2000).

Brief biographies of the justices on the High Court during this period can be found in Kermit L. Hall, et al., eds., *The Oxford Companion
to the Supreme Court of the United States* (1992), and Melvin I. Urofsky, ed.,
The Supreme Court Justices: A Biographical Dictionary (1994). A number of
political scientists, law professors, and biographers have written books
on the justices involved. These include the essays in Herman Schwartz,
ed., *The Burger Years: Rights and Wrongs in the Supreme Court, 1969–1986*
(1988); Robert Goldman, ed., *Justice William J. Brennan, Jr.: Freedom First*
(1994); David E. Marion, *The Jurisprudence of Justice William J. Brennan,
Jr.* (1997); Frank I. Michelman, *Brennan and Democracy* (1999); Michael
D. Davis and Hunter R. Clark, *Thurgood Marshall: Warrior at the Bar,
Rebel on the Bench* (1992); Nancy Maveety, *Justice Sandra Day O'Connor*
(1996); Donald E. Boles, *Mr. Justice Rehnquist, Judicial Activist: The Early
Years* (1987); Sue Davis, *Justice Rehnquist and the Constitution* (1989),
Richard A. Brisbin Jr., *Justice Antonin Scalia and the Conservative Revival*
(1997); Christopher E. Smith, *Justice Antonin Scalia and the Supreme Court's
Conservative Moment* (1993); and the comments after Justice Scalia's own
essay, *A Matter of Interpretation: Federal Courts and the Law* (1997); Scott
Douglas Gerber, *First Principles: The Jurisprudence of Clarence Thomas*
(1999); and Dennis J. Hutchinson, *The Man Who Once Was Whizzer White:
A Portrait of Justice Byron R. White* (1998). A firsthand account of Justice
Blackmun's way of thinking is Pamela S. Karlan, "Bringing Compassion into the Province of Judging: Justice Blackmun and the Outsid-
ers," 71 *North Dakota Law Review* 173 (1996). On the solicitors general,
see Lincoln Caplan, *The Tenth Justice: The Solicitor General and the Rule
of Law* (1987).

Given the importance that abortion had in the selection process for
judges and justices after 1971, one would expect the accounts above to
give a good deal of space to *Roe* and abortion in general. In fact, abortion and *Roe* usually rate only a few scattered references. This suggests
that although abortion was a critical issue in the politics of the period

and both sides accused the other of making it into a "litmus test" for appointment of judges after *Roe*, gender as a way of analyzing legal concepts did not become part of the core jurisprudence of the justices.

By contrast, we have argued that not only did the participation of women lawyers as chief counsel for plaintiffs in *Roe* and *Doe* help make those cases more visible, but that women lawyers defending privacy and choice made those concepts the centerpiece of what we have called the new paradigm of women and the law. Analysts of the justices' opinions should take greater note of the gendered nature of the legal discourse, giving readers a sense of the distinctions between the two paradigms of law. Surveys of women's rise in the legal profession include Ronald Chester, *Unequal Access: Women Lawyers in a Changing America* (1985), and Virginia G. Drachman, *Sisters in Law: Women Lawyers in Modern American History* (1998). Women lawyers are a small part of the now dated but still very useful Leo Kanowitz, *Women and the Law: The Unfinished Revolution* (1970). Two revealing articles by women who participated in post-*Roe* women's litigation, Ruth Bader Ginsburg, "Some Thoughts on Autonomy or Equality in Relation to *Roe v. Wade*," 63 *North Carolina Law Review* 375 (1985), and Sylvia Law, "Rethinking Sex and the Constitution," 132 *Pennsylvania Law Review* 955 (1984), reveal core values of that new paradigm of women and the law. Other articles that helped us understand the new paradigm include Nancy Ehrenreich, "The Colonization of the Womb," 43 *Duke Law Journal* 492 (1993), a thorough review of the literature on doctors and female patients, and Eileen L. McDonagh, "My Body, My Consent: Securing the Constitutional Right to Abortion Funding," 62 *Albany Law Review* 1057 (1999), featuring arguments on abortion as self-defense.

As the almost identical lineup of justices on the Supreme Court in abortion and civil rights cases in the years 1971–2000 indicates, there is a strong tie between a justice's opinions on women's rights and abortion on the one hand, and on race and racial discrimination on the other hand. See, e.g., Michael Dorf, "In Praise of Justice Blackmun," 99 *Columbia Law Review* 1397 (1999). On race prejudice in the nineteenth century, see George M. Fredrickson, *The Black Image in the White Mind: The Debate on Afro-American Character and Destiny, 1817–1914* (1987); Richard Hofstadter, *Social Darwinism in American Thought* (1944); Reginald Horsman, *Race and Manifest Destiny: Origins of American Racial Anglo-*

Saxonism (1981); and Charles A. Lofgren, *The Plessy Case: A Legal-Historical Interpretation* (1987).

The drive for the purification of the "race" that connected sex and race discrimination also figured in the eugenics movement. On it, see Daniel Kevles, *In the Name of Eugenics* (1990) and Edward J. Larson, *Sex, Race, and Science: Eugenics in the Deep South* (1995). Manliness, feminism, and race also came together at the turn of the century. See Gail Bederman, *Manliness and Civilization: A Cultural History of Gender and Race in the United States, 1880–1917* (1995).

The legal issues discussed by the Court have become part of every constitutional law course, and in a departure from the usually balanced approach to controversial subjects that law commentators adopt, abortion seems to bring out our disputatiousness. Lawrence Tribe's *Abortion: The Clash of Absolutes* (1990) and Mark Tushnet's *Abortion: Constitutional Issues* (1996) are liberal defenses of *Roe*. Abortion is one of the many subjects in Joan Hoff's *Law, Gender and Injustice: A Legal History of U.S. Women* (1991), an attack on the limitations of so-called liberal legal views. Essential surveys are Celeste M. Condit, *Decoding Abortion Rhetoric* (1991) and Karen O'Connor, *No Neutral Ground? Abortion Politics in an Age of Absolutes* (1996). Law professor and litigator Catharine A. MacKinnon's *Feminism Unmodified: Discourses on Life and Law* (1987) fits abortion into the larger scheme of radical feminism. MacKinnon was instrumental in formulating the legal notion of "sexual harassment" and winning the first sexual harassment cases.

Arguments against abortion rights appear in philosopher Peter Kreeft's *The Unaborted Socrates* (1983); Mary Ann Glendon, *Abortion and Divorce in Western Law: American Failures, European Challenges* (1987); Kevin C. McMunigal, "Of Cases and Clients: Two Tales of *Roe v. Wade,*" 47 *Hastings Law Journal* 779 (1996); and Lynn D. Wardle, "The Quandary of Pro-Life Free Speech: A Lesson from the Abolitionists," 62 *Albany Law Review* (1998), among a myriad of other publications.

The line between politics and law in these cases is hardly clear, and, as is true for the jurist and law professor, the scholarly balance of the political scientist and historian is severely tested when abortion is the subject. A fine clear survey of the politics of the cases is Donald T. Critchlow, *The Politics of Abortion and Birth Control in Historical Perspective* (1996). Other essays and collections of essays that combine legal and political insights include Robert M. Baird and Stuart E. Rosenbaum, ed., *The Ethics of Abortion* (1989); Faye Ginsburg, *Contested Lives: The Abortion Debate in an American Community* (1989); Malcolm Goggin, ed., *Understanding the New Politics of Abortion* (1993); Barbara Hinkson Craig and David M. O'Brien, *Abortion and American Politics* (1993); and Ted G. Jelen, ed., *Perspectives on the Politics of Abortion* (1995).

On the relation between abortion and the so-called Christian Right see Sara Diamond, *Not by Politics Alone: The Enduring Influence of the Christian Right* (1998); Michele McKeegan, *Abortion Politics: Mutiny in the Ranks of the Right* (1992); and James Risen and Judy L. Thomas, *Wrath of Angels: The American Abortion War* (1998). Susan Faludi, *Backlash: The Undeclared War Against American Women* (1991) documents the many ways in which women found their legal gains under attack in the 1980s. Charles R. Morris's *American Catholic* (1997) is a balanced and well-documented account of abortion politics, among many other topics. Insights into the relations between politics and women's bodies abound in Claudia Dreifus, ed., *Seizing Our Bodies: The Politics of Women's Health* (1978), and Susan Brownmiller, a journalist who "was there," writes brilliantly of the origins of the "women's movement," or rather, the many women's movements of the 1960s and 1970s, in *In Our Time: Memoir of a Revolution* (1999).

The history of abortion is as fascinating as the law surrounding it, and we have argued that the two are inextricably bound. A technical essay arguing that abortifacients in the pre-modern world were also used to regulate the menstrual cycle is Etienne van de Walle, "Flowers and Fruits: Two Thousand Years of Menstrual Regulation," *Journal of Interdisciplinary History* 28 (1977): 183–205. Prof. John M. Riddle, a University of North Carolina historian, is convinced that not only were the plants used for abortions, they were successful, particularly the now extinct giant fennel, silphium. His views are controversial, however. Mary Beth Norton records cases of suspected abortion in her *Founding Mothers and Fathers: Gendered Power and the Forming of American Society* (1996). Cornelia Hughes Dayton tracks the Hallowell case in "Taking the Trade: Abortion and Gender Relations in an Eighteenth-Century New England Village," *William and Mary Quarterly*, 3rd ser., 48 (1991): 19–49. Laurel Thatcher Ulrich's *A Midwife's Tale: The Life of Martha Ballard, Based on Her Diary* (1991) is a magnificent re-creation of the work of a midwife. Hoffer and Hull have studied early modern infanticide in *Murdering Mothers: Infanticide in England and New England, 1558–1803* (1981).

Among the excellent books on abortion and birth control are Janet Farrell Brodie, *Contraception and Abortion in 19th Century America* (1994), an exceedingly able and readable tour through the ideas and personalities on both sides of the birth control and abortion question; Linda Gordon, *Women's Body, Women's Right: A Social History of Birth Control in America* (1976), a powerful and argumentative account of the struggle that women faced to gain control of their own bodies, told with many stories of individual women; James C. Mohr, *Abortion in America: The Origins and Evolution of National Policy* (1978), still the standard narrative of the changing legal and medical treatment of abortion in the nineteenth century (Mohr was the consultant in the so-called historians' amicus brief in *Webster*); Leslie J. Reagan, *When Abortion Was a Crime: Women, Medicine, and the Law in the United States, 1867–1973* (1997), a detailed indictment of the anti-abortion forces; and James Reed, *The Birth Control Movement and American Society: From Private Vice to Public Virtue*, 2nd ed. (1983), a subtle and well-argued biographical approach to birth control and abortion issues, as well as David Kennedy's *Birth Control in America: The Career of Margaret Sanger* (1977). On the impact of Comstock and his program, see Helen Lefkowitz Horowitz, "Victoria Woodhull, Anthony Comstock, and Conflict over Sex in the United States in the 1870s," and Andrea Tone, "Black Market Birth Control: Contraceptive Entrepreneurship and Criminality in the Gilded Age," in *Journal of American History* 87 (2000): 403–434 and 435–459, respectively. An account of many of the same events from the anti–abortion rights side is Marvin Olasky, *Abortion Rights: A Social History of Abortion in America* (1992). Olasky, a senior fellow at the Progress and Freedom Foundation, takes direct aim at Mohr. The story of infertility is tracked in Margaret Marsh and Wanda Ronner, *The Empty Cradle: Infertility in America from Colonial Times to the Present* (1996).

The history of abortion practices and prohibitions in modern America continues to be a window into social, cultural, religious, and political attitudes as well as the history of women. Throughout the twentieth century, magazines of opinion such as *American Mercury, Commonweal, Forum, Harper's Magazine, Literary Digest, Nation, New Re-*

public, and *Time* regularly carried reports on birth control and abortion issues. Elaine Showalter's edition of *These Modern Women: Autobiographical Essays from the Twenties* (1979), reprints a series of firsthand accounts by feminists from the *Nation*'s pages, in 1926 and 1927, covering a wide range of reproductive issues. Medical journals and professional newsletters, scholarly periodicals in sociology and economics, and law reviews also followed these subjects, the latter providing excellent summaries of the state laws and cases at particular points in time. (We counted over 400 major law review pieces on *Roe* and its descendants published during the period 1982–1999.) From 1972, *Ms. Magazine* carried articles on abortion and other feminist issues. On *Ms. Magazine,* see Amy Erdman Farrell, *Yours in Sisterhood: Ms. Magazine and the Promise of Popular Feminism* (1998).

The abortionist Ruth Barnett's tale is the subject of Rickie Solinger, *The Abortionist: A Woman Against the Law* (1994). Josephine Gabler's abortion practice is traced in Reagan, *When Abortion Was Against the Law.* Mid-twentieth-century surveys on abortion include those prepared by Drs. Carl Taussig and Alan Guttmacher, and the collections of essays that psychiatrist Harold Rosen based on conferences in the 1950s and 1960s. See, for example, Rosen, ed., *Therapeutic Abortion* (1954). These highly detailed, scientifically sound reports show the changing view of doctors toward abortion. Comparing these with the doctors' lectures and essays in David J. Rothman and Sheila M. Rothman, eds., *Family in America: Birth Control and Morality in Nineteenth Century America: Two Essays* (1972), and Charles Rosenberg and Carroll Smith-Rosenberg, eds., *Sex, Marriage, and Society: Abortion in Nineteenth-Century America* (1974), shows how much changed in a century.

The twists and turns of AMA policy on women and child care are the subject of the final chapter of Richard A. Meckel, *Save the Babies: American Public Health Reform and the Prevention of Infant Mortality, 1850–1929* (1990). Donald Critchlow, *Intended Consequences: Birth Control, Abortion, and the Federal Government in Modern America* (1999), follows the path of federal family planning policy in the 1960s, '70s, and '80s. Jane Kaplan, *The Story of Jane: The Legendary Underground Feminist Abortion Service* (1995), Carole Joffe, *Doctors of Conscience: The Stuggle to Provide Abortion Before and After Roe v. Wade* (1995), and Rickie Solinger, ed., *Abortion Wars:*

A Half Century of Struggle, 1950–2000 (2000), bring the story up to date. The essays include firsthand accounts by lawyers such as Kathryn Kolbert, doctors such as Elizabeth Karlin and Jane Hodgson, and activists such as Loretta J. Ross, as well as scholars such as Amy Kesselman (writing on the Connecticut abortion rights case).

Of course, one cannot study abortion in isolation from more general issues in women's history. As it happened, the *Roe* era was an especially fruitful one for general histories of American women, for the history of women and the contemporary women's movement were inextricably tied. Some of these early studies include William H. Chafe, *The American Woman: Her Changing Social, Economic, and Political Roles* (1972); Mary P. Ryan, *Womanhood in America: From Colonial Times to the Present* (1975); and June Sochen, *Herstory: A Woman's View of American History* (1974). Barbara Deckard's *The Women's Movement* (1975) tried to chart the course of abortion politics. A more recent treatment is Ruth Rosen, *The World Split Open: How the Modern Women's Movement Changed America* (2000).

Particular topics in women's history are especially relevant to abortion. Domestic relations law is the subject of Hendrik Hartog's beautifully nuanced *Man and Wife in America: A History* (2000). The relation between abortion and medicine in the nineteenth century was the subject of G. J. Barker-Benfield, *Horrors of the Half-Known Life: Male Attitudes Toward Women in Nineteenth-Century America* (1976); John S. Haller Jr. and Robin M. Haller, *The Physician and Sexuality in Victorian America* (1974); and Regina Morantz-Sanchez, *Conduct Unbecoming a Woman: Medicine on Trial in Turn-of-the-Century Brooklyn* (1999).

On women's attitudes toward men and sexuality, see Nancy Cott, "The Modern Woman of the 1920s, American Style," in *A History of Women in the West*, vol. 5, *Toward a Cultural Identity in the Twentieth Century*, ed. Françoise Thébaud (1994), 76–91; Carroll Smith-Rosenberg, "The Female World of Love and Ritual," in *A Heritage of Her Own: Toward a New Social History of American Women*, ed. Nancy F. Cott and Elizabeth H. Pleck (1979), 311–342, Judith R. Walkowitz, "Dangerous Sexualities," in *A History of Women in the West*, vol. 4, *Emerging Feminism from Revolution to World War*, ed. Geneviève Fraisse and Michelle Perrot (1993), 399–426; and Nancy Woloch, *Women and the American Experience*, vol. 2, *From 1860*, 2nd ed. (1994).

On women in the Depression-era south see James Agee and Walker Evans, *Let Us Now Praise Famous Men* ([1941] rev. ed. 1988), and Margaret Jarman Hagood, *Mothers of the South: Portraiture of the White Tenant Farm Woman* (1939). On the roles assigned to women and women's responses in the 1950s, two excellent collections are Brett Harvey, *The Fifties: A Women's Oral History* (1993), and Elaine Tyler May, *Homeward Bound: American Families in the Cold War Era* (1988). A broader survey is David Halberstam's *The Fifties* (1993).

The enduring mythos of motherhood in women's history is the subject of Donna Bassin, Margaret Honey, and Meryle Mahrer Kaplan, eds., *Representations of Motherhood* (1995), and Shari L. Thurer, *The Myths of Motherhood: How Culture Reinvents the Good Mother* (1994). A wide-ranging collection of essays on pregnancy is Annette Lawson and Deborah L. Rhode, eds., *The Politics of Pregnancy: Adolescent Sexuality and Public Policy* (1993).

Two books from the 1960s–1970s period that crossed over all lines of primary and secondary sources, combining personal experience, research, and contemporary comment, are Betty Friedan, *The Feminine Mystique* ([1963] rev. ed. 1983), and Adrienne Rich, *Of Woman Born: Motherhood as Experience and Institution* ([1976] rev. ed. 1986). Friedan's *It Changed Everything* (1976), a collection of journalistic pieces on the movement, reveals something of Friedan's achievement and the opposition she faced. Her *Life So Far* (2000) offers additional reflections on the women's movement. Judith Hennesse's biography, *Betty Friedan: Her Life* (1999), punctures some of the myths about Friedan but in the end makes us admire its subject all the more. Joyce Gelb and Marian Lief Palley, *Women and Public Policies* (1982), puts some of the feminist agenda in context. On the ERA, see Mary Frances Berry, *Why ERA Failed* (1986), and Jane J. Mansbridge, *Why We Lost the ERA* (1986).

As we indicated in the final chapter and the conclusion, we are still in the middle of the story of *Roe,* and no one can predict the ending. To keep up with current events, one might consult three Web sites. A superb source of legal materials, including courts' opinions and briefs of cases submitted to the Supreme Court, is *www.lexis.com.* Lexis also has a news service that covers most of the major dailies, magazines of opinion, and testimony before congressional committees. More narrowly focused on abortion matters, the Web site of the National Abortion Rights Action League (NARAL) is *www.naral.org.* On the other side of these issues, the National Right to Life Committee's Web site is *www.nrlc.org.* NOW, Operation Rescue, Planned Parenthood Federation of America, and various health advisory and church groups also have Web sites that focus on abortion. Some of these Web sites also serve fund-raising and political action functions.

We decline here, as in the text, to explore comparative international aspects of abortion law. In some ways, particularly the role of women's groups in changing the law, comparisons would be revealing, but in each country unique social, cultural, and political conditions determined the course and outcome of legal change. A fine article whose notes supply some of what is missing from this bibliography is Stephen Brooke, "'A New World for Women'? Abortion Law Reform in Britain during the 1930s," *American Historical Review* 106 (2001): 431–460.